Public Sector Economics

for Developing Countries

Michael Howard

Public Sector Economics

for Developing Countries

UNIVERSITY OF THE WEST INDIES PRESS

Barbados • Jamaica • Trinidad and Tobago

University of the West Indies Press
1A Aqueduct Flats   Mona
Kingston 7   Jamaica

05   5   4   3

CATALOGUING IN PUBLICATION DATA

Howard, Michael
Public sector economics for developing countries / Michael Howard
p. cm.
Includes bibliographical references and index.
ISBN: 976-640-091-1

1. Finance, Public – Developing countries. 2. Fiscal policy – Developing countries. 3. Taxation – Developing countries. 4. Structural adjustment (Economic policy) – Developing countries. 5. Developing countries – Economic policy. I. Title.

HJ1620.H68 2001   336.091724 – dc20

Cover and book design by Alan Ross.

COPYRIGHT ACKNOWLEDGEMENTS

The author gratefully acknowledges the permission of Greenwood Publishing Group, Inc., Westport, Connecticut, to reproduce the following pages from his book *Public Finance in Small Open Economies*, Prager Publishers, © 1992 by Michael Howard, pages 16–18, 37–42, 59, 61–63, 110–11, 130–33, 146–47.

The author also acknowledges with thanks the permission of the Institute of Social and Economic Research, Cave Hill campus, University of the West Indies, to reproduce the following articles: "Barbados: Tax Reform of 1992 Compared with 1986", *Bulletin of Eastern Caribbean Affairs* 19, no. 3 (September 1994) and "Theoretical Aspects of Fiscal Harmonization in CARICOM", *Bulletin of Eastern Caribbean Affairs* 20, no. 3 (September 1995).

To my students, past and present

Contents

Tables

Preface

This book has been inspired by Richard Goode's *Government Finance in Developing Countries*. Since the publication of this work the fiscal systems of developing countries have changed significantly. Tax reform has altered the tax systems, placing emphasis on neutral taxes, especially the value-added tax (VAT). Further, these countries have undergone stabilization and structural adjustment programmes which focus on privatization and market liberalization. The text presents a discussion of the major concepts in public sector economics, with particular reference to developing countries.

Perhaps a more important reason for writing the book is that most public sector economics textbooks, written in highly industrialized economies, hardly mention the fiscal problems of developing countries. Fiscal analysis for developing countries can be found in the publications of the World Bank and the International Monetary Fund, literature surveys, monographs and edited books. The present work, while not neglecting the received theory which has evolved in highly industrialized economies, draws on the literature mentioned above. As a result, it is hoped that this book will provide a guide to aspects of the literature on fiscal issues in developing countries.

The book is intended for students in developing countries who are taking semester courses in Public Sector Economics, Public Finance, Fiscal Policy for Developing Countries and the Economics of Taxation. The work is also of value to students of Development Economics. But the text should also appeal to a wider audience as well. Practitioners will find this work a source of useful reference material. The general reader from other disciplines will find the book easy to read. The text requires some familiarity with micro-economic theory as well as macroeconomics. I have tried to keep the exposition as simple as possible, with major emphasis on conceptual clarity.

The first six chapters of the book are concerned with the role of government in the economy, and the determination of public expenditure. Chapters 1 to 3 look at the basic theory of market failure, public goods and externalities, and the role of government. Chapters 4 and 5 discuss the relevance to developing countries of public choice theory and the theories of the political business cycle. These have been neglected areas of research in developing countries. Chapter 6 is concerned with the growth and structure of public expenditure in selected developing countries.

Chapters 7 to 9 provide introductions to highly specialized topics, namely, income distribution and poverty, cost-benefit analysis and the regulation of public utilities. My approach in these chapters outlines the basic conceptual framework for further analysis. This approach appears appropriate primarily because of the extensive empirical and specialized theoretical literature on these topics. Chapters 10, 11 and 12 examine the nature of budget deficits, stabilization policy and structural adjustment in developing countries. The presentation describes a number of country examples of stabilization and structural adjustment. I believe that these areas of enquiry were perhaps the two most important problem areas for governments in developing countries during the 1980s and early 1990s.

Chapters 13 to 20 deal with theoretical and institutional issues in taxation, with special reference to developing economics. Chapters 13 and 14 provide the conceptual foundation for analysing tax issues in any market economy. The equity principle, incidence and the efficiency costs of taxation are discussed there. Chapter 15 explores the main issues in tax reform, while chapters 16 and 17 outline the major institutional and theoretical aspects of taxes on income, wealth and consumption. Chapter 20 is concerned with a survey of the main problems of tax administration such as tax evasion, tax compliance cost, and the special problems of administering the VAT. Wherever possible, I have made reference to empirical examples to support the theoretical discussions.

This book is more comprehensive than Goode's. I discuss government failure, privatization, structural adjustment, public choice and political business cycles. Topics such as public utilities pricing, tax reform, fiscal harmonization and tax administration were not principal concerns of Goode's book.

I am heavily indebted to my students at the University of the West Indies, Cave Hill campus, for their help in conceptualizing and writing this work. Over the years they have helped me to clarify my views on the various areas of public sector finance.

I also owe a great debt to Dr Delisle Worrell and Dr Roland Craigwell for their incisive and constructive criticisms. They helped me to reformulate certain chapters, improve my attention to detail and enhance the overall quality of the work.

I especially want to thank Jennifer Hurley, my secretary in the Department of Economics, Cave Hill, who typed the entire manuscript. Her work was of the highest quality, and her corrections to various drafts were performed with great speed and accuracy. I am also highly appreciative of the assistance of my wife June. Any errors of analysis or content are my own.

Abbreviations

ADP	Automated data processing
AWT	Annual wealth tax
BT	Brown tax
CARICOM	Caribbean Community
CET	Common External Tariff
CIF	Cost, insurance and freight
ECLAC	Economic Commission for Latin America and the Caribbean
ERP	Effective rate of protection
ESAF	Enhanced structural adjustment facility
FF	Fixed fee
FOB	Free on board
GCT	General consumption tax
GDP	Gross domestic product
GNP	Gross national product
HPI	Human poverty index
HRIT	Higher rates of proportional income tax
IDB	Inter-American Development Bank
IMF	International Monetary Fund
IRR	Internal rate of return
ISER	Institute of Social and Economic Research
MNC	Multinational corporation

MPR	Marginal revenue product
MRS	Marginal rate of substitution
MRT	Marginal rate of transformation
MRTS	Marginal rate of technical substitution
NAFTA	North American Free Trade Agreement
NGO	Non-governmental organization
NPV	Net present value
OECD	Organization for Economic Cooperation and Development
OLS	Ordinary least squares
PAYE	Pay as you earn
PBC	Political business cycles
PPBS	Planning programme-budgeting system
PRT	Progressive rent tax
PT	Partisan theory
RPBC	Rational political business cycles
RPT	Rational partisan theory
RRT	Resource rent tax
RST	Retail sales tax
SAF	Structural adjustment facility
SAVD	Specific or *ad valorem* duty
SDR	Shadow discount rate
SHS	Schanz-Haig-Simmons (Definition of Income)
SER	Shadow exchange rate
SOCC	Social opportunity cost of capital
SRTP	Social rate of time preference
SWR	Shadow wage rate
TRA86	Tax Reform Act of 1986 (United States)
UNDP	United Nations Development Programme
UNIDO	United Nations Industrial Development Organization
VAT	Value-added tax
WTO	World Trade Organization
ZBB	Zero-base budgeting

Chapter One

Introduction to Public Sector Economics

Government plays a very important role in all market economies. In recent times public finance economists have been concerned about the extent of government involvement in developing countries. The analytical focus of this work is the economics of the public sector, with special reference to developing countries. The book does not attempt to provide a detailed review of the fiscal systems of these countries. As in existing textbooks, the received fiscal theory is discussed and the constraints on its application to developing countries are shown. Specific country experiences are described in various chapters.

The term *public sector economics* is used here interchangeably with *public finance* and *public economics*. I have never been able to rationalize the distinction between these terms. It is generally recognized that public finance is an older term emphasizing the taxation side of the budget, although it is now also used to discuss the determination and impact of fiscal expenditures. Generally speaking, public sector economics can be defined as the impact of government revenues and expenditures on economic activity. The sources of revenue, as well as the factors influencing public expenditures, also constitute a substantial component of public sector economics.

The objective of this chapter is to provide the conceptual framework to understand the rationale for government intervention in a market economy. The concepts of Pareto optimality and market failure are discussed. Some consideration is given to the constraints on public policy in developing countries. The chapter closes with a brief description of fiscal instruments and government operations. This overview sets the stage for more detailed investigations into the nature of public goods, public expenditure and taxation policies.

PARETO OPTIMALITY

The starting point of my analysis of government intervention is the assumption of a free-market economy. That is, the conventional theory sets out the conditions for the functioning of efficient markets in the absence of government, as well as the reasons for departures from these efficiency conditions. Only then can we provide an economic rationale for the intervention of government. This approach is entirely neoclassical in its orientation, with its overriding emphasis on the efficiency of resource allocation. The discussion of Pareto optimality is not intended to be mathematically rigorous. Microeconomic textbooks already provide excellent derivations of the Pareto optimal conditions. The reader is also referred to Kogiku (1971), and Brown and Jackson (1990).

Pareto optimality is defined as an allocation of resources such that no individual can be made better off without another person being made worse off.[1] This efficiency model makes highly restrictive assumptions. First, there must exist "a full set of markets for all relevant dates in the future and for all risks" (Atkinson and Stiglitz 1980: 7). Second, there should be no externalities in the utility function of the consumer or the production function of the firm. Third, market prices are known with certainty and perfect information should exist in all markets. Fourth, consumers maximize utility and their indifference curves are characterized by diminishing marginal rates of substitution. The factors of production have positive marginal products and operate in the context of a given state of knowledge and technology. These assumptions are guaranteed under perfect competition which ensures that consumers and firms are price takers and that price equals marginal cost. Departures from the $P = MC$ rule are Pareto inefficient. The standard model assumes for analytical convenience two products and two factors of production.

There are three necessary conditions for Pareto optimality: efficiency in consumption, efficiency in production and optimal allocation of output. Under perfect competition, these conditions are satisfied when the following rules are applied:

1. The marginal rate of substitution (*MRS*) between two goods must be the same for the two consumers who buy those goods. That is, $MRS_{xy}^{1} = MRS_{xy}^{2}$ where x and y denote the two goods and the superscripts denote the first and second consumer.
2. The marginal rates of technical substitution (*MRTS*) between two factors of production, must be the same in the production of goods x and y. That is, $MRTS_{lk}^{x} = MRT_{lk}^{y}$ where l denotes labour and k denotes capital.
3. The marginal rate of transformation (*MRT*) for goods x and y must equal the MRS_{xy} for the two consumers, the $MRTS_{lk}$ and the price ratio. That is, $MRT_{xy} = MRS_{xy}^{1} = MRS_{xy}^{2} = MRTS_{lk} = P_x/P_y$

These marginal conditions are based on static assumptions and full employment of the factors of production. Pareto optimality also ignores the income distribution. The inability of the economy to achieve a Pareto-efficient allocation is known as market failure. To the extent that perfect competition does not apply in most real world situations, Pareto optimality can be regarded as an ideal state.

SOURCES OF MARKET FAILURE

Market failure is said to exist when the Pareto optimality conditions break down. That is, consumers can no longer equalize their marginal rates of substitution, and producers offer goods for sale at prices higher than the marginal costs of production. Market failure is widespread in developing countries. In these economies goods and factor markets are in a state of disequilibrium leading to inefficiency in the allocation of resources. Goods markets are characterized by shortages and surpluses, while factor markets exhibit high levels of unemployment and capital scarcities. In most cases the market price does not reflect the marginal costs of production.

Imperfect Competition

Imperfect competition is a cause of market failure. Under this market structure the firm faces a downward-sloping demand curve for its product. Marginal revenue diverges from average revenue and price no longer equals marginal cost. In this scenario a monopolist charges a price that exceeds marginal cost, in order to maximize profit. This leads to an output which is much lower than produced by the perfectly competitive firm, operating under similar cost conditions. The consumer has no sovereignty in terms of resource allocation under monopoly. The operation of the monopolist is said to be inefficient because it leads to a less than optimal allocation of resources.

Natural monopolies and other firms that experience decreasing average costs over a wide range of output are a source of market failure. An unregulated natural monopoly fixes its output at a price that is greater than marginal cost. This output level is not Pareto optimal. If the firm attempts to price its product at marginal cost, the loss has to be financed either by taxation or price discrimination. The pricing policies of natural monopolies are examined more closely in chapter 8.

The same tendency for price to diverge from marginal cost is seen in market situations dominated by oligopolies and multinational corporations (MNCs) in developing countries. Oligopoly is a market structure characterized by a few firms. Although each firm has market power, the alteration of price by one firm causes a response by other firms. The activities of firms are therefore interdependent. No single model can be advanced to explain the reaction of firms to changes in price, and different models exist. There is no guarantee, however, that the market mechanism will equate price to marginal cost under oligopoly.

MNCs are overseas extensions of oligopolies, which originate in most cases in highly industrialized countries.[2] Domestic markets do not determine the price of the products of MNCs in developing countries. These firms allocate resources to maximize global profitability. The neoclassical marginalist analysis, with its emphasis on marginal cost pricing, disregards international transfers of technology and problems which arise from foreign ownership and control of developing economies. MNCs use transfer pricing, which is a form of pricing to facilitate the movement of materials between subsidiaries in order to maximize profits and minimize tax liabilities. Transfer pricing is discussed in more detail in chapter 16. Since MNCs allocate resources globally rather than nationally, their pricing strategy is independent of the domestic price mechanism. This is a source of domestic market failure. The high level of incalculability in their pricing means that the value of sales between subsidiaries is also manipulated. As a result it is very difficult for governments to tax these firms in a manner that would ensure a fair and efficient contribution to government revenue. Girvan (1971) and Plasschaert (1979) give detailed analyses of the pricing strategies of the MNCs.

Public Goods and Externalities

Public goods are those goods and services which exhibit the characteristics of non-rivalry in consumption and non-excludability. The literature makes the distinction between pure and impure public goods. The latter exhibits partial rivalry in consumption. Public goods include defence, national parks, weather advisories, agricultural extension services and so forth. Non-rivalry in consumption implies that one person's consumption of the good does not reduce the utility of the good to others. Non-excludability means that it is impossible to exclude any persons from benefiting from the good, as long as the good is available. These two conditions imply that the market will not be able to provide the goods or services efficiently, since markets function by excluding individuals who cannot pay for the good. Budgetary provision of public goods is therefore required in the presence of market failure.

Externalities exist when the activity of one economic agent affects the utility or production of another without being priced. Beneficial external effects are known as positive externalities. External diseconomies or negative externalities are costs which are borne by consumers or producers. Public goods such as publicly funded medical research and education are a source of positive externalities. Pollution is the classic case of negative externalities. The market or the price system cannot reflect these external costs and benefits. This provides a rationale for government intervention, either to promote positive externalities or regulate negative externalities. Public goods and externalities are discussed in more detail in chapter 2.

Institutional Failure

Gillis, Perkins and Roemer (1992) have identified institutional failure as a leading cause of market failure in developing countries. This is based on the view that underdeveloped institutions exclude many persons from the market. In many countries money and capital markets are small and underdeveloped, and are inefficient mobilizers of savings. Further, money markets in these countries do not respond quickly to interest rate signals.

Gillis, Perkins and Roemer. (1992: 540) also regard institutional failure as a cause of environmental degradation in developing countries. They argue that even though governments own the property rights over most of the forest areas in developing countries, they are incapable of enforcing regulations in these areas. The forest becomes a common property resource. This institutional arrangement leads to extensive damage of the forest areas. The market mechanism is unable to regulate the use of common property resources. This market failure is sometimes known as the "tragedy of the commons". See, for example, Brown and Jackson (1990: 30–33) for a discussion of government intervention in the case of common property resources.

Information Failure

Perfect competition, which guarantees Pareto optimality, assumes perfect knowledge of goods and prices in the market. In many developing countries consumers and workers have incomplete knowledge of goods and services and job opportunities. Gillis, Perkins and Roemer (1992: 104) indicate that investors, producers and traders are unable to hedge against risks because financial, commodity, and insurance markets are underdeveloped or missing. A reduction in market inefficiency can be achieved if government intervenes to provide the infrastructural facilities to ensure the development of money and capital markets. Some developing countries have pursued the policy of liberalizing inefficient markets. Economic liberalization is discussed in chapter 12.

Stiglitz (1994) discusses the problems of imperfect information or incomplete markets in the context of money and financial markets. He argues that some degree of government intervention can improve the efficiency of financial markets in developing countries. Investors are concerned about the solvency and management of financial institutions. In some cases information about these variables is difficult to obtain. Appropriate monitoring of the management performance of firms by the state can improve market efficiency.

Two other types of information failure stem from the problems of moral hazard and adverse selection. For example, in the market for insurance information, failure can result from the fact that those individuals taking out insurance have information that insurers do not possess. This leads to a less than optimal allocation of resources. The first type of problem is that of moral hazard. A person insured against illness may overuse medical facilities because his private marginal cost may be less than the social cost of providing the facility. As a result, insurers may increase costs to all persons thereby leading to market failure.

Adverse selection occurs in insurance when the insurer cannot distinguish between high risk and low risk individuals based on the information available to him or her. The insurer ends up with an adverse selection of persons, and it may be necessary to devise different premiums in an attempt to deal with different risk factors. Information failure may also occur in stock markets where insider trading, which is a strategy for minimizing risks, may prevent the market from achieving an efficient allocation among traders. Insider trading occurs when a privileged group of individuals has access to stock market information which other traders do not have.

Inman (1987: 660) has discussed the types of market institutions to overcome the problem of informational asymmetries. First, contingent contracts such as warranties can be offered whereby the good is paid for only if the quality of the commodity reaches a previously defined standard. He argues that contracts may act as signals for seller characteristics. Government certification of sellers is another way of dealing with market failure. This requires that certification be costless, leading most qualified sellers to become certified, thereby resulting in market efficiency. Certification can be regarded as a public good with positive externalities, providing information about sellers to consumers in the market.

CONSTRAINTS ON PUBLIC POLICY

We have discussed some of the sources of market failure in developing countries. This section looks briefly at the principal structural and institutional problems which impose serious constraints on public policy in developing countries, and the attainment of economic efficiency. According to Gandhi (1987b: 13), developing countries have special circumstances which make the neoclassical model of efficient resource allocation difficult to apply to real situations. He notes that many of these countries suffer from the following well-known economic disadvantages:

1. A highly skewed distribution of income
2. High levels of absolute poverty
3. High levels of structural unemployment
4. Instability of export prices
5. Lack of adequate infrastructure
6. A deficiency of adequate human resources.

These structural characteristics mean that public policy has to focus on a wide range of issues besides the attainment of static efficient resource allocation.

In addition to the above economic problems, two important constraints on public policy discussed by Howard (1992: 8–13) are size and

7

foreign exchange. In small countries, size limits the range of policy options available to government. Further, the size constraint operates by limiting the size of the domestic market, and the economy is forced to look outward to generate its growth dynamic. Howard also argues that small size may increase the administrative costs of government because of the lack of economies of scale in public administration.

Most developing countries suffer from a balance of payments or foreign exchange constraint. The rate at which government can increase its expenditure growth is limited by the country's ability to earn foreign exchange. Excessive government spending, not supported by an expansion in export earnings or an inflow of capital from abroad, may lead to serious balance of payments problems.

An effective constraint on the impact of public policy in many developing countries is the presence of large "underground" or "informal" economies.[3] Primarily because of the high level of illegal trading and self-employment, it is difficult for government to collect taxes from the underground economy. Chapter 20 analyses the serious problem of tax evasion in developing countries. In addition, illegal foreign exchange transactions in the underground economy limit the flow of foreign exchange into the official economy. The presence of large informal economic transactions makes it difficult for governments to plan their economies on a long-term basis. Development plans are usually public sector plans rather than plans which incorporate private sector investment decisions.

FISCAL INSTRUMENTS

In the context of the constraints outlined above, governments in developing countries use basically the same fiscal instruments as governments in developed countries. The fiscal instruments used by governments on the revenue side are taxes, licences and fees, loans from external institutions and domestic borrowing. Of these instruments, taxes constitute the major part of government's domestic revenue and help to transfer resources from the private sector to the public sector. Increased borrowing is required when expenditures exceed tax revenues. Various types of taxes and borrowing will be discussed in detail in later chapters.

On the expenditure side, the major fiscal instruments are expenditure on goods and services, transfer payments and net lending. Government expenditures can be categorized as either current or capital expenditures.

Current expenditures finance the housekeeping activities of government and include wages and salaries, transfer payments and outlays on a wide range of services and goods. Capital expenditures are outlays on fixed assets such as buildings and equipment, and they contribute to overall investment in the economy. Subsequent chapters will analyse the determinants of government expenditures.

The current account deficit or surplus is calculated by subtracting current revenue from current expenditure. If the current account records a surplus, this is a measure of government saving. The size of the overall fiscal deficit will depend on the magnitude of capital spending and net lending by government. The total budget deficit is financed by a combination of domestic and foreign financing. When liquidity in the domestic banking system is high, government may borrow more money from commercial banks. Net foreign financing is the difference between gross foreign borrowing and external amortization payments by the government to service the external debt. Deficit financing is further discussed in chapter 10.

SUMMARY

Public sector economics is concerned with the impact of government revenues and expenditures on economic activity. The standard approach to public sector economics starts with the no-government economy, and examines efficient resource allocation in such an economy. Market failure provides an important rationale for government intervention. Market failure is widespread in developing countries, and government has to deal with a wide range of economic issues which may not be as important for governments in highly industrialized economies. Some of the issues relate to the inefficiency of markets, missing markets, and low levels of institutional development. Small size, foreign exchange insufficiency, and the presence of large informal or underground economies impose serious constraints on the conduct of fiscal policy in developing countries.

Chapter Two

Public Goods and Externalities

T he analysis of public goods and externalities is pursued here in order to provide the conceptual framework for our examination of government intervention in both developed and developing countries. We have seen that public goods and externalities cause market failure. Public goods also generate externalities. This chapter discusses the concept of a pure public good, and the demand for various types of public goods. Some attention is devoted to the causes of externalities, the various types of externalities and the methods government can use to internalize externalities. This chapter highlights the main theoretical issues on these topics, but it is not intended to provide an exhaustive literature survey.

THE PUBLIC GOODS CONCEPT

This analysis briefly looks at the early contributions defining the concept of the polar case of a pure public good. Head (1972) summarizes the approaches to the problem by Samuelson (1954, 1955) and Musgrave (1959, 1969a). Steiner (1974) also provides an interesting discussion on collective goods. In more recent times, Oakland (1987) reviewed a wide range of situations affecting the provision of public goods. Some of these issues will be dealt with in the next section.

Samuelson's contributions to the theory of public goods in the 1950s initiated the modern discourse on the concept of a pure public good. Samuelson was concerned with the polar case of a pure public good which he described as being fully and equally consumed by all members of the relevant group. Musgrave (1959) describes the concept of pure social wants which are consumed in equal amounts by members of the society. Head (1972: 4) argues that the approaches of both Samuelson and Musgrave suggest that joint demand is a predominant characteristic of a pure public good.

The early debate established the following characteristics of the polar case of a public good.

1. Non-rivalry in consumption means that the same physical output of the public good is enjoyed by all members of the relevant group.
2. Non-excludability from consumption implies that it is not possible to prevent consumption of public goods by some, while allowing their consumption by others.
3. The public good is a source of externalities whereby "the full amount of the benefits spills over and can be enjoyed by all persons without payment" (Head 1972: 6).
4. The pure public good in the Samuelson case reveals "jointness" or "indivisibility" of supply in the sense that "any given unit of the good can be made available to all" (Head 1990: 178).

Dasgupta and Pearce (1978: 130) have criticized Head for the use of the term "joint supply" which refers historically to joint production supply. They argue that "joint supply"used by Head is really "joint user supply" or non-rivalry in consumption. However, from the previous quotation it seems to me that Head meant joint production supply. Dasgupta and Pearce further argue that the conditions for public goods given by Samuelson really refer to "user jointness". For a discussion of "joint supply" and "user jointness" see Buchanan (1966) and Samuelson (1969).

The original Musgrave/Samuelson polar case has been criticized on the grounds that few if any public goods and services correspond to the original definition. Defence has been often cited as the nearest approximation to the polar case. However, the polar case can be regarded as significant in the sense that it provides an ideal or standard against which one can analyse public goods in the real world. Musgrave's concept of a merit good has more operational significance than the polar case concept, especially in developing countries. Services such as health care, education, sanitation, low-cost housing and so forth are considered meritorious, and in many poor countries government has an obligation to provide them. Merit goods are subject to the exclusion principal, so that their allocation depends heavily on the political mechanism.

Steiner (1974) has advanced a provocative definition of collective goods. "Any publicly induced or provided collective good is a public good" (Steiner 1974: 247). A collective good can be a collective consumption good or a "bundle of goods and services"demanded by a "segment of the public" which cannot be provided by the free market. Public provision does not make a good a collective good, but "it provides an analytical framework for considering the various sources of public goods" (Steiner 1974: 248). Steiner goes on to classify public goods on the basis of (1) their externality characteristics; (2) those arising from imperfections in the market mechanism which lead to market failure; and (3) those arising from the nature of the environment of the society, including national defence, law and order, and public health. Steiner's broad definition would include all those goods demanded collectively by different segments of the population. These would include impure public goods and local public goods.

The analysis of public goods spans an extensive literature. Our approach in the following sections summarizes and interprets the principal aspects of the public goods theory. We also hope to draw some implications of the theory for developing countries. The issues to be discussed concern the demand for public goods, conditions for the optimal provision of public goods, impure public goods, the theory of clubs, and the Tiebout model.

DEMAND FOR PUBLIC GOODS

Most textbooks compare in some detail the demand for public goods with the demand for private goods using partial-equilibrium analysis. The demand for private goods is based on the competitive market clearing model where market demand is found by summing horizontally the individual demand curves. A single equilibrium price prevails on the market, and consumers have different effective demands for the good. Goods are assumed to be divisible and the price mechanism can exclude individuals who are unable to pay.

Public goods, as we have seen, are subject to the non-excludability principle. The demand for public goods is found by adding the demand curves vertically. The demand curves reflect consumers' willingness to pay a particular tax price for the public good. Samuelson has described these curves as "pseudo-demand curves" or "marginal rates of substitution curves", because they assume that each person reveals his willingness to pay for the output of the public good. Equilibrium is found when the total willingness to pay equals the tax price of the public good. This equilibrium therefore reflects the summation of the marginal rates of substitution which is equal to the marginal rate of transformation. In a real world situation, the estimation of "pseudo-demand curves" in the large group case would require considerable information which it may be impossible to provide. Estimation of demand is compounded by the free-rider problem which arises when individuals do not reveal their preferences, but still consume the public goods. It is difficult to force all individuals to reveal their true preferences. Sometimes compulsory taxation is necessary to finance the provision of the public good.

OPTIMAL PROVISION OF PUBLIC GOODS

Samuelson (1955) advanced a model of the optimal provision of public goods, which was a neoclassical formulation influenced by the earlier work of Wicksell and Lindahl. Samuelson argued that in the two-good case where one good is public, efficient allocation requires that

$$MRS_{xg}^1 + MRS_{xg}^2 = MRT_{xg}$$

where x = private good
       g = public good

This is compared to Pareto optimality for private goods which requires that

$$MRS_{xy}^1 + MRS_{xg}^2 = MRT_{xy}$$

where x and y are private goods.

Kogiku (1971: 115–16) has shown that the above Samuelson efficiency conditions can be derived if the first individual's utility function is maximized subject to the second individual's utility being held constant, and subject to the implicit production function. The model assumes two

13

consumers, and one private good and a public good. Brown and Jackson (1990: 70) also give a diagrammatic derivation of the Samuelson conditions.

The Samuelson efficiency conditions rest on certain highly restrictive assumptions. First, the model assumes the existence of a planner who knows the tax prices each individual is willing to pay for public goods. That is, the planner must have information on the pseudo-demand curves of the individuals. Second, since the model assumes preference revelation by individuals, it takes no account of the free-rider problem. Third, the model is subject to information failure since the costs of collecting information in the large group case would be prohibitive.

Wicksell and Lindahl's approach to public goods provision was based on the benefit principle of taxation which states that people should pay taxes in relation to the benefits they receive from the consumption of public goods. The Wicksell/Lindahl approach was normative in that it attempted to determine a just level of the supply of the public good based on a just distribution of the tax burden among individuals. According to Musgrave (1985: 13), the Wicksell model begins with a just distribution of income, which is necessary for the voting process to arrive at a just and efficient distribution of tax prices. Voting for tax shares and goods in the Wicksell model is based on the unanimity rule whereby a hundred percent voter support is required. However, given the difficulties which would arise from the application of this rule, Wicksell acknowledges that approximate unanimity would suffice (Musgrave 1985; Musgrave and Peacock 1964: 92).

Lindahl was concerned with finding an equilibrium which would reflect just tax shares and public good output. Our discussion of the Lindahl equilibrium leans on Musgrave (1985: 10). Lindahl assumes two consumers who determine their tax shares through a tatonnement process. Unanimous agreement is assumed. The higher the proportion of tax paid by A the lower the proportion paid by B. The tax shares are plotted along A's demand curve which B views as a supply curve for the public good. The intersection of the two demand curves determine the equilibrium quantity of the public good and equilibrium tax shares. The sum of the two tax prices equals the cost of providing the public good.

The Lindahl equilibrium, like the Samuelson model, is based on the view that individuals reveal their preferences. The failure of individuals to reveal their preferences becomes a problem in the large-group case. Also, Lindahl's assumption of unanimous agreement among individuals may not be realistic for large communities. Further, Rubinfeld (1987: 679) has maintained that the unanimity rule grants a veto to the low demand individual "who can stop the process unless compensated by a lower tax share". Assuming an auctioneer regulates the voting process, the low demand veto can manipulate the auctioneer.

IMPURE PUBLIC GOODS
AND THE THEORY OF CLUBS

The concept of an impure public good lies between the case of the private good, where exclusion and rivalry in consumption are possible, and the pure public good subject to non-rivalry in consumption and non-excludability. The impure public good contains elements of both. Impure public goods can be non-rival in consumption, but after a certain point these goods become congested, and sometimes are known as congested public goods. Goods such as highways and other public facilities are subject to congestion as more persons use the service.

Local public goods and public intermediate goods are two other forms of impure public goods. The benefits of local public goods accrue to individuals located near to such goods. In some countries these goods are provided by local governments and financed by local taxation. The Tiebout model, discussed later, is concerned with the fiscal variables explaining why persons choose to live in certain local communities, which provide benefits and services in keeping with their preferences. By "voting with their feet" such individuals reveal their preferences. The Tiebout model is one of spatial mobility, and efficiency is achieved if it is assumed that individuals in the same community have similar tastes.

Public intermediate goods are inputs into the production processes of firms producing private goods for the general public or segments of the public. These include government information services, agricultural extension services and weather reports. It is difficult for the market mechanism to impose a price for these services. Oakland (1987: 493–94) has shown that the efficiency conditions for final public goods can apply to public intermediate goods. He advances a model assuming that each firm produces the same private good using an intermediate public good which is subject to non-rivalry in its use by other firms. Efficiency is attained by summing the marginal valuation of firms using the public good inputs. This compares with summing the marginal rates of substitution of consumers in the Samuelson model of pure public goods.

A club good is a special case of an impure public good. Tennis courts, swimming pools and golf courses are club goods for which exclusion is possible. Club goods can be privately owned and produced, or publicly owned and produced. The theory of clubs is concerned with the optimal output and congestion costs of club goods. According to Sandler and Tschirhart (1980: 1482) "club theory can also be used in determining the need for exclusionary zoning; the efficacy of bussing; and the optimal sizes of communities and cities".

Our analysis here presents the Buchanan model of clubs (Buchanan 1965), and summarizes some of the main issues in club theory (Sandler and Tschirhart 1980). Buchanan assumes that individual homogeneous members share the benefits and the costs of the club. Sandler and Tschirhart (1980: 1482) define a club as "a voluntary group deriving mutual benefit from sharing one or more of the following: production costs, the members characteristics, or a good characterized by excludable benefits". Buchanan attempts to determine the size of the most desirable cost- and consumption-sharing arrangement.

We now present the Buchanan model as summarized by Sandler and Tschirhart (1980: 1484). The model assumes an impure public good (*X*) and a *numeraire* good (*y*). The identical members denoted by (*s*) aim to maximize utility (*U*) subject to a cost constraint (*F*), where (*i*) represents the *i*th member. The problem is stated as follows:

$$\text{Maximize } U^i\ (y, X, s) \text{ subject to } F^i(y^i, X, s) = 0 \tag{1}$$

where y^i is the *i*th member's consumption of the private good, and $x^i = X$ for all *i*, where x^i is the utilization rate of the *i*th member. Marginal utility increases up to a point and then falls as more members join the club. Optimality requires the following first-order conditions:

$$MRS_{xy}^1 = MRT_{xy}^1 \tag{2}$$

$$MRS_{sy}^1 = MRT_{sy}^1 \tag{3}$$

Equation (2) is similar to the Samuelson condition for pure public goods. Equation (3) indicates the equality between the marginal benefits and marginal costs of having an additional club member.

The original theory of clubs has been modified to include heterogeneous membership and transaction costs, and the efficiency of mixed clubs. Oakland (1972) has dealt with the problem of congestion and exclusion costs. The literature on the theory of clubs and its applications is extensive. The club model is applicable to the optimal provision of public goods within communities (see Rubinfeld 1987).

THE TIEBOUT MODEL

The Tiebout model assumes a mobile population and communities, whose local governments offer public goods and services at minimum average costs which satisfy the individual's preference patterns. This local government model makes the following assumptions (see Tiebout 1990: 569).

1. Consumers are fully mobile and move to communities satisfying their preferences.
2. Consumers have perfect information on revenue and expenditures.
3. There is a large number of communities.
4. All individuals live on dividend income.
5. There are no external economies or diseconomies between communities.
6. There is an optimal commodity size. Communities below the optimum try to attract new residents to lower average costs. The converse is true for communities above the optimum.

Rubinfeld (1987: 575) has added additional assumptions to those above. These are that "public goods are financed by lump-sum taxation" and "there is no land, no housing, and therefore no capitalization". We found no evidence of the absence of land in the Tiebout model, because Tiebout assumed that some factor of production or resource is fixed. Tiebout maintained that the factor may be limited land area of a suburban community, or a local beach (Tiebout 1990: 569).

The original Tiebout model has been subject to a large number of criticisms particularly stemming from its highly restrictive assumptions. Buchanan and Goetz (1972), for example, criticize the model on the grounds that it disregards "locational fixity" and assumes the absence of "proprietary entrepreneurship". Brown and Jackson (1990: 260) argue that "the Tiebout equilibrium could be highly unstable if all factors are free to move". High set-up costs and adjustment costs may be necessary to create disincentives to move. The assumption of homogeneous labour is also unrealistic. Despite these criticisms, the Tiebout model may help to explain why some individuals move to zoned tourism enclaves or low-tax havens, and why governments provide a pattern of local public goods in these areas, to satisfy the demands of persons with similar, though not identical tastes.

EXTERNALITIES

In chapter 1 the concept of externalities was defined by closely differentiating between negative and positive externalities. It is appropriate to identify the reasons for externalities, different types of externalities, as well as methods for internalizing externalities. Externalities are internalized when the marginal value of the externality is priced, that is, when the private marginal costs of carrying out the activity are equal to the social costs resulting from the activity.

The lack of property rights, or difficulty in enforcing them constitutes a cause of externalities. Property rights consist of the right to use a resource or asset, to convert the asset or resource into an alternative use, or to sell the resource. In the case of common property resources, it is difficult to prevent other persons from using the resource. In the case of pollution for example, individuals cannot enforce rights to the use of the atmosphere.

There are three major types of externalities: producer-producer externalities, producer-consumer externalities and consumer-consumer externalities. Producer-producer externalities occur when the output or inputs used by one firm affect those employed by another, and the effect is unpriced. For example, the output of an upstream firm may pollute the water downstream, thereby destroying fishing resources and affecting the fishing industry. In developing countries the operation of hotels near the coast may lead to pollution of the marine resources, thereby damaging the fishing industry as well as underwater scenic beauty.

In the case of producer-consumer externalities the utility function of the consumer is dependent on the output of the producer. This type of externality occurs in the case of noise pollution by aircraft, and the effects of emissions from factories. Consumer-producer externalities are rare in practice, but involve the effects of consumer activities on a firm's output. The latter type of externalities are regarded as unimportant (see Dasgupta and Pearce 1978).

Consumer-consumer externalities occur when the activities of one consumer affects the utility of another consumer without being priced. According to Dasgupta and Pearce (1978: 120) a distinction must be made between "envy" and "non-envy" externalities. In an envy situation, there is a welfare loss because the consumer becomes envious of another consumer's acquisition of goods. In the non-envy situation, one consumer's utility is positively affected and he is likely to imitate the other consumer.

We can also distinguish between pecuniary and technological externalities. Technological externalities refer to the effects described above where the production function or utility function is affected. Following Dasgupta and Pearce (1978: 120), a pecuniary externality refers to output or utility effects on a third party due to changes in demand. These effects are reflected in changes in prices and profits of the producer, but do not alter the technological possibilities of production. A negative pecuniary externality can result when an increase in production of one industry causes an increase in the price of inputs used by other industries.

Externalities lead to a divergence between private benefits and social costs resulting in a breakdown in Pareto optimality. Government often has to intervene to correct negative externalities. Pigou (1920) suggested a method of internalizing externalities. His method known as the Pigouvian tax/subsidy solution is as follows: When marginal social benefits exceed marginal private benefits a subsidy should be paid to producers or consumers to allow for benefits not reflected in market demand. The subsidy leads to a reduction in the price of the commodity. When marginal social costs exceed marginal private costs a tax should be levied on producers. A tax causes an increase in the price of the commodity, and a reduction in the quantity demanded. As a result, producers suffer a welfare loss, and marginal social cost equals marginal private cost.

Government can also subsidize the producers to reduce damages. In this case the producer gains in terms of the subsidy, and the society gains in terms of the reduction in damages. However, the subsidy has to be financed which implies a tax on some segments of the population. It is sometimes argued that subsidization might encourage other firms to participate in the activity producing the negative externalities.

In some cases where property rights can be assigned to the party receiving the damages, the agent producing the diseconomy can be legally liable for the damage, and compensation can be paid to the damaged party. However, Coase (1960) has argued that in a world of complete information and zero transactions costs, the two agents can come to an efficient bargain for the level of the external activity, once property rights have been well established. In this case, the externality can be internalized without legal intervention, or government taxing the producer of the spillover. This solution is known as the Coase theorem.

The Coase theorem applies to a small-group case, and is most applicable in the case of two persons, assuming full information. The Coase theorem therefore has very limited application in the real world. Inman (1987) has argued that the Coase theorem is not a sufficient argument for no government intervention, and some form of "minimal state" is required to enforce property rights agreements.

Government can also deal with negative externalities by regulating the activity. This involves setting ceilings to permissible levels of pollution. In the United States, for example, considerable legislation is passed to increase quality control in industry, and to regulate noise pollution from aircraft, automotive emissions and so forth. Regulation also requires information and research, the costs of which are borne by the society. In addition, enforcement costs can be quite high.

The internalization of positive externalities requires subsidies. Governments in many developing countries subsidize higher education, because of the externalities in terms of increased earning capacity of the individual, and increased productivity in the economy as a whole. In highly developed countries subsidization of health research also yields social benefits to persons in developing countries.

APPLICATIONS TO DEVELOPING COUNTRIES

Let us consider a few applications of public goods theory and externalities to developing countries. Some of the views mentioned here are developed further in the chapters on the role of government, privatization and cost-benefit analysis.

Howard (1992: 4) has argued that though the provision of merit goods provides a case for government intervention, the modern arguments for privatization have led to some rethinking on public goods provision. Some public goods can be produced by the private sector operating through government contracts, but certain public goods such as specialized health services, refuse disposal and urban transport can be provided by the private sector. Many developing countries have been persuaded by the

International Monetary Fund (IMF) and World Bank to encourage private sector provision of certain services, because heavy state involvement in the past has led to huge fiscal deficits and balance of payments problems.

According to Dasgupta and Pearce (1978) the existence of public goods also have implications for cost-benefit analysis. This applies to developing countries where a large number of government projects comprise schools, sewage disposal plants, airports, highways and so forth. The provision of these goods has implications for government budgets. Financial resources have to be drawn from the private sector in the form of bonds and debentures, taxation or foreign borrowing. We argue in chapter 10 that different types of borrowing have implications for the balance of payments.

The existence of externalities also justifies the need for cost-benefit analysis. There has been great concern in the modern era over "ecological externalities" and sustainable development (see Gillis, Perkins and Roemer 1992: chap. 19). Some government projects can lead to the destruction of trees, producing ecological damage. Other projects like the building of highways can uproot people from their ancestral lands, resulting in negative social externalities. The same highways can encourage positive externalities in terms of enhancing commercial activity in the areas. External effects and public goods are therefore highly significant in the developing countries.

SUMMARY

The provision of public goods and the occurrence of externalities provide a rationale for government intervention. Many public goods can be provided by the private sector. Much of the literature is devoted to the optimal provision of public goods, although this theoretical approach may not be very rewarding in the real world. We noted that Musgrave's merit good concept may have more operational significance in developing countries. The externalities concept is very important especially in the context of ecological and environmental economics in developing countries. In these countries, considerable pressure is also placed on governments to produce positive externalities in education and health as well as infrastructure.

Governments can take certain measures to deal with negative externalities. In some cases a tax can be imposed on the producer of the externality in order to reduce the damage. In other cases compensation can be paid to affected parties. In circumstances involving small numbers, the individuals can arrive at a solution by bargaining. Charges and fees, as well as the imposition of quality control standards are also effective techniques for internalizing negative externalities. Governments should promote positive externalities, for example, the benefits of health research.

Chapter Three

The Role of Government in Market Economies

T his chapter looks at the role of government in both developed and developing countries. In chapter 1 we stated that market failure provided a rationale for government intervention. The market failure approach emphasized departures from economic efficiency. Government's role, according to this neoclassical view, is to ensure that the price mechanism works well and allocates resources efficiently.

Our analysis here starts with the views of economists who wrote in the context of developed industrialized economies. These include libertarians like Adam Smith and Nozick. Musgrave presents the neoclassical view suggested by the market failure approach. However, we are primarily interested in the writings of development economists on the role of government. We examine some of these views without claiming to provide a review of development policies or strategies. For such information the reader is referred to Gillis, Perkins and Roemer. (1992). The chapter closes with some comments on market-oriented development, and looks at privatization as one manifestation of this new approach to development thinking after 1980.

LIBERTARIAN VIEWS ON THE ROLE OF THE STATE

Adam Smith, the founder of classical economics, was a leading proponent of the pre-eminence of the market mechanism. According to Musgrave

(1985: 3), "the operation of the public sector, as developed by classical economists, is seen in the context of a natural order which calls for reliance on and non-interference with the market". Although Smith was against governmental interference with the market, he had a theory of government sometimes known as the "duties of the sovereign". The system of natural liberty required the sovereign to perform three duties: defence, the exact administration of justice, and the erection and maintenance of public works. Even though he was a libertarian, Smith realized that the market could not provide certain public goods which were too expensive for provision by private individuals.

An extreme libertarian view is that of Nozick (1974). He starts his analysis from the "state of nature" or pure anarchy. Man has individual rights but he also recognizes that other persons have the same basic rights. This recognition of the rights of others allows peaceful co-existence (Gordon 1976: 579). In this condition of anarchy, an agency called the state emerges with a monopoly of protective services. This is the minimal state. This state, because of free-rider problems, has to adopt coercive taxation to supply protective services. The minimal state offers only one public good, that of protection against force, theft, fraud, and enforcement of contracts. Any development of coercive power beyond the minimal state is illegitimate. Redistribution of income is limited to the finance of outlays on the only public good. Additional redistribution is illegitimate (see Gordon 1976: 580; Atkinson and Stiglitz 1980: 337). This concept of the state is a utopian view which completely ignores redistribution. We have mentioned it here in order to contrast it with more comprehensive realistic approaches discussed in the following sections.

The Neoclassical Role of Government

Musgrave (1959) identifies three functions of government: allocation, distribution and stabilization. The allocation role occurs when government intervenes to correct economic distortions caused by market failure. When the market fails to provide an adequate distribution of income, government's task is to redistribute income. Stabilization is necessary when the market is plagued by instability, unemployment and inflation. To the extent that Musgrave's three functions are a response to market failure, and are designed to guarantee economic efficiency, we can define this approach as the neoclassical role of government.

The allocation role of government is concerned with the attainment of static efficiency of resource allocation. Chapter 2 discussed how government needs to correct externalities and provide public goods and services which may not be efficiently provided by the private sector. Another area of government intervention concerns the use of common property resources for which property rights cannot be assigned. An example of a common property resource is pasture land where free access is guaranteed to each individual for cattle grazing. Common property resources are subject to overuse since each individual pursues his own self-interest. Common property resources deteriorate as the size of the users increases. The market mechanism fails to guarantee an optimum allocation of resources.

Pareto optimality says nothing about the prevailing distribution of income. In considering the distribution of income, we are concerned with the concept of equity or fairness. Economists speak of an equitable distribution of income. The income distribution depends on a country's history, laws of inheritance, education, social mobility, economic opportunity and other factors. In many developing countries, the legacy of slavery has been a major cause of the highly unequal income distribution.

Governments attempt to redistribute income by a wide range of fiscal measures. Social security and national insurance are systems whereby government provides pensions and other types of benefits such as sickness, unemployment and maternity. Such schemes have been established in many developing countries and are based on payroll taxes whereby the worker contributes part of his salary and the employer contributes a percentage of the required tax payment.

Government also redistributes income through its expenditure policy. For example, expenditure on education creates human capital and improves the earning capacity of the individual. Public expenditure on low-cost housing is a means of redistributing real income to the poor. The state can also interfere with the market mechanism by the provision of subsidies, price controls, and taxation of luxuries. The impact of indirect redistribution through the market is more difficult to quantify than the effects of direct expenditures or national insurance schemes. These measures are discussed in more detail in chapter 7.

Stabilization is a short-term function of governments and is the subject of intense theoretical discussion ranging from Keynesian to monetarist and new-classical prescriptions. Stabilization policy attempts to achieve an adequate trade-off between price stability, employment, balance of payments equilibrium and growth. In this section we briefly outline why stabilization is needed and the broad policies that can be adopted. Chapters 10 and 11 discuss budget deficits and stabilization policy in the context of developing countries.

Stabilization is vital in small, open economies which can be viewed as disequilibrium systems (Balassa 1982). Disequilibrium arises out of a number of situations. The terms of trade (the ratio of import to export prices) can deteriorate leading to a deficit in a country's trade balance. Excessive government spending and excessive consumption by citizens can also cause a drain in foreign exchange and balance of payments disequilibrium.

The government therefore has to adopt policies to correct the disequilibrium. Broadly speaking, there are two types of stabilization policies: demand management and supply-side policies. Demand-side policies attempt to reduce levels of domestic demand and spending. These include fiscal measures such as heavier taxation, and monetary policies such as credit restrictions and higher interest rates. Supply-side policies are designed to increase the volume of output in the community. These comprise measures to improve the efficiency of capital and labour. Demand management policies are short term, whereas supply-side adjustments are more long term, since they attempt to increase supply capacity through tax incentives, the better use of technology and so forth.

GOVERNMENT REGULATION

Regulation is often described as a separate function of government. Regulation can be defined as "the government (or the state) directly prescribing and proscribing what private sector agents can and cannot do, so that their actions do not contradict the public interest" (Chang 1997: 704). Government regulation in this sense is achieved through the implementation of rules sanctioned by legislation (Brown and Jackson 1990: 48).

A well-known theory of regulation is the so-called capture theory developed by Stigler (1971), Posner (1974) and Peltzman (1976). This theory advances the view that regulatory agencies are captured by interest groups including producers, consumers and public interest groups such as environmental lobbyists. The theory suggests that the regulatory agencies will promote the interests of producer groups rather than the public interest (Chang 1997). This allows producer lobbyists to pursue wealth maximizing activities which may lead to a misallocation of resources.

There are various aspects of government regulation and each area has an extensive literature. For instance, in chapter 9 we examine some issues in the regulation of public utilities. Financial regulation comprises legal constraints imposed on commercial banks and other financial institutions. These include stock market and credit controls observed by commercial banks (see Williams 1996; Stiglitz 1994). Labour market regulation involves measures to protect the rights of workers such as minimum-wage regulation, severance payment requirements and measures to regulate the length of the work week, holidays with pay and so forth. Our analysis in this section looks at the changes in the approach to regulation in the post–World War II period.

Chang (1997) identifies three phases of government regulation in the post–World War II period. These are the age of regulation (1945–70), the transition period (1970–80) and the age of deregulation (1980 to the present). These changes took place in both developed and developing countries.

The immediate post–World War II era was characterized by an increased involvement of the government in most economies. Frequent nationalizations and the growth of public enterprises were accompanied by increased regulatory practices especially in public utilities. The age of regulation also saw new developments in the theory of public goods, externalities and welfare economics which sanctioned increased state intervention and regulation.

According to Chang (1997: 708), the transition period (1970–80) "witnessed an upsurge in pro-market theories which challenged the postwar orthodoxy of 'regulated capitalism'". This period was characterized by economic crises in the world economy (for example, the economic problems caused by the "oil crisis" of 1974 and the economic recession of 1981) which led to a questioning of the theory of heavy state involvement. Moreover, state involvement led to "government failure" whereby governments became influenced by rent-seeking interest groups which diverted resources into wasteful activities. We will discuss in more detail the concept of "government failure" in a later section.

The early 1980s were characterized by a new emphasis on market-oriented development, structural adjustment, privatization and deregulation, as solutions to the massive government failures of the 1970s. This movement was also strong in the developing countries and was encouraged by institutions such as the IMF and World Bank that were involved in bailing out many developing countries which had encountered severe balance of payments and debt problems.

Chang (1997: 714–15) asserts that the impact of deregulation is difficult to assess because it took place at the same time as privatization and other structural adjustment policies. He argues that the United States and United Kingdom, two of the leading countries in deregulation, had not succeeded in markedly improving their economic performance after they implemented deregulation measures. Latin American countries such as Argentina, Bolivia and Mexico failed to raise their trend rates of growth. In subsequent sections, we consider in more detail the changes in the role of government in developing countries in relation to market-oriented development.

THE GROWTH AND DEVELOPMENT ROLE OF GOVERNMENT

Many development economists as well as some public finance economists have identified a growth and development role of government. Although some of the functions of government suggested by these economists can be subsumed under Musgrave's classification, the emphasis is on the institutional and structural factors which influence long-term development and growth. Development economists argue that development involves much more than static efficient resource allocation emphasized by the neoclassical economists. Distribution should also be regarded as part of the long-term development process. The development approach to the role of government has been stressed by Lewis (1955), Stiglitz (1996), Goode (1984), Howard (1992) and Tanzi (1991). Before discussing the development approach, it is necessary to elaborate the concepts of economic growth and development.

Meaning of Growth and Development

Rodney (1972) states that a society develops economically as its members jointly increase their capacity for dealing with the environment. This improved capacity depends on the application of science and technology and the organization of work. Rodney's definition of development also implies that human society has experienced constant economic development. Further, development is not a purely economic process since it involves social interaction in dealing with the environment. Rodney's approach is holistic in that it regards development as a process characterized by interaction between the mode of production and the superstructure of human society which includes social relations, classes, forms of government and sociopolitical institutions generally.

Rodney's analysis provides a general conceptual framework of reference. However, the concept of economic development used in this chapter is more specific and operational because it is intended to provide a guide for economic policy. Economic development is defined here as a dynamic process of structural change which guarantees a rise in real output, a more equitable income redistribution and increased welfare levels for the poor majority of the population. Structural change relates to the diversification of the productive base, reflecting a movement of factors of production and output among primary, secondary and tertiary economic activities (see also Howard 1989b, 1992).

Development also implies increased local decision making in the economy. The acquisition of a reasonable degree of local ownership and control of productive sectors aids the development process. Governments need to stimulate local entrepreneurship and mobilize domestic savings. However, the development process should not exclude foreign resources. External resources are necessary to provide foreign exchange and stimulate capital formation.

Economic growth is defined as the increase in real output. Economic development should guarantee growth, although growth by itself is not development. Endogenous growth theorists have been concerned with identifying the main sources of growth.[1] One of the main sources of growth is savings which accelerate the capital formation process. The propensity to save is determined by income levels, cultural patterns and the development of institutions to encourage the savings habit. An increase in thrift may stimulate investment if the savings are effectively mobilized, but too high a level of thrift may retard investment. Governments must also save by increasing the surplus on its current account. Governments therefore need to reduce wasteful expenditures. Dissaving by government leads to the printing of money to finance public sector activities. Money creation causes inflation and balance-of-payments deficits. If government imposes tax rates which are too high, these may also reduce the level of savings.

The accumulation of physical capital is not the only source of growth. Endogenous growth theorists devote considerable attention to the role of human capital. The development of human resources can lead to an outward shift in the production function. Human resource development depends on education and training, the use of information technology and so forth. Human resource development enables workers to become more productive thereby raising the level of real output.

29

Small, open economies also need foreign exchange to achieve reasonable rates of economic growth. Foreign exchange is necessary to supplement domestic savings and to finance imports. Such foreign exchange can be acquired through foreign borrowing. In an effort to accelerate their rates of economic growth, some developing countries import high levels of raw materials and capital goods. This sometimes leads to large balance of payments deficits and a depletion of foreign reserves. Severe losses of foreign exchange can cause economic embarrassment for developing countries, forcing them to seek assistance from the IMF. Developing countries should therefore attempt to achieve a growth rate which is consistent with their ability to earn foreign exchange.

The natural resource base of a country also provides a source of growth. However, it is the efficient use of these resources which determines the expansion of the production function. Some countries with huge petroleum and bauxite resources have low rates of economic growth. On the other hand, a country like Japan with a limited natural resource base has been one of the fastest growing economies since World War II.

Proponents of the Growth and Development Role of Government

The views of Lewis (1955), Tanzi (1991), Goode (1984) and Stiglitz (1996) are outlined here. Lewis (1955) saw the state as a catalyst for development by creating the appropriate institutions and incentives to stimulate the growth of a productive capitalist class. Capital accumulation depends on the institutions, values and beliefs of the society.[2] Lewis (1955: 57) observes that "institutions promote or restrict growth according to the protection they accord to effort, according to the opportunities they provide for specialization and according to the freedom of maneuver they permit".

Lewis regarded the safeguarding of property rights as a condition for capital formation. It was therefore necessary to protect private property from public abuse and public property from private abuse. He argues that without property "the human race would have made no progress whatsoever, since there would have been no incentive to improve the environment in which one lived" (Lewis 1955: 60). The importance of property rights and capital formation for economic growth is elaborated in his model of unlimited supplies of labour (see Howard 1989b: 9–11).

Lewis (1955: 376–77) lists nine functions of government which are relevant for economic growth and development. They are as follows:

"maintaining public services, influencing attitudes, shaping economic institutions, influencing the use of resources, influencing the distribution of income, controlling the quantity of money, controlling fluctuations, ensuring full employment and influencing the level of investment". Only two of these functions really differ from those in Musgrave's classification. These are the influencing of attitudes and shaping economic institutions. Lewis' real contribution to our understanding of the role of government therefore highlights the role of attitudes and institutions in public policy.

Tanzi (1991) regards economic growth as perhaps the most important objective of government in developing countries. "The developed countries do not have to concern themselves excessively with growth. To them stabilization and equity may be more worthwhile pursuits. For the developing countries, however, where per capita incomes are generally very low, growth must be the overriding objective" (Tanzi 1991: 11). Goode (1984) also stresses the importance of growth and development and outlines the types of strategies used to promote these objectives, including export promotion, tax incentives, investment in infrastructure and so forth.

Stiglitz (1996) sees the role of government in developing countries as establishing infrastructure in its broadest sense to allow markets to fulfill their central role in increasing wealth and living standards. This broad-based infrastructure includes six roles: promoting education, promoting technology, supporting the financial sector, investing in infrastructure, preventing physical degradation, and creating and maintaining a social safety net (Stiglitz 1996: 13–15). These roles apply to all types of economies. However, he believes that market failure is more severe in developing countries and as a result, these government policies are more urgent in correcting serious market failure.

GOVERNMENT FAILURE

The foregoing analyses emphasized the importance of government intervention as a means of correcting market failure as well as stimulating development and growth. However, government can also be inefficient. The imperfections of government can be described as government failure. Many government civil services are notoriously incompetent and some economists have noted the tendency for productivity in the government sector to remain constant compared with rising productivity in the private

31

sector. The causes of government failure are now discussed and suggestions made to improve the functioning of government.

One of the best known areas of government failure is short-sighted regulation. Government regulation may focus on a very specific area of activity without considering some of the social or environmental effects of the activity. Public transport may be regulated by creating bus terminals in certain city areas thereby leading to congestion and pollution problems.

Regulation may also impose significant implementation costs on the economy. These costs include the administrative costs of monitoring the system as well as the compliance costs imposed on individuals. Regulation costs can be financed by taxes which make some individuals worse off in terms of a reduction in welfare. Therefore, by interfering with the market mechanism, government may reduce the welfare of citizens. The failure of government regulation is often due to imperfect knowledge of the type of technology to apply in order to achieve the best results. Government may apply inappropriate and costly technology because of a lack of research on the part of the bureaucracy (see Albrecht 1983: 65).

Albrecht (1983: 62) puts forward a number of reasons to show why voter ignorance and short-sightedness are causes of government failure. When voters are ignorant of the real benefits and costs of public policies, they may oppose beneficial projects and support costly and inefficient ventures. Voter ignorance may lead to overspending and overtaxation. Voter ignorance persists because citizens do not have the time to carry out the type of research necessary to evaluate government projects. Additionally, many voters are myopic, preferring policies with short-run benefits. Politicians often present a package to the electorate with short-run goals such as the reduction in unemployment or the lowering of inflation, even though these objectives may impose a heavier tax burden on the electorate in the short run. Again, overspending may distort resource allocation.

Tollison (1982) analyses other causes of government failure stemming from the problems posed by special interest groups and lobbyists. These groups may be able to influence government to pass legislation or implement policies in their own interests rather than in the interests of the economy as a whole. Rent-seeking is an important activity of special interest groups. Rent can be defined as a return in excess of a resource owner's opportunity cost. Rent-seeking is a normal feature of economic activity in competitive markets. However, government can create rents for certain interest groups by granting legal rights to certain firms or individuals to pursue specified activities or perform certain services. For example, government can grant firms franchises to operate services, or licences to sell certain goods. Further, contracts can be assigned to particular businesses to build highways or implement housing projects. In this way, government creates property rights for favoured individuals which lead to barriers to enter certain industries or businesses.

Rent-seeking is the study of how various business interests compete for artificially created rents. Firms sometimes bribe government or spend large sums of money to induce public sector officials to give them the right to operate a service. Such competition often leads to a misallocation of scarce resources. Very often contracts and franchises are not rewarded to the lowest bidder, and government projects are allocated on the basis of political preference. Rent-seeking by monopoly interests is a cause of government failure.

Another cause of government failure is low productivity in the civil service and the lack of incentive for technological efficiency. Government inefficiency is characterized by bureaucratic red tape. The public sector in many ways resembles Baumol's non-progressive sector which experiences zero productivity growth. Baumol (1967) asserts that the labour intensive nature of public services offers less scope for technological change that improves productivity. Peacock (1979) has also observed that because of the non-profit nature of many government services there is a lack of incentive to introduce innovations.

Public sector reform has been advanced as a means to reduce government failure. Important suggestions have been made by Blackman (1992). First, there should be an upgrading in the quality of management in the public service in the Caribbean, with greater emphasis on strategic planning. Second, in public utilities and other productive services, efficiency can be increased by reducing political interference in day-to-day management. Third, productivity can be enhanced by the implementation of incentive systems based on productivity gains. This calls for the establishment of performance criteria for departments. Finally, the public sector in the Caribbean needs to improve its information system to ensure that relevant information is fed to managers to improve decision making.

GOVERNMENT AND MARKET-ORIENTED DEVELOPMENT

Rationale for Market-Oriented Development

The market-oriented approach to development is a worldwide strategy which gained ground in the 1980s as a response to government failure. The resurgence of the market was facilitated by the collapse of many socialist command economies. The command approach to development inhibited enterprise and slowed economic growth. In the contemporary period many governments have introduced deregulation measures, and there has been a pronounced movement towards privatization and liberalization of the market in developing countries. However, market-oriented development can only be accomplished if there is institutional reform. For example, property rights have to be enforced to enable markets to work efficiently.[3]

In developing countries, there were many factors which led to greater reliance on the market. First, the nationalization and state ownership which characterized the economies of the 1960s and 1970s did not work well (Howard 1992). State-owned corporations accumulated significant losses and were unable to adjust to the risks of a changing world economy. The inefficient management of these enterprises also contributed to large fiscal deficits forcing government to borrow heavily from abroad. The heavy regulation of the economies also encouraged corruption, as firms resorted to rent-seeking behaviour in order to acquire lucrative contracts from the governments.

The industrialization policies pursued were also too inward looking. These policies based on import substitution relied heavily on the protection of the domestic market by means of tariff barriers. It was found that with import substitution, the term used to describe the domestic production of a good which was previously imported, utilized large amounts of foreign exchange to import raw materials. Further, protectionism encouraged inefficient production because investors were sheltered from external competition. The market-oriented approach to development emphasizes outward-looking strategies to promote exports.[4]

The new emphasis on market-oriented development was also aided by the revival of neoclassical economics. Supply-side economists argued that the free flow of market forces and reduction in the size of government would lead to increased productivity and investment. Low tax rates and tax incentives to investors were necessary to stimulate investment. The neoclassical revival also led to a new emphasis on productive efficiency in order for firms to achieve higher levels of domestic and international competitiveness.

The process by which some developing countries have introduced market-oriented development is known as structural adjustment. The policy reforms include deregulation of the economy by the removal of price controls and subsidies and the removal of ceilings on interest rates, a process known as financial liberalization. The abolition or reduction of exchange rate controls and the sale of state enterprises to the private sector are all attempts to improve the functioning of the market mechanism. The purpose of structural adjustment is to increase overall productive and allocative efficiency and stimulate economic growth. This policy approach, which forms the basis of structural adjustment, is sometimes known as the "Washington Consensus" because it is strongly supported by the IMF and the World Bank. Some of the weaknesses of this paradigm are discussed in chapter 12.

Market-oriented development has been facilitated by the rise of globalization. This is a concept used to describe the integration of free markets, international capital transfers and information. Globalization also involves increased direct foreign investment. These trends in the world economy meant that government's economic policies had to be more outward looking, always attempting to increase international competitiveness.

Privatization and Efficiency

The process by which government sells 51 percent or more of certain properties to the private sector is known as privatization. This can be done by direct sale or through the selling of shares to the private sector. Privatization is an aspect of market-oriented development. Privatization attempts to reduce the size of government, relieve the public sector of burdensome enterprises and stimulate competition in the market. Privatization is therefore a partial solution to government failure. A weaker form of privatization can be achieved by contracting out certain government services to the private sector. The analysis here focuses on the theory and potential impact of privatization, rather than on detailed empirical investigation of privatization in various countries. Chapter 12 makes some observations on privatization in Mexico. For empirical analyses of other developing countries the reader is referred to Ramanadham (1989).

A central argument used to support privatization is the "inefficiency" of public enterprise. Various explanations for such "inefficiency" have been advanced by economists, such as Vernon-Wortzel and Wortzel (1989), Hanke (1987), and Hemming and Mansoor (1988). First, they argue that the performance of a state enterprise is not only a function of state ownership per se, but also a function of the type of management and the appropriate culture in the firm. Some state-owned enterprises function

35

efficiently. Nevertheless, the organizational culture of state enterprises tends to be government oriented rather than customer oriented. This is reflected in political interference in day-to-day decision making, which in many cases prevents public sector managers from pursuing strategic planning.

Second, a view is advanced from property rights theory. According to Hanke (1987), different forms of property ownership give rise to different economic incentives and different economic results. Private enterprises are free to use and exchange their private property rights, which give individual owners a claim on the assets of the enterprise. Private sector managers ultimately face the bottom line, which measures the profits or losses that owners claim. On the other hand, public managers and employers allocate assets that belong to taxpayers. Such managers do not bear the costs of their inefficient decisions, nor do they gain from efficient behaviour. Only the politicians are ultimately accountable to the taxpayers. The political interference and property rights theories are generally strong in explaining the managerial drawbacks of public enterprise. Privatization is seen as a means of improving the efficiency of enterprises by limiting the scope of political interference.

The main argument in support of privatization is that of efficiency. Property rights theory suggests that public enterprises operating in competitive markets should be privatized. The argument applies to manufacturing industries, airlines, and other competitive service industries. Competition provides greater incentive to private managers to increase allocative and productive efficiency.

The replacement of a public monopoly by a private monopoly may not necessarily lead to significant efficiency gains. However, it is generally recognized that privatization can reduce political interference and enhance the quality of management. In any case, a private monopoly in the field of public utilities has to be regulated, to guarantee social efficiency by way of equitable pricing arrangements.

The above arguments need some modification. Some governments are not inclined to privatize, by way of divestiture, enterprises which are profitable or socially efficient, where social efficiency is a highly valued objective. A socially efficient allocation is one which increases overall welfare. It is contended that privatization should be considered mainly for those commercial enterprises which have become a financial burden on the taxpayers. Continued maintenance of such loss-making enterprises also increases their financial inefficiency, because public sector firms have easy access to credit and government subsidies and are protected from competition.

There are also political constraints involved in privatization. The political directorate may regard certain public utilities as employment agencies. Privatization reduces such political influence. Trade unions, too, may fear that privatization would result in increased unemployment, thereby reducing their political influence. One must, therefore, address the political economy of privatization, rather than confine the analysis mainly to economic efficiency arguments.

Although economic theory gives general guidelines to privatization, the political decision to privatize an enterprise should be based on the application of specific economic and political criteria to the special case. Such criteria would include economic and social efficiency, financial viability, managerial performance, and the perceived impact of the privatized enterprise on employment, prices, and output.

Privatization may not be recommended for certain public goods or public utilities in small developing countries, where social efficiency is the objective function of government. This argument applies to the areas of water management, primary and secondary education, health and social security, sanitation, infrastructure and rural transport. These services are subject to market failure, and government has a responsibility to provide them in the interest of social efficiency and income distribution. The private sector can complement the government's provision by contracting certain services, for instance, low-cost housing.

The theory of property rights suggests that financial institutions develop more efficiently when left to the private sector. Historically, financial institutions tend to be more operationally efficient in competitive markets driven by the profit motive. However, a private development bank is not likely to be socially efficient if it attempts to maximize profits in pursuit of its shareholders' interests. Privatization of an ailing development bank may not be the solution to the problem of long-term development finance in small systems. Alternative solutions are necessary.

A number of lessons can be learnt from the British experience (see Wiltshire 1987). These are important for developing countries considering privatization. The first lesson of the British privatization process is the concept of "dressing up" the enterprise for sale. This involves restructuring the enterprise until it can compete in the private sector. Dressing up normally involves a cost, since revenues are taken from the consolidated fund. It also necessitates a redistribution of income from taxpayers to ultimate shareholders. However, in many developing countries, a government with a heavy fiscal deficit is not likely to undertake any substantial restructuring of an enterprise before sale. The dressing up process is also likely to encounter serious political opposition.

The other issue in the British experience concerns the price at which the enterprise is sold to the private sector. British enterprises were usually sold on the share sale method. Wiltshire (1987) maintains that this type of pricing has been intensely criticized because of the rapid rise in share prices after the sale. Criticism of the process implies that in order to give the privatization programme increased momentum, the British government undervalued the enterprises before sale by underpricing the shares.

Although the share sale method helps to broaden the structure of private ownership, as well as enable employee shareholding, there is one constraint on this method in small Caribbean countries. The share capital market is relatively small, and the countries' stock exchanges are embryonic. Therefore, if privatization is pursued on a large scale using this method, efforts will have to be made to increase the capacity of the markets to take the float. In the Caribbean the promotion of a regional stock exchange has been one step in the direction of overcoming the small size of national stock exchanges.

Another criticism of the British process is that privatization failed to ensure competition thereby appearing to convert public monopolies into private monopolies (Wiltshire 1987: 58–103). As we have seen an argument for privatization is that it increases efficiency by fostering competition. However, privatization of a public monopoly can hardly ensure increased competition. The possibility of increased competition after a privatization programme usually depends on the type of market in which the industry operates. In the case of developing economies, this will depend on whether the industry is import-substitutive or export-oriented, on the degree of protectionism offered to the industry in reducing external competition and so forth. Given the high levels of protectionism in Caribbean manufacturing, the greatest opportunities for competition offered by privatization seem to be in the area of services.

One disadvantage of privatization is that it may "sell the family silver". This means that the revenue from the sale of a public asset should not be placed in the consolidated fund, but should be earmarked for future generations and future public uses (Wiltshire 1987: xiii). There is some support for this position in developing countries, in the sense that a sale of real assets should not be used to finance current expenditures such as wages and salaries, but should be placed in a fund for further capital accumulation. The British experience also suggests that in the pursuit of privatization, the governments of small countries should adequately safeguard their national interest from foreign influences. Selling the family silver to the local private sector is preferable to selling a country's assets to foreigners.

SUMMARY

The allocation, stabilization and distribution roles of government identified by Musgrave are widely acceptable in public finance theory. We have included three other functions: regulation, growth and development. Even though Musgrave's classification has some applicability in developing countries, the growth and development roles of government appear to be more important. Issues such as human resource development, foreign exchange insufficiency, low rates of savings growth, widespread poverty, and limited institutional development are more important in the calculus of decision making in poor countries than in the rich. Although developing countries have to pursue some degree of efficient resource allocation, institutional and structural issues must be given priority. Governments in many developing countries have adopted a market-oriented approach to development in order to reform their economies, thereby reducing the heavy hand of the state in regulating economic activity. Some of the constraints on this approach will be considered in chapter 12.

Chapter Four

Public Choice

The focus of my discussion here is the theory of public choice from a developing country perspective. This approach to the analysis of the growth of government budgets, which was first developed in the United States, spans a wide literature. My analysis identifies the main elements of public choice theory to gauge whether it has any relevance in explaining budgetary outcomes in developing countries.

The public choice literature is heavily philosophical and qualitative in orientation, and is concerned with the application of economics to political analysis. The political business cycles theory, which is discussed in the next chapter, is more amenable to quantitative testing, and examines the economic behaviour of governments in election years, especially in exploiting the Phillips curve trade-off between inflation and unemployment. Political business cycles theory is an extension of public choice theory since it focuses on the interaction between economics and politics, by employing the Downs (1957) model of political parties. This chapter does not claim to be a survey of the literature on public choice theory. The reader is referred to Orchard and Stretton (1997) for a critical survey of this school of thought.

Are public choice theories relevant to the analysis of the economic behaviour of governments in developing economies with democratic political systems? How far can the institutional bias of public choice theory in the United States help us to understand political realities in these developing countries? This chapter helps to answer these questions.

I am not aware of much research done on public choice theory in developing countries. There are elements of public choice in the work of Jones (1987, 1992). He is concerned with the politico-administrative aspects of bureaucracy in the Caribbean, and the political influence of pressure groups in the colonial period. However, he does not identify his work as falling within the ambit of public choice theory. His contribution does not attempt to analyse the relationship between pressure groups and the determination of public goods, or the growth of public expenditure. It is hoped that my analysis will provide a framework for further work on the non-market approach to public goods determination in market economies.

PUBLIC CHOICE: DEFINITION AND SCOPE

Public choice theory is concerned with the positive analysis of public goods determination. Employing the definition of Boadway and Wildasin (1984:138), "it treats the political mechanism, especially voting behaviour as the means by which the preferences of individuals for public goods are rationally transmitted to policy makers and, as such, is an extension of economic analysis into political decision making". Buchanan and Tulloch (1962) are credited with being the founders of modern public choice theory. Buchanan and Tulloch examined the structure of American politics with a view to applying the tools of economics to political analysis.

The scope of public choice theory is quite broad. One aspect of the public choice approach focuses on voting models as the means by which individual interests of citizens are transformed into political outcomes. My presentation also discusses log rolling or vote trading, the role of political parties, interest groups, and the importance of bureaucracy as determinants of the provision of public goods. Much of the work on public choice has been done in the United States and the assumptions of a large part of the theory relate to social and political institutions in the United States. Political theories of economics have also generated some influence in the United Kingdom.

The major assumption of public choice theory is that voters, politicians, bureaucrats, interest groups and rent-seekers are motivated primarily by self-interest (Orchard and Stretton 1997). Voters put pressure on government to reduce taxes and grant higher subsidies and welfare. Bureaucrats desire increased perquisites and status. Politicians aim to maximize votes and power. Interest groups and rent-seekers demand special favours from government. These demands lead to budget maximization and higher government spending. Budget maximization may also result in inefficient allocation of resources and government failure.

In the neoclassical price-auction model, individuals and firms are also motivated by self-interest in the sense that individuals maximize utility and firms maximize profits. This model results in an efficient allocation of resources in the provision of private goods. Given their characteristics, most public goods cannot be efficiently provided by the market mechanism, and government becomes a substitute for the market. Non-market provision of public goods causes competition for political influence by various interest groups. Government also becomes a utility maximizer. Government failure has led some economists to argue that some public goods may be allocated efficiently by the market mechanism, thereby reducing the political influence of rent-seekers and pressure groups. Deregulation and privatization in the contemporary period are consequences of government failure.

Central to the work of Buchanan and Tulloch (1962) is the concept of the "fiscal constitution". The view of Jackson (1993:26) is that "a fiscal constitution can be thought of as a set of policy rules: but a set which is bounded by an appeal to notions of justice, liberty and freedom". The rules defining the fiscal constitution are chosen under conditions of uncertainty. This means that the rules must be chosen to minimize risks for individuals. The rules should also be based on a clear concept of justice. Fiscal constitutional rules therefore set certain limits on the political process. Buchanan and Tulloch looked at the economic aspects of the American constitution with a view to analysing the economic implications of certain voting rules.

Buchanan and Flowers (1975) have applied the notion of fiscal constitution to the determinants of tax share choices in a democracy. Tax shares are constitutional in the sense that taxes are "quasi-permanent" fiscal devices. Tax structures should be conceived as inherent parts of a fiscal constitution which must guarantee that taxation is equitable. In this respect, Buchanan's emphasis on justice as a determinant of the rules of the fiscal constitution is a precursor to Rawls' (1971) theory of justice. In Rawls' view, the distribution that is justifiable is one which maximizes the benefits to those individuals who are most disadvantaged in the society. Political authorities will therefore select a set of constitutional rules for taxation which will not penalize unduly persons in unfavourable positions. These rules will determine the degree of progressive taxation and the balance between direct and indirect taxation.

THEORIES OF PUBLIC CHOICE

Majority Voting and Cyclical Majorities

This section outlines the simple textbook model of majority voting and the problem of cyclical majorities. My exposition closely follows that of Buchanan and Flowers (1975: 113–16). The purpose of majority voting is to determine a political equilibrium for the provision of public goods according to established constitutional rules.

Let us assume a three-person community with individuals V_1 V_2 and V_3. They vote on three alternative proposals as follows:

- Proposal A – spend nothing on a school
- Proposal B – spend $1,000 on a school
- Proposal C – spend $2,000 on a school

The three voters have an ordinal preference ranking. Individual V_3 prefers proposal C, and he prefers the middle proposal to no spending at all. Individual V_2 prefers the middle spending proposal B to each of the other extremes. Individual V_1 prefers proposal A but he would vote for proposal B if for some reason proposal A is unattainable.

An individual's preference is said to be single-peaked, if as he or she moves away from the most preferred outcome, his or her utility falls consistently. Proposal B will gain the majority of the votes against all other proposals. If put against C, both V_2 and V_3 will vote for B. If put against A, both V_1 and V_2 will vote for B. Hence majority voting will favour B. The preferences of V_2 are therefore median for the group of voters. V_2 is therefore the median voter. As a result, a political equilibrium will be reached because proposal B (spending $1,000 on a school) will be chosen.

The model outlined above is known as the median voter theorem. It states that if all preferences are single-peaked, the result of majority voting will reflect the preference of the median voter. The median voter theorem holds if the voter's preferences are transitive. If a person's preferences are double-peaked or multiple-peaked, a phenomenon known as cycling will occur, and the process will not lead to a majority vote. If a voter prefers A to B and C to B his preferences will be double-peaked.

The median voter theorem has been used to investigate the demand for public goods and the growth of public expenditure. Following Atkinson and Stiglitz (1980: 322–26), the standard model investigated is

$$Log\ G = a + b\ log\ Y_m + c\ log\ P_m$$

where G is the level of public spending, Y_m is the after tax income of the median voter, and P_m the price of the public good to the median voter.

Atkinson and Stiglitz (1980) and Jackson (1993) have identified a number of problems associated with the estimation of this model. The first problem is that of identifying the median voter. Even though the median voter earns the median income, differences in taste may lead to different voting behaviour by the median voter. Jackson (1993) sees the median voter model as a crude approximation to political behaviour which does not capture the essence of complex voting systems.

The second problem is that of measuring the price of the public good, that is, the cost to the median voter of purchasing an extra unit of G. This depends on the tax share of the median voter. The tax share of the median voter will be determined by distortions in the tax structure and may not affect the price of public goods.

Third, Romer and Rosenthal (1979) have argued that the model is rarely set against an explicit alternative. Despite these criticisms, studies have been carried out by Bocherding and Deacon (1972) and Bergstrom and Goodman (1973) using the median voter model.

Bureaucracy

Public choice theory departs from the view of the bureaucrat who always obeys orders and carries out instructions relating to the budget/expenditure process. The approach adopted to the study of bureaucracy is that bureaucrats are utility maximizers. Niskanen (1971) advanced a model of bureaucracy which employed a utility managerial function approach. The bureaucrat's utility function includes his salary, his public reputation, perquisites, and power. Since these components of the bureaucrat's utility function also relate to the size of the budget, Niskanen's theory holds that bureaucrats are also budget maximizers.

Buchanan and Flowers (1975) have argued that the most useful framework for understanding the operation of bureaucracy is one which allows comparison of the supply characteristics of public versus private sector production. These sectors are characterized by three important differences. First, public bureaus do not compete in supplying the same service. Second, government bureaucracies do not operate for profit. Third, public services are produced by lump-sum taxes. The lack of competition to supply goods by public bureaus leads to reduced incentive for the production of the service. Bureaucrats, therefore, do not maximize profits but maximize their own utility. Bureaucrats become monopoly suppliers of public services which lead to allocative inefficiency as a result of the excessive supply of these services. Thus, the absence of competition in the public sector supports Niskanen's model.

Jackson (1993) has criticized Niskanen's model as being too crude. Bureaucrats serve the public interest, in the Weberian model, just as much as they serve their own interests. Brown and Jackson (1990: 202) have argued that in the United Kingdom bureaucratic salaries do not depend upon the size of the budget administered by top civil servants. In the Caribbean, top civil servants generally carry out instructions handed down by ministers of government. In Barbados, in the context of an incomes protocol during the 1990s, top civil servants had no influence on the determination of their own salaries.

Niskanen's approach has been developed by Romer and Rosenthal (1979) in a study which shows how bureaucrats will develop a budget proposal to put before voters, and thereby influence the size of the budget. This model advances the view that "bureaucrats who spend the money not only prefer to maximize expenditures but also achieve considerable monopoly power over the alternative expenditures available to the political decision makers, legislators, or voters" (Romer and Rosenthal 1979: 563). This monopoly model is developed in the context of "direct democracy" referendum voting on public expenditures. In this model, bureaucrats control the referendum voting agenda, and voters have a choice between the bureau's proposal or some institutional defined "reversion expenditure". The "reversion point" may be the current level of expenditure or some alternative level of expenditure if the proposed expenditure level by the bureau fails to command the majority vote (Romer and Rosenthal 1979: 566).

Like the Niskanen model, Romer and Rosenthal's monopoly model of bureaucracy is irrelevant for the Caribbean. Referendum voting on public expenditures is not a feature of the Caribbean political environment. This approach may have more relevance to referendum voting in municipalities in the United States, but not in the Caribbean where expenditures are controlled by ministers of finance according to rules governing the fiscal constitution.

The role of Caribbean bureaucracies in influencing the growth of public expenditure cannot be understood without a firm grasp of the operation of the Westminster-Whitehall model of bureaucracy. This model imported from Britain during the colonial period, essentially carried out decisions made by ministers and therefore facilitated the provision of public goods. The model was not an entrepreneurial model as sometimes suggested for the operation of bureaucracy in American public choice theory. That theory assumes bureaucrats have a high degree of autonomy. Jones (1992) used the historical method to interpret the role of the Westminster-Whitehall model in the contemporary era. Jones' analysis is more concerned with the strictly politico-administrative aspects of this model, rather than with its economic implications for the growth of public expenditure.

Jones (1992) contends that the state and the bureaucracy in the colonial period were highly centralized. However, the bureaucracy was heavily dependent on external forces, especially the policy directions and fiscal supports from the colonial office. The Westminster model was based on free-market capitalism, and the political bureaucracy lacked an entrepreneurial focus. The bureaucracy was committed to constitutionalism and the rule of law, and the principle of ministerial responsibility.

This model was modified in Jamaica and other Caribbean countries in the post–World War II period. Ideological factors expanded the state bureaucracy as well as para-statal institutions especially in Jamaica. The ideology of democratic socialism adopted by the Jamaican government in the 1970s led to an extensive para-statal movement to provide public goods and services. This new welfarism, according to Jones (1992: 18), institutionalized a different administrative culture. Whereas the Westminster model stressed that budgetary allocations should be financed from local taxation and that welfare should be used as a palliative, the democratic socialist experience forced a revision of this model. The new welfare concept now embraced extensive provision of housing, education, health, and employment. The new bureaucratic style was also linked to "democratic participation, community development and self-management" (Jones 1992: 18). In this context, we differ from Niskanen in arguing that bureaucrats in the democratic socialist model of bureaucracy were not purely utility maximizers, but were interested in community welfare.

This model experienced a crisis in the 1980s forcing a downsizing of the state bureaucracy, and extensive IMF intervention. In Barbados and Trinidad and Tobago, democratic socialism led to similar modifications of the para-statal arm of the state bureaucracy. However, it is true that in most of these countries the civil service still operated in the Westminster mode, with constitutionalism, ministerial responsibility and the absence of entrepreneurial focus providing the rules of the game.

Downs' Economic Theory of Politics

Downs' (1957) theory of political competition is one of the most influential contributions to public choice theory. Downs emphasizes the role of political parties as vote maximizers. Even though he retains the assumption that voters are utility maximizers, individual voters do not vote on every budget issue. This makes it possible for politicians in office to pursue their own goals, the most important of which is to maximize votes in the next election. The political utility function consists of power and prestige, and politicians are not really interested in achieving an efficient allocation of resources. However, this may be possible if political competition forces the government to move the economy closer to a Pareto optimality. Even though politicians may introduce economic reforms, when in power, they will need to maximize votes before this can be accomplished.

The median voter theorem is central to the Downs' model. Political parties must identify the preferences of the median voter in order to maximize votes. The vote-maximizing party will choose economic policies to persuade the median voter. However, Brown and Jackson (1990) have argued that the median voter model is a "naive behavioural specification of politics". They further contend that voters and politicians have asymmetric information. Voters are not well-informed about budgetary outcomes and politicians do not know who the median voter is. The election process is also characterized by less than full voter participation. This limits the median voter model because it is necessary to know the probability of the median voter participating in elections. Further, vote maximization is too strong an assumption of the Downs' model. A majority of votes matters more than maximization of votes. The existence of pressure groups and lobbies also mean that politicians will attempt to appeal to a wide cross-section of interests other than the median voter (Brown and Jackson 1990).

Although the Downs' model sheds some light on the influence of economics on political behaviour, it cannot explain the complexities of voting behaviour in the developing countries or the nature of political competition. Ideological factors, for example, played an important role in developing countries such as Jamaica and Guyana, and have influenced the size of budgets in those countries, especially during the 1970s. In many Caribbean territories, notions of social democracy advanced by populist leaders were important in mobilizing voter participation (Howard 1992). The concept of the median voter is far too limited to understand complex politico-economic processes in many developing countries.

Logrolling

Buchanan and Tulloch (1962) made an important contribution to the analysis of logrolling, which is a form of vote trading common to the US Congress. In this process, a legislator agrees to trade his vote for another legislator's in exchange for the latter's vote on a measure which the former legislator prefers. Logrolling enables politicians to advance bills that are important to their own constituencies, while spreading the taxation costs nationally. Parochial issues and local projects are pushed through by logrolling. Logrolling is therefore a process by which intensity of preferences can be registered. However, logrolling favours minority interests because if a fiscal measure is supported by the majority of legislators, logrolling would not be effective. By promoting minority interests, logrolling also leads to larger budgets than may normally be the case.

In democracies where pre-eminence of the party is emphasized, logrolling may not be effective. In the Caribbean, logrolling is not a feature of the political process because the adversary system of government stresses party loyalty. In the Caribbean, it is uncommon to find opposition politicians trading votes with government members. This aspect of public choice theory is therefore not relevant to economic decision making in the Caribbean.

Special Interest Groups

Special interest groups can exert pressure on democratic governments, thereby raising the level of public expenditure. I outline briefly Gary Becker's (1983) theory of pressure groups competing for political influence, and the work of North and Wallis (1982) for the United States. It is also well known that rent-seeking interest groups can increase social costs, thereby leading to government failure, in their attempts to secure monopolies in certain economic activities.

Becker's theory rests on the view that individuals belong to interest groups, defined by industry, income level, geography and other characteristics. These groups use political influence to advance the economic power of their members. Pressure groups compete for political influence in order to determine the equilibrium structure of taxes and subsidies. The competition for political influence is determined by the number of persons in the group as well as the deadweight costs of certain taxes and subsidies. According to Becker (1983:373) "deadweight costs stimulate efforts by taxed groups to lower taxes, but discourage efforts by subsidized groups to raise subsidies". Each group can exert greater pressure if it minimizes the number of free riders in the group. Control over free riding therefore increases the efficiency of the group. Becker further argues that efficient methods of subsidization raise subsidies and the number of benefit recipients, but have negative effects on tax payers. He cautions that "cooperation among pressure groups is necessary to prevent wasteful expenditures or political pressure that results from the competition for influences" (1983:388).

North (1985) and North and Wallis (1982) have advanced an explanation of the growth of government in the United States and the role of interest groups in influencing government expenditures. Their argument is as follows: The revolutionary change in technology in the United States in the nineteenth century led to a rapid growth in the transactions sector of the economy, and an expansion in specialization and the division of labour. These developments led to an increase in the provision of government services to reduce the costs of transactions between various members and groups in the society, as well as to redistribute income between groups. These "transaction cost-reducing services" include transportation, justice, police, postal services, and so forth.

The growth of specialization also stimulated the development of new interest groups which led to political pluralism. This was reflected in the formation of new organizations to replace functions previously undertaken by the family and traditional economic institutions. Voluntary organizations could not fulfil the demands of special interest groups given the new specialization and division of labour. The demand by special interest groups for public goods and income redistribution therefore were significant determinants of the expansion of government to undertake these activities.

North's theory is a partial explanation of the growth of government. Interest groups and lobbies play an important role in any democratic society. However, their activity is only part of the complex socioeconomic process influencing government growth. With the exception of Jones (1987), I am not aware of any empirical studies on the impact of pressure groups on government growth in the Caribbean. It is well known that trade unions in the Caribbean have exerted a major influence on the wage component of government expenditure (Howard 1992). The role of the trade union is examined in the next section. Further, lobbies in the hotel and manufacturing sector in some Caribbean economies have been successful in securing high levels of subsidization of those industries by way of income tax concessions and duty-free allowances. The economic impact of these incentives has been discussed by Howard (1992: 126–28).

Jones' (1987) analysis of political pressure groups in the colonial period helps us to understand the emergence of pressure groups in the Caribbean and their influence on public expenditure. Jones identifies seven major groups, namely, the merchant-plantocratic lobby, the administrative bureaucracy, the lobby of organized labour, professional associations, the lobby of organized religious bodies, community associations, and the peasantry. Perhaps the most influential of these in terms of public policy in the colonial period was the business lobby and the state bureaucracy.

The business lobby's influence on public policy has extended into the contemporary period. The business lobby in the colonial period was a homogeneous elite group closely linked with the Westminster-based administrators. They sought to perpetuate the plantation system and institutionalize public policies relating to taxes, subsidies, contracts, and manpower (Jones 1987:49). The political influence of the planter class business lobby in the colonial period perpetuated an economic system based on class and privilege. The influence of the present-day business lobby will be analysed in the next section.

EXTENTENSIONS OF THE PUBLIC CHOICE APPROACH

I critically evaluated the main components of public choice theory as it developed in the United States. The view is advanced here that the public choice approach can be modified in the context of the histories of developing economies. Our analysis here uses the Caribbean region as an example. This interpretation draws on Howard (1989a) who stressed the importance of politico-historical analysis for understanding budgetary outcomes. My approach is influenced more by the historical thesis of North (1985), North and Wallis (1982), and Jones (1987, 1992), than by the static theories of Downs (1957) and Buchanan and Tulloch (1962).

The application of public choice theory in the Caribbean includes a consideration of the following:

1. The emergence of mass-based political parties after 1937 led by populist leaders;
2. The importance of ideology particularly before 1980;
3. The importance of the business lobby and trade unions as pressure groups;
4. The impact of the IMF as an external pressure group after 1980.

Of course, the last three of these factors had relevance not only in the Caribbean but in other developing countries as well.

The above developments appear to be the most important politico-historical factors influencing budgetary outcomes in the Caribbean. The period between 1937 and 1960 in the Caribbean was significant for the achievement of adult suffrage, decolonization, the emergence of representative government, the rise of populist leaders, and political independence from Britain. This constellation of factors meant that political parties were able to articulate the interest of lower income groups. It is argued that even though political parties were interested in maximizing votes, as in the Downs model, they were also concerned with improving the social welfare of the masses and political independence. They also had a strong sense of anti-imperialism and anticolonialism. The change in the character of the state as a result of political decolonization gave impetus to the growth of budgets which emphasized social welfare and development projects (Howard 1989a, 1992).

Public choice theory in the United States assumes the capitalist ideology as given. Public choice is exercised within the framework of the market mechanism. In the Caribbean after World War II with the emergence of democratic socialism, there was greater emphasis on the role of the state as a catalyst of development, and a reduction in the importance of the market mechanism as an allocator of resources. This movement was characterized by a massive intrusion of the state bureaucracy in all aspects of economic activity especially in Guyana and Jamaica (Howard 1992). The budgets in the 1970s and 1980s were based on a new welfarism enshrined in the manifestos of political parties. These budgets reflected the growth in the size of government, characterized by heavy expenditures on statutory corporations and public goods.

The business lobby in the postindependence period embraces a number of interest groups compared with the plantocracy of the colonial period. It now comprises employers' confederations, manufacturers' associations, small businesses, agricultural interests and the hotel lobby. These various groups are able to influence government budgets by securing certain fiscal benefits and subsidies. For example, the hotel lobby in Barbados has been very successful in influencing the heavy subsidization of the tourist industry by government. Rent-seeking has become more widespread than in the colonial period as the party in power is forced to reward certain firms and interest groups who finance its political campaigns.

The trade union has been one of the most formidable interest groups in the Caribbean after 1937. Analyses by Henry (1972) and Nurse (1992) examine the historical evolution of the unions as well as their political and organizational behaviour. Many trade unions in the Caribbean had a political base, or were attached to political parties. Nurse refers to this feature as "political unionism", which was fostered by the emergence of middle class political leaders during the decolonization movement in the 1950s. Unions were involved in the passage of labour legislation and securing high wages both in the public and private sectors. The effectiveness of the unions in the growth of government budgets was considerably curtailed during the 1990s by government wage cuts, the legislation of salaries for civil servants, downsizing of the labour force, and the formation of wages and incomes protocols. The growth of trade unions was also significant in other developing countries.

It is important to examine the role of the IMF as an external "pressure group" in the language of the public choice approach. Indeed, our analysis can be applied to any country which has implemented IMF stand-by arrangements or extended fund facilities. The nature of these facilities will be discussed in chapter 11. It is suggested here that when the IMF imposes its conditionalities on a country, public choice theory breaks down. Even though governments are democratically elected, the budget is determined by the conditionalities set out by the IMF, rather than by the will of the people or the choices of politicians. The role of the IMF is not even mentioned in the North Atlantic-based public choice or political business cycles theories. This is why the institutional basis of these theories is so misleading in the Caribbean context. Under the rule of the IMF, in many instances, the fiscal constitution is suspended. Interest groups, especially trade unions, are immobilized because the primary goal of the IMF is to reduce the size of the government. The IMF has played a central role in the politics and economics of the Caribbean and many other developing countries since the end of World War II.

It is reasonable to argue that the application of public choice theory in the Caribbean must modify the rigid self-interest assumption of the American public choice theory. Self-interest played a part in motivating politicians, voters and bureaucrats. However, the new welfarism model of the postwar period was a primary determinant of the growth of government budgets in the Caribbean.

SUMMARY

Public choice theory is a school of thought rather than a unified theory of public expenditure growth. The propositions of this school, which have a strong bias to American political institutions, have not been tested and quantified for a large number of developing countries. Much of the American approach is static and abstract, often ignoring changes in the political philosophies of governments over time. My analysis argued that the theory can be extended to the Caribbean, but this requires a historical approach. Even though politicians and voters were motivated by self-interest in the Caribbean, they were also motivated by a philosophy of social welfarism, which was a response to centuries of colonialism. My work did not focus on the specific details of the operation of the public choice approach in other developing countries. My observations on the Caribbean can provide a focus for future empirical work in other market economies on the budgetary impact of pressure groups, bureaucracy, and the role of political parties. The historical approach is preferable to static analysis.

Chapter Five

Political Business Cycles

Political business cycles theory, which emerged in developed countries, attempts to explain the role of political parties in influencing the Phillips curve trade-off between unemployment and inflation. Political business cycles theory assumes that governments can use monetary and fiscal policies to fix the desired level of unemployment and inflation, in a manner which would facilitate their re-election to power. This chapter examines this body of thought and assesses its relevance to developing countries. Following Alesina's (1989) classification of political theories of the business cycle, we distinguish between four variants of the theory, namely, political business cycles (PBC), rational political business cycles (RPBC), partisan theory (PT), and rational partisan theory (RPT). These are briefly discussed in the following sections.[1] To the extent that political business cycles can only work if governments exercise control over central banks, I also comment on the issue of central bank independence.

THEORIES OF THE POLITICAL BUSINESS CYCLE

PBC Theory of Nordhaus

The theory of the political business cycle has been popularized by Nordhaus (1975). The idea underlying the political business cycle is that governments seek to maximize votes in the next election, by implementing policies which would lead to favourable economic outcomes just before the election. After the election, governments pursue less favourable economic policies. Nordhaus assumed that voters were backward looking and short-sighted and voted for the incumbent political party if its policies before the election emphasized low unemployment. Nordhaus' model analysed the political business cycle in relation to the choice between inflation and unemployment. At the time of his writing, the conventional macroeconomic theory stressed a trade-off between the rate of inflation and the level of unemployment. Low inflation rates were associated with high levels of unemployment. This was the famous Phillips curve. However, despite his emphasis on the trade-off between inflation and unemployment, Nordhaus asserted that his model could also be directly applied to other problems of choice such as public investment in capital goods, or balance of payments policies.

Nordhaus' model rests on a number of crucial assumptions. First, he assumes that unemployment is a control or policy variable and governments can set unemployment rates at any desired level. His second assumption is that even though households are rational in their preferences, they are ignorant of the relationship between unemployment and inflation. Immediately after the elections, the government raises the level of unemployment to combat inflation. Just before the next election, unemployment will be lowered thereby exploiting the Phillips curve. Nordhaus tested his model in nine countries and found that the model worked reasonably well for the United States, Germany and New Zealand. However, a political business cycle was implausible for Australia, Canada, Japan and the United Kingdom. There were very modest implications of a political cycle for France and Sweden.

Most work on political business cycles has been carried out for developed countries. There are many reasons why the theory as presented by Nordhaus and others have to be seriously modified in developing economies. First, the concept of a Phillips curve in these countries is implausible. High levels of inflation exist with chronically high levels of unemployment, especially in some countries which have undergone devaluations. This process is sometimes known as stagflation. Second, governments in developing countries cannot fix the rate of unemployment to desired levels, nor can they target the rate of inflation which is usually imported. This is because many developing economies are highly open. Even though politicians may try to reduce unemployment around election time, there is no precise trade-off between unemployment and inflation.

Rational Political Business Cycles,
Partisan Theory, and
Rational Partisan Theory

These theories are not mutually exclusive since they include elements of Nordhaus' theory. There exists an extensive literature on these approaches and our discussion can only identify representative models. These various approaches have been described as politico-economic models (Frey 1978). Most of these models build on the self-interest assumptions of public choice theory. The RPBC introduces rational expectations into PBC by assuming voters are rational and not easily fooled by well-timed pre-electoral expansions (Alesina 1989: 58). Even if voters are rational, governments could still manipulate short-run budget cycles. These views are represented in the work of Rogoff and Sibert (1988).

Partisan theory is based on the original work of Hibbs (1977). The PT assumes partisan politicians and examines policies pursued by right-wing and left-wing governments, such as the conservative and labour parties in England. Using data drawn from 12 west European and North American countries, Hibbs showed that the preference of leftist governments has been for relatively low unemployment and high inflation, while right-wing governments have pursued policies to guarantee low inflation and high unemployment. These differences in policies were based on the "objective economic interests and subjective preferences of their class defined core political constituencies" (Hibbs 1977: 1468). Alesina and Sachs (1988) have adapted Hibbs approach by assuming ideological politicians and rational voters (RPT). This theory predicts expansion at the beginning of a left-wing government and a recession at the beginning of a right-wing government. Other theories, such as the analysis of Frey and Schneider (1978) for the United Kingdom, seek to combine the PT and PBC theories.

Theoretically, the politico-economic models derived for industrialized economies can be criticized on two levels. First, the models are partial in the sense that they examine a specific part of the economy, mainly the relationship between the government budget, inflation, and unemployment. Private sector investment and savings functions are largely ignored. Second, most models ignore open economy variables like the balance of payments. This is particularly so for models of the United States where it is assumed that the balance of payments constraint is not binding. However, Frey and Schneider's model (1978) for Britain contains a balance of payments constraint. This constraint ought to be included in models for developing countries where a different type of specification is needed.

The econometric methodology also has specification problems since the Phillips curve hypothesis is not applicable to the stagflationary conditions of the 1970s. During this period both developed and developing countries experienced high inflation and high unemployment rates, related to the oil crisis of 1974 and its recessionary effects, and not necessarily to government policy variables per se. The econometric method is illustrated here by briefly examining a representative model by Frey and Schneider (1978). This model estimates the *LEAD* or popularity function of the British government. The *LEAD* function is of the following form:

$$LEAD = a = b_1 LEAD_{t-1} + b_2 I_t + b_3 U_t + b_4 GDY_t + b_5 NE_t + b_6 DEP_t$$

where

LEAD$_t$ = Lead of government popularity over the popularity of the main opposition party in percentage points as indicated by the Gallup survey.

I$_t$ = The index of retail prices

U$_t$ = The unemployment rate

GDY$_t$ = Rate of growth of real personal disposable income

NE$_t$ = Dummy variable to measure number of quarters to the nearest election

DEP$_t$ = Dummy variable to measure depreciation of the government's popularity.

The signs of the coefficient of the **GDY** variable and **LEAD$_{t-1}$** are expected to be positive, and all other variables are expected to have negative signs. Frey and Schneider found that government's lead over the opposition is determined by the state of the economy as indicated by **GDY, I** and **U**, and election cycle variables.

Frey and Schneider argue that government would change its policy instruments for re-election purposes depending on the size of the **LEAD** function. The government pursues an expansionary policy to raise popularity when re-election is uncertain, that is, when **LEAD$_t^*$ > LEAD$_{t-1}$** where **LEAD$_t^*$** is some critically low level of popularity. When government is confident of winning the election, that is, **LEAD$_t^*$ < LEAD$_{t-1}$**, government pursues ideological goals. Government's economic behaviour is subject to a balance of payments constraint.

Chrystal and Alt (1981) contend that both the popularity and ideological policy functions of Frey and Schneider's model contain specification errors. They argue that the popularity function may not hold for the years after 1974 when they were high levels of inflation and unemployment. Second, there are difficulties of specifying ideological differences between parties. We also note that Frey and Schneider's popularity function may be difficult to apply to most developing countries, in the absence of regular surveys like Gallup to measure the performance of government.

Perhaps a more serious problem for modern-day econometricians is that the PBC models of the 1970s and 1980s may contain spurious regressions, since the models were based on the classical OLS (ordinary least squares) econometric knowledge at that time. The unit root and cointegration revolution in econometrics casts doubts on the usefulness of these models because many variables such as output and money have been found to be non-stationary, which means that the means and variances of those variables change over time.

The foregoing discussion says nothing about the underlying assumption of central bank independence. PBC theory cannot be discussed in abstraction from the issue of central bank independence. The manipulation of monetary and fiscal policy is predicated on the view that the government has some policy control of the central bank. No attempt is made here to review the literature on central bank independence. Empirical analyses in this area have been carried out by Cukierman and Webb (1994) and Alesina and Summers (1993). The conclusion of this literature is that central banks can be ranked in terms of the degree of their political vulnerability (Cukierman and Webb 1994).

In highly developed money markets, the central bank needs greater policy independence to anticipate market changes and enter the market as a competitor. The money market must therefore be highly developed for monetary policy to play an active role. In many developing countries, the absence of these conditions reduces the potency of monetary policy, and therefore the policy independence of the central bank. The primacy of fiscal policy and the accommodative role of monetary policy explain the dependent role of central banking in most developing countries. However, even though government can use fiscal policy to influence job creation, the overall employment rate is influenced by the behaviour of the private sector. Government cannot fix the employment rate. We argue later that although the theory of the Phillips curve is not strictly relevant to developing countries, one can still advance a theory of the political budget cycle under the assumption that the central bank is a policy dependent institution.

In their contribution to the debate on central bank independence, Worrell and Belgrave (1997) advance a valid argument that the pursuit of central bank independence may not be the appropriate path for central banks in the Caribbean to follow. Their focus is on policy independence. The literature on central bank independence is predominantly concerned with inflation control. Worrell and Belgrave maintain that central banks have multiple objectives, and Caribbean central banks cannot focus exclusively on price stabilization. In the pursuit of the central bank's multiple objectives the treasury may easily frustrate the central bank if their objectives differ. Worrell and Belgrave posit the view that Caribbean central banks should seek a consensus with the treasury on economic policy. The central bank should provide information and analysis to shape a consensus around that strategy. They assert that it is not the central bank's business to determine national economic objectives, but to ensure that public choices are fully informed. Therefore, rather than pursue policy independence, the central bank would promote national consensus on economic policy.

RELEVANCE OF POLITICAL BUSINESS CYCLES TO DEVELOPING COUNTRIES

Following Alesina (1989), it may be more useful to examine the data in developing countries for political "budget cycles" rather than PBCs employing the Phillips curve trade-off between employment and inflation. The purpose of this exercise would be to observe whether the budget deficit deteriorated in the election year when compared with the previous year. Such analysis assumes that (1) politicians are rational in that they seek to maximize votes, (2) the central bank is a policy dependent institution, (3) the Phillips curve is not operational, and (4) the balance of payments constraint is binding. Political "budget cycles" can be observed from time series data. Our discussion below is not a model of the political business cycle. My argument is that PBC models need to integrate private sector variables in order to have any plausibility as an explanation of unemployment and output levels.

An examination of the Barbadian data in the Central Bank's *Annual Statistical Digest* reveals high budget deficits for some election years. The deficit rose in the election year 1976 and remained high in 1977. In the election year 1981, central bank money creation led to a large deficit of

Bds$154.8 million. This deficit occasioned the intervention of the IMF. In the year after the 1986 election, the deficit rose to an all-time high of Bds$219.8 million and then fell sharply. In the fiscal year 1990/91, the deficit also rose to Bds $248.2 million and then declined. The election year was 1991. Again the IMF intervened. The deficit fell between 1992 and 1995. The evidence seems to show a tendency for high deficits in some election years. However, the series is too short to speak of a well-defined budget cycle.

However, even though increased government spending in election years may lead to growth in short-term employment, small developing economies do not show a pronounced business cycle determined either by the government budget or private sector activity. Output and employment levels in these economies are normally determined by seasonal and external factors affecting the export of staples such as sugar, tourism, bananas, and petroleum. Therefore, even in election years, governments may be unable to offset recessionary factors affecting the performance of export sectors, and may have to resort to satisfying the demands of rent-seekers, as well as pursue partisan economic policies in order to achieve majority votes in the next election.

Howard (1992) has shown that the consequence of such budgetary expansion financed by money creation led to balance of payments deficits in Barbados and Jamaica. It is difficult, however, to observe concurrent budget and foreign exchange cycles because balance of payments deficits have also occurred in non-election years.

I also examined whether there was an election "money creation cycle" in Barbados, by observing the evidence on central bank money creation (central bank claims on the government) between 1973 and 1994. There were peaks in money creation in the election years 1981 and 1991. Central bank claims on government rose to $266.0 million by the end of election year 1991 when there was a budget and money creation crisis. The government was forced to resort to the IMF for finance. Although we cannot speak of a pronounced cycle because of the short series, it is reasonable to say that politicians have dominated the central bank in Barbados in two election years.

I am aware of two studies applying PBCs to developing countries using econometric techniques. These are Schuknecht (1996) and Edwards (1994). Schuknecht (1996) examined 35 developing countries that held elections during part of the period 1970 to 1992. His analysis found empirical support for fiscal policy cycles, with governments pursuing expansionary fiscal policies which led to increased fiscal deficits before elections. This pattern was particularly noticeable for countries with a relatively small share of external trade. Edwards (1994) looked at aspects of the political economy of inflation and stabilization in developing countries. He also applied the PBC theory to Chile.

Schuknecht found that the Nordhaus approach was more relevant than the partisan approach to political budget cycles. He tested four hypotheses as follows:

1. Output rises and unemployment declines,
2. Fiscal deficits increase before elections,
3. Trade-oriented economies exhibit less pronounced cycles than less trade-oriented economies,
4. IMF-supported programmes result in lower fiscal deficits and short-term recessions. (Schuknecht 1996: 158–61)

Schuknecht's econometric results were that elections do not have a significant impact on output. The latter was more influenced by a country's openness and improved terms of trade. The impact of elections on the fiscal deficit was strong especially in relation to the expansion in government expenditure. The more inward-looking countries showed very strong election and budget cycles. The estimations did not support the hypothesis that IMF-supported programmes had a significant recessionary effect on output. Schuknecht's work paves the way for future research. In Caribbean countries with trade-oriented economies, expansionary fiscal policies have been pursued regardless of the degree of openness and the resulting balance of payments costs.

Schuknecht's analysis contains a number of weaknesses. First, he does not assume an explicit balance of payments constraint in his model. He distinguishes between trade-oriented and less trade-oriented economies, but most developing countries are trade-oriented either as exporters of staples such as petroleum, coffee, bananas, and sugar, or as importers of high levels of consumer and intermediate goods. The use of the trade openness measure may not be a good statistic to test the political business cycle hypothesis. It is better to assume that fiscal expansion will have significant repercussions on the balance of payments of most developing countries.

Second, Schuknecht's model is partial in the sense that it ignores the behaviour of the private sector with respect to savings, investment, and consumption. Therefore, it suffers from the same weakness of other PBC models. The omission of private sector variables means that it is difficult to identify all the sources of output and employment changes in the economy.

Third, it is not clear why Schuknecht included the IMF in his model, and proceeds to argue that IMF policies had no negative impact on output. The real impact of IMF stabilization policies can only be determined by time series analysis for individual countries. He measures the IMF influence by the use of dummy variables. This approach does not seem appropriate, given the comprehensive nature of IMF programmes and the macro impact of massive devaluations.

Edwards (1994) provides an econometric analysis of PBCs in Chile from 1952–73. He included dummy variables to account for the political orientation of the government, that is, whether the government was a right-wing or left-wing government. Dummy variables were also specified for presidential and congressional elections. He found that inflation tends to increase in the period preceding both presidential and congressional elections. He also reported that for a number of developing countries, governments tend to implement devaluations early in their tenure of office. Although the work of Edwards documents well-known political trends, the importance of his work is the application of economics to political analysis in developing countries by using econometric techniques.

SUMMARY

My analysis contended that the PBC theory, which incorporates some of the postulates of public choice theory such as rationality, self-interest and majority voting, was more testable using the econometric methodology. However, our principal criticism is concerned with the partial nature of these models, and the assumption of the Phillips curve trade-off. I believe that the inclusion of variables such as elections and political popularity constitutes an innovative departure from standard macroeconomic models which include mainly economic variables such as income and prices. Government in the standard models is usually treated as an exogenous variable.

This chapter produced evidence to show that although there is not a political business cycle for Barbados, politicians have augmented public spending in some election years. We were unable to advance a partisan theory of the ideological differences between the two major parties in Barbados. The British partisan approach to PBC theory, which assumes a left-wing and right-wing government (labour and conservatives), is therefore not strictly applicable to Barbados.

This chapter can be regarded as an attempt to discuss the relevance of politico-economic models in developing countries. The challenge for future research is the production of models which integrate election behaviour and the standard macroeconomic approach to modelling the behaviour of output and employment, as well as the government's budget constraint.

Chapter Six

Public Expenditure Analysis

This chapter looks at theories of expenditure growth, the structure of government expenditure in selected developing countries, and the relationship between government expenditure and economic growth. Various chapters discuss other aspects of government expenditure. Chapter 7 will outline how government spending influences the income distribution, especially through expenditure targeting. Previous analysis also dealt with public choice theory which attempts to explain the size of government and the growth of public expenditure. We shall also discuss an approach emerging from the public choice literature dealing with government deficits as a cause of public expenditure growth.

APPROACHES TO PUBLIC EXPENDITURE GROWTH

Wagner's Law

Early work in the 1960s examined public spending by the use of cross-sectional regression analysis. This empirical approach to the determination of public expenditure growth has focused primarily on the testing of Wagner's law of increasing state activity. Wagner's law suggests that the share of the public sector in the economy will rise as economic growth proceeds. Many of these tests used cross-sectional as well as time series analysis. The 1960s approaches by Williamson (1961) and Thorn (1967) tested the proposition that a relationship exists between per capita income and the size and pattern of government expenditures. These studies were based on the view that the "stage of development" can be represented by the amount of per capita income. The studies concluded that (1) the share of government expenditure in the gross national product (GNP) tends to increase with per capita income; (2) current expenditures as a whole increase their share of the national product with rising income; and (3) social expenditures tend to rise as a percentage of total government expenditure.

Cross-sectional studies revealed serious drawbacks. It should be noted that income per head is not a good indicator of development, since it says nothing about the distribution of income. Statistically, it is not good to extrapolate from cross-sectional studies for the purpose of time series analysis; that is, cross-sectional analysis may give misleading indicators for individual countries. Another shortcoming of these studies is that sociopolitical variables play no part in some regression analyses. A study for the Caribbean by Goffman and Mahar (1971) identified other influences on public expenditure growth, including openness and changing internal political philosophies. However, as Odle (1976) notes, these studies put forward no systematic theory to explain the role of the state.

Sackey (1980) also used regression analysis to explain expenditure determination in the Caribbean. Sackey's study provides an empirical investigation of Wagner's law, utilizing time series data on 12 less-developed countries. The results support Wagner's law in the long run. Sackey examines various expenditure elasticities and expenditure growth rates. The weakness of Sackey's analysis is that it concentrates almost exclusively on the measurement of statistical magnitudes. He does not advance an explanation of the causes of the behaviour of the expenditure variable. Sackey completely excludes non-economic factors. Further, he specifies real per capita government expenditure as a function of the level of real per capita income and the previous year's real expenditure per capita, ignoring political explanations of expenditure growth.

More recent investigations into Wagner's law for developing countries include work by Murthy (1993) for Mexico and Alleyne (1996) for Jamaica, Barbados, and Trinidad and Tobago. These studies used more advanced econometric techniques than earlier studies. Alleyne (1996) found that there was no evidence of Wagner's law in Jamaica and Guyana. The lack of cointegration between the variables implied that there was no long-run relationship between public expenditure and per capita income in Jamaica and Guyana. Wagner's law was confirmed for Barbados where there was cointegration between the variables. The value of Alleyne's work is that it questions previous studies not using cointegration techniques.

Stages of Development and Displacement Thesis

The stages of development approach to the growth in government spending are exemplified by Musgrave (1969b) who focused on demand-side influences on expenditure patterns. Different types of expenditures play a more important role at different stages of development. On the other hand, Peacock and Wiseman (1961) utilized a supply-side approach, treating changes in government expenditure as consequences of social disturbances or wars. It is necessary to look closely at Musgrave's analysis, since it offers some insight into expenditure determination in small countries like those in the Caribbean.

Musgrave (1969b) distinguishes between (1) the determinants of public expenditure development and (2) conditioning and social factors. According to Musgrave, allowance must be made for the political, cultural, and social factors that determine the environment in which budget policy operates. Musgrave concentrates his analysis on public capital formation, public consumption, and transfer payments. Capital formation in the form of infrastructure tends to he high in the early stages of development. As the economy develops, basic social overheads are created and additions are made at a slower rate. The structure of social overhead capital declines as a share of net capital formation. Therefore, the ratio of public to total capital formation may be expected to he high in the early stages of development and to decline, at least temporarily, after the "take off" is reached. However, there may be later periods in which capital expenditure rises as a share of total capital formation.

Musgrave's analysis is not conclusive with regard to public consumption and public redistribution. There is no clear theory that public consumption will rise as a share of government outlays. Furthermore, public redistribution depends on the objective of distributional policy, which varies from country to country.

Musgrave's analysis rests on safer ground with respect to the conditioning factors. Demographic factors are important influences on public expenditure growth, for obvious reasons. Expansion in the absolute size of the population leads to expansion in the level of public services. This is particularly so in urban areas, especially when population growth is combined with rural-urban migration. The age structure of the population also has an impact on distribution of services. For instance, an age structure which is highly skewed toward the very young will lead to more emphasis on primary and second education. As the population ages, pensions and various welfare services become more important.

Other factors, such as technological change and sociopolitical factors, are all discussed in a very generalized way by Musgrave. Musgrave proceeds to regress expenditure/GDP ratios on per capita income, a procedure which leads to misleading conclusions because the econometrics ignores the political factors. Musgrave's approach, while identifying some of the factors which influence government expenditures, is too general to provide a rigorous theory of public expenditure growth.

Peacock and Wiseman's (1961) displacement thesis maintains that public expenditure shows a gradual upward trend under normal conditions, but that increased outlays during war or social upheavals permit permanently higher postwar civilian expenditures. Public expenditure is financed by higher taxation during periods of stress, and this expenditure is displaced upward after the war or social upheaval. Peacock and Wiseman's analysis is essentially short term, since it explains the upward displacement of the expenditure function, but does not provide a firm theory of the determinants of the displaced function.

Politico-Historical Stages Approaches

The politico-historical stages thesis is perhaps the strongest explanation of the magnitude and growth of government spending in the Caribbean during the post–World War II period. I accept the thesis that the change in the role of the state was a dominant determinant of public expenditure growth. This approach is embodied in the work of Odle (1976), which is the first comprehensive analysis of the evolution of public expenditure in the Caribbean. Odle's work concentrated on Guyana, but had theoretical application to the entire Caribbean (Odle 1975). Odle's stages theory is applicable to the Barbadian case (Howard 1979, 1982). This section discusses the work of Odle and its wider applications, to pave the way for an examination of the structure of public expenditure in the Caribbean.

Odle (1975) distinguishes three major periods of public expenditure growth: the traditional period, the transitional period, and the postcolonial period. The traditional period is the colonial period (pre-1960), when the tax system and the allocation of public expenditure in the Caribbean were designed to assist the operations of the foreign-owned plantations. In Barbados, Jamaica, and Trinidad, a heavy proportion of expenditure was allocated to road building, to link the sugar estates and aid the extraction and internal transportation of sugar. There was also considerable spending on ports and harbours to facilitate shipments of sugar. The share of government spending on education and health was relatively low. Public expenditure patterns were modified after 1937, when the British government adopted a more benevolent approach to public policy in the colonies. This was seen in the passing of the Colonial Development and Welfare Acts of 1940 and 1945, which provided for increased loans and grants to improve the social and economic infrastructure. This provision for minimum social welfare and infrastructure increased the share of expenditure in the domestic product.

During the stage of internal self-government in the 1950s or the transitional period before full political independence from Britain, emphasis was placed on reducing monoculture in the Caribbean. Governments adopted industrialization programmes based on liberal tax incentives. There was an increase in the public expenditure share of public goods and infrastructure to support private enterprise. Statutory corporations were established during this period, including development boards, and marketing and financial corporations. Thus, the change in the character of the state gave the political directorate more autonomy in economic management, which was reflected in rising public expenditures.

The postindependence period, which began in Guyana and Barbados in 1966, was characterized by sharp increases in public expenditures owing to the internal and external responsibilities of nationhood. This included increases in administrative expenditures to finance new ministries; increases in defence spending; and increased spending in areas which were neglected during the colonial period, such as secondary and university education, and health. This increase in expenditures was financed by heavy income taxation, which began to rival import duties in importance.

In some territories, like Guyana, Jamaica, and Trinidad and Tobago, the state established a large number of public enterprises to counterbalance certain foreign-owned interests. These efforts were supported by the establishment of cooperatives in some territories to increase local participation in economic activity. This heavy emphasis on state ownership increased the share of government expenditures.

Howard (1982) has applied the stages theory to Barbados, with the colonial and postindependence periods differentiated. In the colonial, period the high level of structural dependence led the government to adopt expenditure policies which reinforced the dominant mercantile class and retarded the emergence of a public policy to diversify the productive base. The existing colonial monetary system during this period was a constraint on government spending, because the colonial government had no control over the money supply, credit, or the structure of interest rates. The government's power to spend was limited by the reserves at its disposal; therefore, the policy makers budgeted for a revenue surplus in times of export boom in order to spend in times of slump.

The political philosophy during colonialism was that secondary as well as tertiary education were privileges set aside for the élite. This explains the low level of capital expenditure on education. Between 1953 and 1964, capital expenditure on education grew at an estimated annual rate of 0.8 percent in Barbados (Howard 1979). The level of current spending was not even adequate. Most schools suffered from an acute lack of accommodation. The class-ordered educational system prevented the emergence of an expenditure policy geared to reallocate human resources.

The most important fiscal achievement of the colonial administration was the building of a deep water harbour, which absorbed a heavy proportion of capital expenditure. Capital spending on economic services grew at the rate of 15.7 percent between 1953 and 1964. The colonial development plans in Barbados recognized the need for improved roads, port facilities, and water resources. Despite this emphasis on infrastructure, the colonial government was concerned with economic growth as it related to sugar output, rather than with the wider concept of economic development which relates to reallocation of resources to increase the flexibility of the economy (Howard 1982).

Political independence of Barbados from Britain brought a change in the role of the state, and an expenditure policy was adopted which was more egalitarian. Further, independence facilitated the inflow of foreign capital from donor agencies, thereby enabling higher levels of public expenditure. The post-independence period in Barbados saw a rapid growth of spending on education, health, and social services. Between 1966 and 1978 education constituted the largest category of current account spending. Government became committed to the concept of "free education" up to the tertiary level. The government of the day stressed the concept of social democracy, by which all citizens should have the right to work, and free education was a vehicle to reallocate human resources. There was heavy spending on social services, with the provision of national insurance and social security.

Governments in the Caribbean had become quite large (Howard 1989a). During the early 1980s they adopted aggressive expenditure policies, partly as a result of the crisis in the major export sectors. In pursuit of the democratic socialist ideal, heavy government expenditure was designed to maintain employment and social welfare levels. These policies led to large fiscal and balance of payments deficits. However, one can argue that structural weaknesses in Caribbean economies played a part in government expenditure growth.

The "Baumol Effect" or Unbalanced Productivity Growth

The "Baumol effect" can be considered as one explanation of public expenditure growth. The Baumol effect may have some significance in explaining the heavy wage bills of some public services in the Caribbean and other developing countries. Baumol (1967) divides the economy into two sectors, the progressive and non-progressive sectors. The progressive sector experiences productivity growth, while productivity in the non-progressive sector is constant. The basic difference between the two sectors resides in the role played by labour in the activity. In some cases, labour is an instrument to produce the final product, while in others, labour itself is the end product (Baumol 1967: 416). Manufacturing is an example of the former type of activity, whereas there are services, such as teaching, where labour is an end in itself. Services tend to be labour intensive and offer less scope for technological change that improves productivity. The concept of a non-progressive sector may apply to public service labour activity.

The Baumol model can be summarized in the following propositions:

1. The output of the non-progressive sector is produced only by labour with constant productivity. The output of the progressive sector is a function of labour productivity which grows at an exponential rate.

2. Wage rates are equal in the two sectors and increase at the same rate as productivity in the non-progressive sector.

3. The cost per unit of output of the non-progressive sector will rise without limit, while the unit cost of the progressive sector will remain constant. This is because productivity in the non-progressive sector is less than in the progressive sector.

Baumol's model, therefore, provides an explanation of expenditure growth in the public sector, if we assume that the public sector is labour intensive and experiences constant productivity, and that public sector wages move at a rate similar to that of wages in the progressive sector, which uses capital intensive technology. Government wage costs are, therefore, the major cause of public expenditure growth in this model.

Baumol's model is intuitively appealing but difficult to quantify in the Caribbean and other developing countries, where the public service is popularly perceived as inefficient and cumbersome, more bureaucracy-oriented than service-oriented. Despite the difficulty of estimating productivity in the public service in the Caribbean, one can still regard the Baumol effect as a plausible explanation of the large wage bills of the public sectors of these countries. Mascoll (1989) empirically tested the Baumol model, and found that increases in real wages in the private sector of Barbados and Trinidad and Tobago partly explained the growth of public expenditures as a proportion of gross domestic product (GDP). Craigwell and Mascoll (1995) provide a more direct way of measuring the Baumol effect. They used real per capita government expenditure as a measure of public sector productivity. They found evidence of the Baumol effect for Barbados.

It is also true that trade unions in the Caribbean have placed heavy emphasis on inflation as the rationale for wage increases in the public sector, rather than relating wage increases to productivity growth. We also note the observation of Peacock (1975a: 105) that productivity of government services may be markedly influenced not so much by the characteristics of supply along the lines of the Baumol effect, but "by the lack of incentive to introduce process and product innovations by bureaucratically organized production". Perhaps this lack of incentive in the public services stems not only from the non-profit nature of many government services, but from the reality that public sector managers are ultimately responsible to politicians. As a result, the managers feel no compulsion to introduce new ideas. Productivity remains constant, and public sector wage costs rise under trade union pressure.

Baumol's thesis of unbalanced productivity growth can explain only one aspect of government expenditure growth related to the costs of government services. It is therefore a supply-side thesis as Mascoll (1989) notes, but it ignores demand-side variables which influence the provision of public goods such as education, health, low-cost housing, and so forth.

Fiscal Deficits and Public Spending

A provocative hypothesis advanced for the United States by Buchanan and Wagner (1977) states that fiscal deficits lead to increased government spending. This thesis, sometimes described as the Buchanan/Wagner hypothesis, is based on the view that voters are ignorant of the level of their future tax liabilities as a result of current deficits, and therefore demand higher levels of spending. This contradicts the notion of rational expectations that "individuals learn about the costs of future as well as present taxes over time and do not systematically hold biased perceptions because of fiscal indulgence in deficit spending" (Borcherding 1985: 368). Niskanen (1978) showed empirically that larger deficits give rise to higher levels of spending in the United States. Niskanen argued that deficits cause a reduction in the "perceived tax price" to the current generation of voters, and lead to increases in federal spending if there is any negative price elasticity of demand for federal services.

The Buchanan/Wagner hypothesis, which was born in the context of fiscal federalism in the United States, has been applied to Barbados by Craigwell (1991). Craigwell's work on Barbados found support for the Buchanan/Wagner hypothesis. However, an unresolved problem is whether Barbadians expect the "perceived tax price" to fall as a result of a fiscal deficit. The principal problem with Craigwell's approach is that he does not evaluate Niskanen's assumptions in the context of the Barbadian economy. However, the econometric analysis used to test the Buchanan/Wagner hypothesis for developing countries can be misleading, because it is highly controversial whether deficits cause increased spending or the latter causes deficits. It is entirely possible, as shown by Howard (1992), that the line of causality could run from increased expenditure to higher fiscal deficits. In developing countries which experience chronic fiscal disequilibrium as a result of structural and political factors (Tanzi 1982a), heavy government expenditures contribute significantly to large fiscal deficits. Further, I am not aware of any valid test of the assumption in developing countries that the "perceived tax price" of government services will fall as a result of a fiscal deficit. Citizens may anticipate higher taxes when governments in developing countries are forced to pursue stabilization programmes to reduce the size of the deficit.

Craigwel, Mascoll and Leon (1994) also found for Barbados over the period 1973–89 that there is a causal influence running from government revenue to total government expenditure. They argue that this result supports the Buchanan/Wagner view that revenue leads expenditure. I still believe that this area of inquiry is controversial despite the application of advanced econometric techniques.

We can infer from the analysis of this chapter as well as the earlier insights drawn from the theory of public choice and PBCs, that public spending can only be explained by a myriad of economic and non-economic factors. Some of these variables are amenable to quantitative analysis such as prices, incomes and population. The activities of special interest groups and bureaucracy have an impact on the government's budget, but cannot be convincingly explained by the econometric analysis. Although some economists have attempted to analyse government spending without reference to public choice theory, Borcherding (1977: 64) warns against this tendency in dealing with "the social dynamics of Leviathan".

ALLOCATION AND CONTROL OF PUBLIC EXPENDITURE

Structure of Government Expenditure in Selected Countries

This section makes a broad comparison of public sector expenditure in developed countries with those of developing countries. Howard (1992) has analysed the structure of public spending for some Caribbean countries noting the heavy emphasis on education, health, and economic services. He also reported that wages and salaries comprised over 40 percent of current expenditures in Barbados and Trinidad and Tobago during the 1980s. Our subsequent analysis will also show whether the allocation of public expenditures in other developing countries is similar to the pattern noted for the Caribbean.

Tables 6.1 and 6.2 report the functional and economic distribution, respectively, of total public expenditure for selected developed and developing countries. The first noticeable feature is that spending on social security is much higher in the developed countries. The social security systems of developed countries are more advanced than those of developing countries. Chapter 16 shows that payroll taxes contribute a higher proportion of tax revenue in the developed countries. The only developing country which showed a similar pattern of spending on social security was Argentina. In recent years, some Latin American countries have improved their social security systems (Mesa-Lago 1997).

Governments in developing countries outlay a greater proportion of their expenditures on economic services than developed countries. This is perhaps due to a higher level of state involvement in the market economy. Developing countries invest heavily in infrastructure and provide a large number of support services in agriculture, manufacturing and tourism.

73

TABLE 6.1: Selected expenditures by function as percentage of total expenditures

Developed Countries	General Public Services	Defence	Education	Health	Social Security and Welfare	Economic Services
United States (1995)	9.72	16.84	1.77	19.20	29.23	5.51
Canada (1994)	10.68	5.81	2.89	4.89	39.79	8.79
Japan (1993)	3.63	4.11	6.03	1.60	36.86	3.35
Australia (1995)	9.47	7.18	7.61	13.43	33.57	7.39
Netherlands (1995)	9.21	3.92	10.63	14.64	37.04	5.88
Spain (1993)	5.74	3.33	4.20	6.15	39.59	8.07
Sweden (1995)	7.86	5.29	5.29	0.26	51.89	10.87
Switzerland (1993)	4.66	2.57	2.57	20.46	48.17	11.32
United Kingdom (1995)	7.10	4.94	4.94	13.96	31.12	5.93
Developing Countries						
Botswana (1993)	18.18	12.05	20.64	5.13	3.78	15.33
Ghana (1993)	14.11	4.85	22.03	6.96	7.10	15.95
Zaire (1995)	50.05	3.71	0.82	0.76	–	36.30
India (1995)	7.25	14.45	1.80	1.65	–	15.14
Indonesia (1994)	8.42	6.90	9.77	32.50	5.27	31.24
Sri Lanka (1995)	9.25	14.59	10.11	5.86	18.06	17.71
Argentina (1992)	13.59	6.59	4.73	1.99	50.70	11.82
Grenada (1995)	22.37	–	16.85	10.44	8.64	28.40
St Vincent (1995)	37.62	–	16.58	13.17	7.69	13.75
Barbados (1995)*	8.75	2.80	20.22	19.45	8.07	14.44

Source: IMF, *Government Finance Statistics Yearbook*, 1996.
*Central Bank of Barbados, *Annual Statistical Digest*, 1996.

TABLE 6.2: Selected expenditures by economic type as percentage of total expenditures and net lending

Developed Countries	Capital Expenditure	Current Expenditure	Goods and Services	Wages and Salaries	Subsidies and Current Transfers
United States (1995)	3.38	96.12	22.87	8.67	58.77
Belgium (1994)	4.75	95.62	18.10	14.53	57.89
France (1995)	4.36	94.14	23.81	16.13	63.53
Germany (1993)	4.78	94.85	30.51	7.98	57.01
Italy (1994)	3.68	93.70	14.60	10.91	57.15
Spain (1993)	6.58	93.65	20.34	14.42	62.23
Sweden (1995)	3.16	96.19	15.25	5.96	72.91
Switzerland (1993)	4.46	92.43	28.77	4.83	60.93
United Kingdom (1995)	5.08	94.86	29.63	8.53	56.40
Developing Countries					
Botswana (1993)	15.18	73.68	48.29	25.67	23.61
Ghana (1993)	14.52	84.51	44.89	27.70	23.21
Zaire (1995)	3.19	96.81	94.50	57.80	1.67
India (1995)	9.78	75.69	18.81	8.00	32.89
Indonesia (1994)	45.75	48.51	25.03	13.28	13.21
Sri Lanka (1995)	21.36	76.24	35.16	18.97	21.13
Argentina (1992)	2.88	92.15	24.74	18.67	58.27
Grenada (1995)	24.55	75.45	62.23	41.61	6.26
St Kitts and Nevis (1994)	10.99	88.89	63.74	–	11.84
St Vincent (1995)	9.08	90.92	–	–	–
Barbados (1995)*	11.34	88.60	–	36.50	26.50

Source: IMF, *Government Finance Statistics Yearbook,* 1996.
        *Central Bank of Barbados, *Annual Statistical Digest,* 1996.

Earlier chapters have shown that developing countries have been part of the movement towards liberalization and deregulation. The proportion of expenditure on education is also higher in some developing countries such as Barbados, Grenada, St Vincent, Ghana, and Botswana. Spending on education and health is lowest in India and Zaire.

Table 6.2 shows that capital expenditure is a much lower proportion of total expenditure in developed countries than in most developing countries. This tendency is a result of a lower ratio of spending on economic services in the developed countries. For most developing countries wages and salaries constitute a higher proportion of their budgets. This can be partly explained by the lack of economies of scale in the public services, some of which are large relative to the rest of the economy.

Subsidies and current transfers constitute a higher percentage of total expenditure in the developed than in the developing countries. Subsidies include payments to enterprises in both the public and private sectors. In many developing countries, subsidies and transfers cover losses by state enterprises. As Gillis, Perkins and Roemer (1992: 298) have pointed out, food subsidies in developing countries have been common in countries such as Sri Lanka, Egypt, and India. These subsidies help to control the price of basic food and improve the income distribution. The higher level of transfers in the developed countries relate to the greater emphasis on social security and welfare.

Expenditure Controls

The analysis in Howard (1992) noted that large subsidies and transfers to public enterprises, as well as increased spending on economic and public services, led to unsustainable fiscal deficits in many developing countries during the 1980s. Structural adjustment and stabilization programmes (see chapters 11 and 12 of this book), were required to increase the efficiency of governments. Expenditure controls are part of structural adjustment and have become necessary in developing countries to ensure discipline in the operation of government. Premchand (1983: 280–86) has outlined the nature of expenditure controls. His observations form the basis of our subsequent discussion. His five techniques of expenditure control are as follows:

1. Across-the-board cuts in expenditures constitute an approach whereby all expenditures are given equal treatment. This technique requires centralized control of budgetary expenditures. Across-the-board cuts may ignore the importance of high growth

sectors leading to a misallocation of resources.

2. Specific sector cuts have the advantage of eliminating or reducing programmes which are unproductive. They are preferable to across-the-board cuts because government can implement and maintain the priority areas in its development plan.

3. Another technique is the selection of quick-yielding projects. Such projects are not often identified in the budget. The problem with this technique is that the benefits of most government projects cannot be evaluated simply in terms of revenue yield. Social and external benefits have to be considered.

4. Public sector wage cuts and reductions in administrative posts constitute another means of reducing the cost of government.

5. The imposition of cash ceilings has been employed in the United Kingdom. This approach indicates the maximum amounts that could be spent on blocks of services. However, frequent revisions may be necessary in the context of inflation. This could lead to uncertainty in planning expenditures.

The implementation of expenditure cuts, especially during a period of structural adjustment, often leads to a slow-down in the growth of social expenditures. The structural adjustment programme in Jamaica, for example, resulted in a decline in social and economic services. Handa and King (1997: 925–28) report that government expenditure on social and economic services between 1988 and 1993 fell by 32 percent in real terms. The reductions in real public spending in education and health also caused a decline in the quality of services provided.

PUBLIC EXPENDITURE AND ECONOMIC GROWTH

An important area of concern in the literature is the relationship between public expenditure and economic growth. Diamond (1990), Tanzi and Zee (1997), Easterly and Rebelo (1993), and Belgrave and Craigwell (1997) are among a growing number of economists examining this issue. Diamond considers the thesis that government spending may actually slow down the accumulation of human and physical capital, if such spending leads to a resource transfer from the private sector to the government. This is the so-called crowding out phenomenon. This argument is also supported by the observation that the public sector is less efficient than the private sector, and therefore economic growth is much slower as a result of increases in public spending.

Government can accelerate growth through spending on human capital and health to expand the productivity of the labour force. Spending on technical and university education enhances the knowledge base of the economy and raises the level of skills. Research and development expenditures and the provision of new technology complement spending on human capital resources.

Diamond's (1990) study used a sample of 38 developing countries to investigate the relationship between government expenditure and economic growth. His work shows, on the basis of regression analysis, that countries with higher levels of government capital expenditure as a share of GDP have higher growth rates. His main conclusions were "that capital expenditures on health, housing, and welfare may boost growth in the short term; capital infrastructure expenditure may have little influence on growth; and directly productive capital expenditures may even negatively influence growth. At the same time, current expenditure in directly productive sectors appears to exert a significant positive influence on growth" (Diamond 1990: 36).

Tanzi and Zee (1997) survey the empirical evidence on the growth effects of public expenditure in developed and developing countries. Much of this evidence is inconclusive. We note the results reached by Easterly and Rebelo (1993: 419) using cross-section and panel data for developed and developing countries. First, they found that the share of public investment in transport and communications was robustly correlated with economic growth. Second, the government's budget surplus was also consistently correlated with growth and private investment. Third, they found that the link between other fiscal variables and growth was statistically insignificant.

Cross-section analysis may not give a true picture of the relationship between government expenditure and growth for individual countries. Belgrave and Craigwell (1997) investigated the evidence for Barbados using historical data. They distinguish between "productive" and "unproductive" government expenditure. "Productive government expenditure is classified as that component of public expenditure, an increase in whose share will raise the trend growth rate of the economy" (Belgrave and Craigwell 1997: 40). Their results indicate that capital expenditure can be considered productive because it was positively related to growth. Health, housing, agriculture, and public works determine economic growth and are considered productive. However, educational expenditure was surprisingly insignificant. Current expenditure was negatively related to growth and can be considered unproductive.

SUMMARY

We have examined the main causes of public expenditure growth in developing countries. They include stages of growth theories, displacement effects, unbalanced productivity growth as well as public choice theories in an earlier chapter. The analysis informs us that it is quite difficult to explain government expenditure growth by employing a single economic model or econometric techniques. There are considerable non-economic and political factors which determine the size of government.

The structure of government expenditure in developing countries reveals some differences when compared with developed countries. First, the developed countries place heavy emphasis on social security expenditure, whereas developing countries spend more money on economic services. This is because spending on social infrastructure is very important in countries at lower stages of development. Developing countries need to control their expenditures because failure to do so results in chronic fiscal and balance of payments problems.

Contributions to the literature on the impact of government expenditure on economic growth were examined. This literature is inconclusive on the nature of this relationship. It is acknowledged that certain types of capital expenditure augment economic growth.

Chapter Seven

Income Distribution and Poverty Alleviation in Developing Countries

D uring the 1990s poverty alleviation programmes were implmented by many governments in developing countries. Public sector economics involves the analysis of the income distribution, inequality, and poverty alleviation. First, we examine the concept and measurement of the income distribution and its relationship to economic development. Second, the discussion focuses on the concept of poverty and its manifestations in developing countries. Third, and perhaps most importantly, the choice of various government policies to redistribute income and alleviate poverty will be discussed.

CONCEPT AND MEASUREMENT OF INCOME DISTRIBUTION

It is important to distinguish between household or personal income distribution and functional distribution. Personal distribution describes the allocation of income among various groups in the society. It is normal to speak of the distribution of income among lower, middle and upper income groups. The lower income group is usually the largest, and one of the tools of government is to raise the level of real income of this group relative to higher income earners. Functional distribution is concerned with the return to various factors of production. This approach is sometimes called the theory of distributive shares, which explains the determination of wages, profits, rent and interest. Wealth or asset distribution refers to the distribution of economic ownership, which also determines overall income distribution.

Conceptually, income distribution has been described as a public good. Thurow (1971) asserts that each individual faces the same income distribution. An individual's welfare will depend on his own income as well as the prevailing income distribution. Government must intervene to provide a more equitable distribution by implementing an appropriate tax/transfer mechanism.

One of the best known approaches to measuring income distribution is the Lorenz curve. This is a technique which consists of plotting along the vertical axis the percentage share of income held by households, and on the horizontal axis the accumulated percentage of households. The line of perfect equality or 45-degree line running from the lower left-hand corner to the upper right-hand corner shows an equal distribution of income. The closer the Lorenz curve is to the line of perfect equality, the more equal income distribution is. For a further discussion and illustration of the Lorenz curve technique, the reader is referred to Brown and Jackson (1990: 387–89).

The Gini coefficient is derived from the Lorenz curve. The coefficient gives a precise measurement of the income distribution at any point on the Lorenz curve. The coefficient is the ratio of the area between the Lorenz curve and the 45-degree line, to the total area under the 45-degree line. The Gini coefficient lies between zero and one. The closer the ratio is to one the greater the degree of inequality. Likewise, the Gini coefficient approaches zero as the income distribution approaches perfect equality.

The use of the Gini coefficient as a basis for comparisons of the income distribution between countries in Latin America and the Caribbean encounters a number of problems. Some countries use census data and others employ household budget surveys. Different income concepts and inadequate data bases also lead to false interpretations of the Gini coefficient (Cardoso and Helwege 1992). Despite these problems, it is important to note the wide variation in the Gini coefficient for Latin American countries in the late 1980s. Psacharopoulos (1993) shows that Brazil, Chile, Guatemala, Honduras, Columbia and Panama reported Gini ratios above 0.5 in 1989 compared with other Latin American countries where the ratios varied between 0.4 and 0.46. The sharp variations in the Gini coefficients were attributable to declining real wages during the recessionary period of the 1980s. In the Caribbean countries of Barbados and Jamaica, Gini coeffi-cients have been reported for specific years during the 1970s and 1980s. Downes (1987) found a Gini coefficient of 0.4638 for Barbados in 1978, while Diez de Medina (1997) reported a lower coefficient of 0.41 for Barbados in 1996. The reported Gini coefficient for Jamaica was 0.526 in 1983 (Wasylenko 1986). Howard (1992) provides detailed explanations of the variations in the income distribution in Barbados and Jamaica during the recessionary conditions of the 1970s and 1980s.

ECONOMIC DEVELOPMENT AND INCOME INEQUALITY

Much of the work on development and income inequality in the 1970s was devoted to testing Kuznets' (1955) inverted U-shaped hypothesis, that as per capita income rises in the early stages of development, inequality also increases. At higher levels of development, the income distribution improves. This relationship has been investigated by Ahluwalia (1976). The major results found in the work of Ahluwalia (1974, 1976), which used cross-section analysis to examine the relationship between the income shares of various percentile income groups and other variables such as education, population growth and economic growth which may influence income inequality, are reported here.

The cross-section analysis of Ahluwalia revealed that the relationship between development and inequality follows the inverted U-shaped pattern observed by Kuznets. This work on inequality and development in the 1970s had important implications for redistribution policy, because it revealed crucial relationships substantially affecting the inequality process. First, education was observed to be positively related to equality. Ahluwalia found that secondary schooling was associated with shifts in income from the top 20 percent income group to all other groups except the lowest 20 percent. Moreover, secondary schooling tended to benefit the middle income group more than the lower income group. Increases in the literacy rate was associated with an increase in the income share of the lowest 40 percent income group (Ahluwalia 1976: 323).

Second, the growth of population tended to increase inequality among the lowest 40 percent income group. This is explained by the fact that population growth is highest mainly in the lowest income groups, so that countries experiencing rapid population growth will show a slower growth of per capita income among low income groups when compared with the rich. This process increases income inequality at a given level of per capita GNP (Ahluwalia 1976: 326).

Third, the cross-section results did not indicate that a faster rate of growth leads to higher inequality at a given level of development. Ahluwalia (1974: 17) asserts that the rate of growth of GDP was positively related to the share of the lowest 40 percent income group.

A study by Anand and Kanbur (1993) using cross-section data, tested the hypothesis that all countries follow the same Kuznets' process. This work rejected the hypothesis. However, the authors admit that time series data may show that the Kuznets' process may or may not operate in some countries.

This analysis of the relationship between development and inequality was not concerned with other significant factors affecting inequality in national economies. The work primarily provided some policy parameters available to governments to influence the income distribution. Obviously, cultural, historical and political factors are important. We argue later that human resource development is one of the most important policy parameters for redistributing income in developing countries.

MEASUREMENT AND EXTENT OF POVERTY

It is important to distinguish between inequality and poverty. Inequality of income relates to relative income levels across the society. The World Bank's *World Development Report* (1990) defines poverty as the inability to attain a minimum standard of living. It is generally recognized that income alone cannot be used to measure a person's standard of living. The attainment of certain consumption levels, the satisfying of basic needs such as education, health care, and the access to resources are the criteria which are widely used to determine poverty levels in a society. My subsequent discussion draws heavily on the World Bank's *World Development Report* (1990) and the United Nations Development Programme's (UNDP) *Human Development Report* (1997).

A distinction has been made in the literature between absolute and relative poverty. Absolute poverty refers to the standard of living of members of society which falls below some absolute or minimum requirement, very often referred to as the poverty line. Relative poverty is closer to the concept of inequality in the income distribution. The World Bank in its 1990 *Development Report* defined an arbitrary global poverty line of US$370.00

defined in constant 1985 prices. The advantage of the concept of a global poverty line permits cross-country comparisons. However, a global poverty line disregards the value placed on various commodities by nationals in different countries. National poverty lines have been used as a basis for national poverty alleviation programmes.

Attempts to measure poverty have relied on either income or consumption as a *numeraire*. The World Bank uses a consumption-based poverty line. This is calculated by gauging the expenditure required to buy a minimum standard of nutrition. Other measures are usually added included life expectancy, infant mortality, and school enrolment rates. National poverty lines vary depending on the criteria used for estimating food energy requirements (UNDP 1997).

The UNDP report (1997) introduced a Human Poverty Index (HPI) to measure more precisely the extent of poverty across countries. The index includes variables other than income and consumption. The HPI includes the percentage of persons expected to die before age 40, the percentage of adults who are illiterate, and the percentage of people without access to health services. Other variables in the HPI are availability of safe water, and the percentage of underweight children under five. Some of the implications of this index for the measurement of poverty in various countries will be discussed later.

The extent of poverty can be estimated by the headcount index and the poverty gap (World Bank 1997). The headcount index indicates the number of poor as a proportion of the population. The poverty gap measures the income transfer necessary to bring each member of the poor up to the poverty line.

The World Bank and the UNDP have employed the various measures outlined above to estimate the extent and characteristics of world poverty. These findings are now briefly discussed. In its 1990 *World Development Report*, the World Bank estimated that in 1985, 1,115 million people in the developing countries lived in poverty, or one-third of the total population of the developing world. Most of the world's poor live in South Asia and sub-Saharan Africa, with very low life expectancy and primary school enrolment rates in sub-Saharan Africa. In these regions, income poverty was more extensive in rural areas. Problems of malnutrition, lack of education, and low life expectancy were most severe in the countryside.

The UNDP report (1997) recognizes that the HPI cannot measure the totality of human poverty. However, the report employed this index to rank 78 developing countries by their poverty status. Trinidad and Tobago, followed by Cuba, Chile, Singapore, and Costa Rica were the countries where human poverty affects less than 10 percent of their people. Human poverty was most severe in seven countries – Niger, Sierra Leone, Burkina Faso, Ethiopia, Mali, Cambodia, and Mozambique. In the latter group of countries, the HPI exceeds 50 percent. The UNDP's analysis came to similar conclusions as the World Bank's, noting that poverty affected a quarter to a third of the people in the developing world, and 40 percent of this poverty was in sub-Saharan Africa and South Asia. The HPI registered 15 percent in Latin America and the Caribbean.

Earlier work by Altimir (1982) and the Economic Commission for Latin America and the Caribbean (ECLAC 1989) measured the poverty lines for Latin American countries by estimating the cost of a minimum food budget, assuming differences in local dietary customs. Given the difficulty of estimating the non-food component of poverty, including the cost of housing, health care, other services, and education, the poverty line for each country was based on the cost of a basic food basket multiplied by two. Altimir estimated that 40 percent of Latin American households were poor in 1970. The incidence of poverty was highest in Honduras, Peru, Brazil, and Colombia (Cardoso and Helwege 1992). Morley (1995) produced other evidence about Latin American poverty in the 1980s. He estimated that the percentage of the poor in Latin America rose from 26.5 percent in 1980 to 31.0 percent in 1989, with most poverty found in the rural areas.

In the Caribbean, the World Bank (1996) has estimated that poverty in the region averages 38 percent of the total population, ranging from 65 percent in Haiti to a low of 5 percent in the Bahamas. The head count index showed that the Bahamas, Antigua and Barbuda, Barbados, and St Kitts and Nevis had the lowest poverty levels. The incidence of poverty was highest in Belize, Dominica, Guyana, Haiti, Jamaica, and Suriname. Poverty rates were also higher than 20 percent in the Dominican Republic, St Lucia, and Trinidad and Tobago (see World Bank 1996: 3–4).

POLICIES TO ALLEVIATE POVERTY AND REDISTRIBUTE INCOME

Policies designed to alleviate poverty also help to reduce income inequality. All policies are not equally effective and depend on the stage of the country's development, the structure of the economy, and the budgetary resources available to the government. In this section, we focus primarily on policies that deal with the poor. These policies include stimulating economic growth, direct government expenditures on a national scale to provide health care, education, and other social services. Social security and the targeting of transfers also deal directly with the poor. Redistribution through the market mechanism is not as effective as the measures above. Programmes designed to reduce poverty by targeting the poor are sometimes known as poverty alleviation programmes.

Spending on Human Resources

The principal rationale for government spending on education and training is that such outlays provide human capital. Ahluwalia's analysis discussed previously implies that improved secondary education benefits middle income groups, while increases in the literacy rate enhance the income share of the lowest income groups. His work leads to the conclusion that government spending to improve the income distribution should be targeted towards primary and secondary education.

Knowledge contributes directly to the development process. Such spending in developing countries results from the existence of a shortage of critical skills such as doctors, agronomists, and technical personnel. The identification of these shortages must be followed by a strategy to overcome them by the provision of appropriate incentives for training and by orienting the educational system to meet the demands of the economy. In many developing economies it may be necessary to increase the share of the budget targeted to the provision of primary education especially in rural areas.

Expenditure on human resource development helps to reduce poverty and inequality by increasing productivity as well as the earnings capacity of the individual. This also fosters upward social mobility. Education also increases national productive capacity thereby stimulating employment and improving the income distribution. The use of education as a redistribution device can be slowed by the lack of absorptive capacity of many developing economies. This refers to the maximum number of persons which can be employed without redundancy or underutilization of skills. A highly abundant supply of education means that the products of the educational system may have to accept jobs at a much lower level of skill than the jobs for which they have been trained. Sometimes intellectual unemployment may result. Therefore, human resource policies have to be closely linked to other policies designed to augment economic growth.

Pattern of Economic Growth

The World Bank's *World Development Report* (1990: 56) proposes a "pattern of economic growth that increases the efficient use of the assets owned by the poor". These comprise long-term rural development schemes and urban employment that increase the earnings of small farmers and wage labour. This approach would include a reduction in agricultural taxation and making technical innovations accessible to small farmers. The Report shows that indirect taxes have a heavy incidence on agriculture in some developing countries. The patterns of agricultural subsidies are also important. However, if pricing supports are biased in favour of large farmers, this may lead to economic growth but worsen the income distribution in the rural sector. Generally speaking, growth can be accelerated by human resource development, increasing both agricultural and manufactured exports, and by using foreign aid and borrowing productively.

Research by the World Bank (1996) showed that high-growth countries in the Caribbean such as Antigua, Bahamas, Barbados, and St Kitts and Nevis had relatively low levels of poverty. Countries with negative or low growth rates like Guyana, Haiti, Jamaica, Suriname, and Trinidad and Tobago had higher levels of poverty. It is suggested that increasing a country's growth rate may reduce levels of poverty by creating jobs and higher income levels among the poor.

Targeting the Poor

The targeting of benefits to the poor is an important means of increasing the impact of direct government expenditures on the income distribution and poverty. Successful targeting relies on the choice of criteria to identify the poor, the administrative feasibility of the targeted programme, and the type of resource transfer such as cash, food or other assets which are being made available to the poor (Shaw 1993). The technical aspects of targeting have been investigated by Atkinson (1995), Kanbur, Keen and Tuomala (1995), Grosh (1995), Besley and Kanbur (1988) and Keen (1992). Sen (1995) considers some of the constraints on targeting as an instrument for alleviating poverty.

Van de Walle (1998b: 232–37) has made a distinction between broad targeting and narrow targeting. Under a strategy of broad targeting, no attempt is made to reach the poor directly but expenditures are allocated towards broad areas which are important to the poor. Such expenditure includes outlays on basic social services such as primary education, health care, and rural development. It is possible to determine the "benefit incidence" of such spending by ranking the population into income per capita groups, and estimating the amount of government spending allocated to each group (see van de Walle 1998a).

Narrow targeting attempts to concentrate spending on well-defined vulnerable groups of poor people. This type of targeting can be based on means testing where the recipient of income transfers or transfers in kind can be identified by a means test. That is, persons above stipulated income levels do not qualify for certain benefits, for instance, medicare, food stamps, and so forth. The World Bank's *World Development Report* (1990: 92) and van de Walle (1998b) also discuss "indicator targeting". Correlates of poverty are identified from sample surveys and benefits allocated, not according to income, but by region of residence, landholding, gender, nutritional status or household size. Another approach known as "self-targeting" subsidizes only those commodities the target group has indicated it prefers. According to Alderman and Lindert (1998: 213), self-targeting is a substitute for generalized food subsidies in order to limit participation to the intended beneficiaries rather than better-off groups.

Alderman and Lindert (1998) discuss how Tunisia transformed its generalized food subsidies to a self-targeting programme based on product quality differentiation. In 1993 the Tunisian government shifted subsidies to narrowly defined food items that were perceived by beneficiaries to be of lower status because of packaging or ingredients. These foods were of identical quality to previous subsidized products, but they were perceived as "inferior goods" by wealthier households. Alderman and Lindert assert that self-targeting substantially reduced the Tunisian government's expenditure on food subsidies, and ensured that subsidized products reached the vulnerable target groups.

Ali and Adams (1996) also assess the impact of the Egyptian food subsidy system on the income distribution. They argue that even though four subsidized foods, namely, bread, wheat flour, sugar and oil, were available to all Egyptians, the system was self-targeted to the poor because it subsidized "inferior foods", particularly bread and sugar. "Inferior foods" are those which are consumed in greater proportion by the poor than by the rich.

The belief that market-wide food price subsidies may benefit better-off groups is also reflected in the Jamaican government's food aid programme. Polanyi-Levitt (1991) analyses this targeted food programme introduced in 1984 to cushion the effects of recession and structural adjustment. Polanyi-Levitt asserts that the Jamaican food stamp programme was designed to support persons who needed basic nutritional support. Beneficiaries of the programme are assessed on the basis of financial need. The poor and elderly under the Public Assistance Programmes automatically qualify for food stamps. Polanyi-Levitt (1991: 47) criticized the food stamp programme as a poor substitute for the direct subsidization of imported food staples. She argues that food stamps were accepted by traders as cash. However, I believe that narrow targeting is preferable as a poverty alleviation programme to subsidizing a broad base of imported food.

Atkinson (1995) has cautioned that though targeting has become politically acceptable, this policy should pay close attention to the objectives of policy, the range of policy instruments, and the constraints of targeting. He argues that the relative efficiency of each policy instrument depends on how poverty is measured and how the poverty objective is defined.

The principal constraints on targeting policies include imperfect information, administrative costs, work incentive distortion, and stigma (Atkinson 1995) and (Sen 1995). The effectiveness of any targeting programme depends on the information available to government. Persons who do not satisfy the criteria for benefits may provide inaccurate information in order to qualify (Sen 1995: 12). Also, the existence of the programme may not be known to all eligible persons. This asymmetry of information often leads to false claims and corruption.

Another problem noted by Sen (1995: 13) and Atkinson (1995: 53) is that persons may be aware of their entitlement but do not make a claim. Some people are afraid of being stigmatized as poor. This problem is usually associated with income-tested benefits. Further, targeted programmes have to be monitored. A person who is entitled to a benefit may cease to qualify if his earnings improve. If he is not monitored he will continue to receive benefits at the expense of an eligible person.

Systems of targeting also involve administrative costs in the form of resource costs and bureaucratic delays. Grosh (1995) has argued that the administrative costs of targeted programmes in Latin America are not as high as generally believed. She further found that targeted programmes had a much more progressive incidence than general food price subsidies, public health, and education services. This implied that the poor benefited proportionally more from targeted programmes than from general policy instruments.

Incentive distortion as noted by Sen (1995: 13) is an important consideration in designing a targeting programme. Incentive distortion arises as a result of reductions in labour productivity. That is, subsidies may induce persons to reduce their labour supply, by removing the incentive to increase their income through their own efforts. Research on this is not conclusive. Moffitt (1992) notes that the disincentive effects of social security benefits in the United States are limited.

Redistribution through the Market

Government can also redistribute real income by manipulating relative prices. This is a more indirect route to deal with the poverty problem. Minimum wage legislation, agricultural price controls, and taxation policies can be used to interfere with the price mechanism to bring about an income distribution which favours the poor. These policies reduce the efficiency of the market mechanism, and the effects on the income distribution are not always predictable.

Minimum wage legislation is designed to attack poverty resulting partly from low wages. Minimum wage policies help to defend the income of wage earners in the face of rapid inflation. Along with the imposition of minimum wages, governments also try to regulate relative wage levels between sectors in the context of a sectoral redistribution policy. Wages should, however, be tied to productivity to maintain levels of economic growth. Although minimum wages can offer workers a small degree of protection, minimum wages cannot be too high because this may generate unemployment among the unskilled. Employers may react to a high minimum wage by restricting employment.

Another method by which government can interfere in the market mechanism to improve the income distribution is the provision of price support schemes for farmers. This policy can be combined with the provision of subsidies for public services such as transport and low-cost housing. In the rural sector, deteriorating terms of trade lead to a worsening of the rural income distribution because many farmers are dependent on staple exports which are subject to price fluctuations. Governments often establish price supports by buying surplus output, therefore allowing farm prices to remain constant. However, subsidies generally lead to economic inefficiency and impose a cost on the government's budget. Additional taxation is often levied on other groups in the society in order to pay for the subsidy. These groups may not necessarily benefit from lower prices.

Heavy indirect taxation on luxury goods and lower taxes on essential goods allow income to be redistributed by changing the purchasing power of various income groups. Taxation is not regarded as an efficient means of income distribution because very often higher income groups purchase similar goods bought by the poor. Price controls on essential goods may be used to achieve the same purpose, but these may lead to black market activity, especially if the controls are placed on a wide range of goods. The present emphasis on market liberalization has led to a reduction in the use of price controls in many countries.

Importance of Social Security

Following Howard (1992: 102), there are three main functions of social security. First, it is a form of insurance against the risk of an uncertain lifetime. The poor find it difficult to save enough money to provide for old age and the problems which arise from disability. The government therefore has to intervene to provide a compulsory tax transfer mechanism known as national insurance to provide pensions for the aged. Second, social security is a redistributive mechanism among the existing workforce. Intragenerational redistribution takes the form of contributions to national insurance schemes in the form of payroll taxes. These contributions are divided between employees and employers. The share of these groups may vary from country to country. In turn, the national insurance scheme pays benefits thereby providing contributors with protection against loss of income arising from old age, disability, or injury. Third, in many countries social security is a savings mechanism which can be used to finance other social services provided by the government.

National insurance schemes have been analysed in relation to their impact on work incentives. It is sometimes argued that these schemes may reduce work effort. People who are on welfare for many years may lose the incentive to work. Other analyses have focused on the incidence of payroll taxes to support these schemes. The argument is that payroll taxes tend to be regressive and fall heavily on workers. These aspects of payroll taxation will be analysed when we consider taxation in more detail.

Social Security in the Caribbean and Latin America

The World Bank (1996) documents the coverage and range of benefits of the national insurance and social security schemes in the Caribbean. Although in all countries the national insurance scheme is compulsory for employees, workers in the informal sector, especially in Belize and Guyana, are not covered. The coverage of the population of pensionable age receiving pensions is 92 percent in Barbados, 82 percent in Trinidad and Tobago, 10 percent in Belize, 26 percent in Dominica and less than 5 percent in Grenada (see World Bank 1996: Annex IV, Table IV.4).

The range of benefits are similar across Caribbean countries, although only Barbados provides an unemployment benefit. All schemes have short-term benefits such as sickness and maternity and in some countries employment injury. The schemes also include long-term benefits such as old-age pensions, invalidity and survivors' benefits. Some schemes also provide non-contributory old-age pensions (see World Bank 1996: Annex IV, Table IV.2).

It is appropriate to consider existing models of social security in Latin America, drawing on the work of Mesa-Lago (1997). My analysis is designed to acquaint readers with Mesa-Lago's contribution. No attempt is made to discuss in a few paragraphs the details of Latin America's social security systems.

Mesa-Lago (1997) suggests that social security reform in Latin America was a response to the fiscal crisis resulting from a heavy external debt burden, as well as a deep economic recession during the 1980s. The existing welfare system in Latin America was not capable of dealing with the social costs of these crises, reflected in a rise in inflation and unemployment, and a decline in real wages.

Mesa-Lago distinguishes between three models of social security reform in Latin America. The first is the Chilean model, characterized by a substantial private sector component. The second was the public sector model, and Cuba was an extreme case of this approach. The third type of model was a mixed system, which incorporated state control and private sector involvement. He argues that the Chilean model was part of an extensive liberal structural adjustment programme initiated under a military authoritarian regime. Cuba's state-controlled social security system was started before the economic crisis of the 1980s.

The Chilean social security system is operated by private competing corporations, and regulated and supervised by a state agency. There is no employer contribution and only insured workers contribute. The state continues to finance the deficit of the older public system which still maintains a large number of pensioners (Mesa-Lago 1997: 509–10).

Cuba, Costa Rica, and Mexico have public security systems which have not been reformed. Coverage in Cuba is universal and employers pay a 10 percent payroll contribution, and the state covers any resulting deficit. Health care is universal and egalitarian in Cuba. In Costa Rica and Mexico, reforms have been designed to strengthen the state-controlled system. Space constraints do not permit a consideration of all the mixed social security systems, and the reader is referred to Mesa-Lago (1997: 510–15).

Informal Safety Nets

Informal safety nets play an important role in alleviating poverty. In the Caribbean, the World Bank (1996) indicates that there has been a strong tradition of self-help and mutual aid. Further, the extended family has provided assistance for its elderly members as well as the young. At the community level, non-governmental organizations (NGOs) and other community-based groups play their part in poverty alleviation. These organizations depend on charitable donations and voluntary service. It has been suggested that these groups perform a central role in community development, and in some countries are quite large. It is estimated that 300 NGOs exist in Haiti, 300 in Guyana and 110 in Belize (see World Bank 1996: 41).

INDIA'S EXPERIENCE WITH POVERTY ALLEVIATION PROGRAMMES

Countries in southern Asia have high rates of rural poverty. Poverty alleviation programmes have been designed to attack poverty directly. We review India's poverty alleviation programmes during the 1980s, by summarizing the evaluations of these programmes by Maithani (1993), Hye (1993), and Rao (1993).

It has been suggested that the adoption of direct poverty alleviation programmes by the government of India arose from the failure of the development and growth process to reduce poverty among the poor. Growth itself was slow and uneven, and the benefits of growth did not trickle down to the poor because of a weak institutional framework (Maithani 1993: 66).

India's attack on poverty utilized the targeting approach. Hye (1993: 73–79) has identified four main strategies. These included land reform measures, wage-employment programmes, self-employment programmes, and social welfare measures. These programmes were regarded as a visible response to poverty by the Indian government in order to bring about immediate benefits. Further, targeted programmes were seen as part of the overall development strategy (Maithani 1993).

Land reform measures adopted in India were designed to redistribute land to assist marginal farmers and share croppers. Hye (1993: 85) asserts that the benefits of land reform were limited, partly because of the entrenched power of the élite, and the failure of the land reforms to effect a more equitable distribution of land holdings.

Wage employment was the second strategy adopted by the Indian government. This programme provided employment for the poor through rural works programmes. The wage employment programmes gave priority to activities which helped to improve land resources and the ecosystem in rural areas, including irrigation, construction of field channels, drainage, and soil conservation measures such as afforestation (Rao 1993: 149).

A well-known example of wage employment is the employment guarantee scheme organized by the Maharashtra State in India since the 1970s. We describe here some of the characteristics of this scheme, but no attempt is made to evaluate the scheme in terms of its coverage and the extent to which it has relieved poverty in the state of Maharashtra.[1] The Maharashtra's employment guarantee scheme was designed to provide unskilled manual labour on small-scale, rural public works projects such as roads, irrigation, and reforestation. The scheme is financed by taxes on the urban sector of the state of Maharashtra (Ravallion and Datt 1995: 418).

An important element of wage employment was the adoption of food-for-work programmes. The first of these was started in 1977 and was designed to employ rural people. Wages were paid partly in kind using food grains stored in government buffer stocks. This was converted into the National Rural Employment Programme in 1980 (see Hye 1993: 76) for details of the various schemes). Hye has criticized these strategies for reaching only a small number of the rural poor.

A third aspect of the poverty alleviation programmes in India was self-employment. One of the self-employment initiatives is the Integrated Rural Development Programme which was designed to reduce poverty through skill formation. Beneficiaries were provided with income-generating productive inputs. Beneficiaries were identified by a baseline survey assessing household income. Wage employment programmes were subsidized by the central and state governments (see Rao 1993: 151).

Social safety net measures were introduced including various welfare programmes such as the Special Nutrition Programme, and a midday meal programme. The Special Nutrition Programme covered pre-school children, pregnant women, and nursing mothers, while the midday meal programme included primary school children. It is estimated that the Special Nutrition Programme covered 11.5 million persons between 1985 and 1990 (Hye 1993: 79). An old-age pension scheme was also introduced for agricultural workers and other unorganized rural workers. Further, the Indian Public Distribution System aimed at guaranteeing essential commodities at subsidized prices to the poor (Hye 1993: 79).

The institutional mechanisms for the administration of the various poverty alleviation programmes were based on the existing infrastructure, as well as the establishment of local government bodies at the community level. The role of these bodies was to plan and implement the various rural employment programmes. The Special Nutrition Programme was bureaucratically administered. Hye (1993: 80) suggests that this programme had a small impact on the nutritional status of the poor because of inadequate community participation.

Maithani (1993: 67) has raised some criticisms of the Indian targeted programmes. He argues that the programmes did not influence the structural causes of poverty, and he questions the sustainability of these programmes. Maithani also contends that most self-employed activity tended to be capital-intensive and skill-intensive, favouring large-scale commercial enterprises, and placing poor farmers at the mercy of market forces. Further, he maintains that wage employment programmes, despite the investment of huge resources, did not generate enough employment in terms of man-days.

Summary

Poverty and inequality are widespread in developing countries. The challenge facing policy makers is to devise a combination of policies which recognize the institutional and structural constraints of individual economies. These policies include human resource development, and the acceleration of the rate of economic growth in a manner which rewards certain economic groups like small farmers and small businesses. Other strategies include expenditure targeting and the improvement of social welfare programmes and social security. The structure of social security systems in Latin America and the Caribbean is varied. Chile is an example of a privatized social system, whereas the Cuban system is completely state-controlled. Other systems in countries such as Costa Rica and Mexico, as well as systems in the Caribbean, show a predominant state involvement. The Indian experience with poverty alleviation programmes shows that it is necessary to generate employment as one means to reduce poverty levels.

Chapter Eight

Introduction to Public Utility Regulation

P ublic utilities are found in both the public and private sectors. Well-known public utilities are electricity, telephone, gas, and water operations. The practice of public utility regulation varies widely in both developed and developing countries. This chapter introduces the reader to the main factors determining the regulation of prices in public utilities. The chapter looks first at the nature of public utilities and the need for a price which should be fair and reasonable to consumers. Second, we consider marginal cost pricing or optimal pricing which is the theoretical approach to public utility pricing, but has serious limitations as a method of pricing in real world public utility rate-making. Third, we examine the institutional approach to rate-making. This approach analyses the criteria used in rate-making to determine the rate base and rate of return to the public utility. The last two concepts are important elements of public utilities regulation.

Many of the issues in public utility economics are highly controversial. However, because of the highly specialized nature of this topic and its extensive literature, the chapter merely gives the reader a guide to the concepts used in public utility regulation, rather than an in-depth discussion of the various controversies. An examination of the differences in the structure of public utilities pricing in various developing countries is also beyond the scope of this book. Many public finance textbooks do not go beyond the standard treatment of marginal cost pricing and peak-load pricing using the neoclassical approach. It is hoped that the analysis of the broad issues in institutional rate-making in public utilities will encourage more research in this area in developing countries.

NATURE OF PUBLIC UTILITIES

Public utilities are large monopolies controlled by government regulations. According to Garfield and Lovejoy (1964), government regulation is a substitute for competition, given the indispensable nature of the service. Government regulation attempts to achieve reasonable prices or rates, reasonable profit, and adequate quality of service. Public utilities are usually described as natural monopolies because of the nature of the service provided, and because their large size leads to economies of large-scale production, as well as declining unit costs. Natural monopolies use large amounts of capital which is usually specific to their operations.

There are two major considerations influencing the demand for public utility services. These are the time pattern of demand and the elasticity of demand. Public utilities experience daily or seasonal peaks in demand and must have excess capacity to service these peaks. Variations in demand considerably influence the price of the service. Elasticities of demand vary for the services of public utilities. For example, the demand for electricity by households tends to be inelastic. However, the public utility is able to practise price discrimination because of differences in the elasticity of demand between consumers.

The monopoly power of public utilities as a result of large size and price discrimination implies that government regulation of their operations is very important if the utility is to achieve a reasonable pricing strategy. A reasonable price is one that is equitable. That is, consumers should not pay more than their fair share to the utility. The price should also provide a stable cash flow to the firm which would enable it to cover its financial obligations. A reasonable price should also be convenient to collect.

The determination of a reasonable price is a highly complex task. Normally, a public utilities board or tribunal is called upon to apply certain legal principles in arriving at such prices. Legal differences exist over definitions of the rate of return to the public utility, the concept of valuation of the utility's property, the treatment of depreciation expenses, and so forth. These difficulties are discussed in a public utilities rate hearing where representatives of the firm and the public can advance arguments for or against price changes.

MARGINAL COST PRICING

In the case of an unregulated natural monopoly, the neoclassical theory of the firm states that the firm will produce at a point where marginal revenue equals marginal cost and price is greater than marginal cost. In this case, the monopoly is not observing the efficiency criterion $P = MC$. However, the public commission cannot charge the monopoly price because profits are excessive and a large number of consumers would be excluded from the service. The firm can pursue average cost pricing. This occurs where average cost equals average revenue thereby ensuring financial autonomy for the firm. Even though average cost pricing occurs at the break-even point, allocative efficiency is still not guaranteed.

Marginal cost pricing which occurs at the point where $P = MC$, is a theoretical first-best criterion to ensure efficiency in public utilities. In order to guarantee marginal cost pricing, the regulatory commission would have to ensure that the loss made by the utility would be financed by raising additional taxation which has welfare implications for consumers. Marginal cost pricing is not often discussed in rate-making hearings by public commissions. However, theoretical economics still considers alternative ways by which the loss would be financed to guarantee optimal pricing.

A loss under marginal cost pricing can be financed by a subsidy from national funds. This is equivalent to an increase in national taxation either by way of direct or indirect taxes. A subsidy has implications for the income distribution. The beneficiaries of the service may not be the same persons who pay the taxes. Subsidization may apply to services such as public transport and government-owned natural gas operations. Subsidies may also inflate the government's budget deficit and may lead to an inefficient allocation of resources.

A two-part tariff is a form of differential pricing to ensure that the public utility covers its marginal as well as fixed costs. A two-part tariff comprises a flat charge, that is, a fixed sum of money paid monthly or yearly to the utility, plus a per unit charge for the service. The per unit charge covers the marginal costs for each unit supplied. The nature of two-part tariffs varies greatly from country to country. They are most widely used in services such as electricity and telephones.

Price discrimination is also a form of differential pricing in public utilities. The firm charges different rates for different users according to cost conditions or varying elasticities of demand. For example, different rates may be charged for commercial and residential users on the basis of elasticity of demand. However, price discrimination should give careful consideration to equity, especially in the case of water usage. The persons least able to pay such as pensioners, the disabled, and the abjectly poor, should be given special rates.

Peak-load pricing is also a type of differential pricing. This type of pricing arises from variations in demand for the use of a service. For example, the demand for electricity may be greater during the day than at night. High demand at peak periods leads to a higher price for the service. This is known as the peak load price. This implies that marginal costs will be greater at peak than at off-peak periods. During the off-peak period, the utility has excess capacity. However, as capacity usage is reached marginal costs rise sharply.

Bonbright, Davidsen and Karmerschen (1988) have identified some of the limitations of marginal cost as a basis for optimal pricing. They argue that the $P = MC$ rule may not be socially optimal if it applied in some sectors of the economy and not in others. When price exceeds marginal costs in some sectors as a result of external diseconomies, heavy taxation, and so forth, an attempt to equate price to marginal cost in another sector may worsen resource allocation. Further, the $P = MC$ rule does not ensure that the distribution of income is equitable. Government may need to adopt different types of taxation and expenditure policies to ensure a more equitable distribution.

One of the difficulties of implementing marginal cost pricing is the large amount of information that would be required. This first-best strategy calls for an estimation of cost curves which shift over time. Also, the measurement of marginal costs will depend on the estimation of various elasticities of demand which determine output. This is relevant also to peak-load pricing where the peaks may fluctuate in response to changes in tastes and technology.

PRINCIPLES OF RATE-MAKING

The Rate Base

A public utility should earn a reasonable rate of return on its capital to be able to stay in business. It is necessary to establish a rate base or property value against which a firm's net profit can be applied. Some basic approaches have been advanced to determine the valuation of physical property. One important question is whether physical property should be valued at original cost or reproduction cost. Another concept used to determine the rate base is the concept of the "fair value" of the property. The last concept is not well-defined but seems to be a combination of different methods.

The original cost can be defined as the actual book value or the price actually paid at the time of the acquisition of the property used for utility services less depreciation. Reproduction cost is the cost of reproducing the facilities at market prices. Some writers have argued that whereas original costs tend to provide more rate stability, reproduction costs reflect current economic conditions and are a better indication of the use of resources (Jarvis and Sampson 1973). The use of these concepts vary from jurisdiction to jurisdiction.

The "fair value" method combines the original cost method, the reproduction method, and other factors affecting the value of the property. Weights are assigned to the two concepts and a judgement is made on what constitutes other factors. The fair value method is therefore a vague approach to valuation which aims to satisfy the diverse interests of consumers and business. Further, many jurisdictions do not define what legally constitutes "fair value".

Another concept used in the determination of the rate base is the end-result concept. This approach has not solved the problems of valuation. The end-result doctrine states that as long as the return to the utility ensures its financial integrity and is regarded as fair and reasonable, then the rate of return cannot be regarded as unjust. It is the result rather than the method which determines whether a rate is reasonable. McClean (1995), in his evaluation of rate hearings in Barbados, has maintained that the end-result doctrine has been used in a judgement pertaining to an appeal by the Barbados Telephone Company against the Barbados Public Utilities Board.

The Rate of Return

In the pricing of public utility services, the regulatory commission must guarantee a fair rate of return to the firm for its use of capital. Garfield and Lovejoy (1964: 116) have described the rate of return as "the amount of money a utility earns, over and above operating expenses, depreciation expense, and taxes, expressed as a percentage of the legally established net valuation of utility property, the rate base". The rate of return is therefore the amount of money earned on the rate base expressed as a percentage in order to facilitate comparisons with other companies.

What are the criteria for a fair rate of return? Garfield and Lovejoy (1964) and Bonbright, Davidsen and Karmerschen (1988) have identified a number of criteria for arriving at a fair rate of return. First, the return should be similar to the return in businesses which have similar or comparable risks. Second, the return should enable the firm to attract capital. Third, the return should be high enough to encourage efficient management. Fourth, the return should provide a stable and predictable price level to rate payers. Fifth, the return should assure confidence in the financial condition of the public utility.

The Hope Natural Gas case in the United States in 1944 established the principles outlined above. These legal guideposts continue to influence the determination of a fair rate of return in developing countries. McClean (1995) has identified the Hope case as providing the foundation for judgements relating to the rate of return to the two largest public utilities in Barbados, namely the Barbados Telephone Company Limited and the Barbados Light and Power Company Limited.

Cost of Service

In order to arrive at a fair and reasonable price for the utility's services, the regulatory commission must determine what are proper and improper expenses. This is important because certain components of the utility's expenditures can be passed on to consumers in the form of higher prices. Expen-ditures normally comprise operating expenses, depreciation, charges and taxes. Operating expenses include all administrative, marketing, energy, and public relations costs. The determination of what constitutes an improper expense can be highly controversial. Thus, the cost of service concept is very significant in public utility regulation. Problems arise when the utility includes certain types of operating expenses which can conceal high profits. Particularly, certain managerial fees and fringe benefits may be questionable. However, most operating costs, such as wages and salaries, pensions, advertising costs, and so forth, are usually regarded as proper expenses (Jarvis and Sampson1973).

Perhaps the most controversial area is depreciation, which is the wear and tear arising from the use of physical capital. Depreciation is sometimes referred to as capital consumption, and is regarded as a cost, thereby affecting a firm's profit levels. Depreciation deductions can be passed on to customers and can lead to significant increases in prices. The method of depreciation is a source of controversy and varies from jurisdiction to jurisdiction. The straight-line and accelerated depreciation methods are discussed in chapter 16.

Pricing Structure

We have already alluded to differential pricing or price discrimination as a feature of public utilities. The cost of service is a determinant of differential pricing because the utility would attempt to distribute its costs efficiently among different classes of customers. However, cost conditions which reflect the supply side of the market alone do not determine differential pricing. Another important concept is the "value of service" concept which considers the demand characteristics of the market.

According to Garfield and Lovejoy (1964: 139), the upper limit of the pricing structure "is a price which reflects the value of service, that is, the conditions of demand which characterize each segment in the total market of a utility". Value of service reflects how consumers value the money spent on the service and the overall conveniences of the service. Utilizing the value of service concept, the regulatory commission would determine a pricing structure which reflects the willingness of customers to bear differential prices. Consumers will demand the service in relation to their perception of its worth. Thus, the upper limit of rates set by the public utilities board will reflect the value of service rendered by the public utility.

SUMMARY

A natural monopoly is characterized by capital intensity and economies of scale which lead to decreasing average costs. Public utilities are natural monopolies which are subject to government regulation in order to ensure a fair and reasonable price to consumers.

Marginal cost pricing is a method of pricing public utility services and has been discussed extensively by economists. This first-best approach to pricing is said to lead to efficient resource allocation. Marginal cost pricing has a number of shortcomings that limit its usefulness. Very important is the subsidy which would have to be used to guarantee its effectiveness.

Institutional rate-making is concerned with the determination of a fair and reasonable price. The major concepts in this regard are the rate base, the rate of return to the utility, the cost of service, and the value of service.

The rate base is the property value against which the business estimates its rate of return. An estimation of too low a rate of return can lead to arguments by the public utility for higher prices. This is why legal arguments are involved in the discussion of these concepts. The cost of service and value of service are determinants of the pricing structure. The regulatory commission must scrutinize the deductions from operating revenue and what constitute improper expenses.

Chapter Nine

Introduction to Cost-Benefit Analysis in Developing Countries

C ost-benefit analysis is a technique used by government for choosing between alternative projects given a budget constraint. Cost-benefit analysis is a highly specialized area and no attempt is made here to give readers an exhaustive treatment of this methodology. The literature contains a large number of technical analyses on shadow pricing and different decision rules for evaluating projects in developing countries. Contributions by Little and Mirrlees (1974), Roemer and Stern (1975) and United Nations Industrial Development Organization (UNIDO 1980) are among the leading sources on project appraisal techniques. Following the procedure in chapter 8, the presentation introduces the main theoretical issues in cost-benefit analysis, and refers readers to more technical treatments of the subject. Cost-benefit analysis is important in evaluating the returns to various public investments, including education and health, as well as the foreign exchange benefits and costs of export and import-substitution projects.

STAGES OF COST-BENEFIT ANALYSIS

The discussion here draws from UNIDO (1980) and Roemer and Stern (1975). The UNIDO manual identifies three stages of cost-benefit analysis, namely, project preparation, project evaluation, and project implementation. Project preparation starts with the identification of a project idea. This is usually the outcome of a political process based on cabinet decisions or development plans. Sectoral plans for the economy identify export projects or areas of investment, such as sewage and irrigation projects, and so forth. If a project appears promising, the preparation stage involves the compilation of a feasibility study which is the final document in the formulation of a project proposal. This is a technical document based, not only on economic data, but also on social and engineering data.

The second stage is project evaluation. This involves the identification of the quality and quantity of physical inputs and outputs. The principal problem of project evaluation is valuing the costs of the inputs, and the benefits derived from the outputs of the project. This means that a set of prices known as shadow or accounting prices must be applied to the resources used in the project to measure the opportunity costs of allocating scarce resources. The opportunity costs of the project are all payments that reduce the availability of real resources to other users. The benefits of a project involves additional goods and services, or the reduction in the cost of a good previously available. External economies must also be included. These are benefits arising outside the boundaries of the project. Project planners also seek to minimize external diseconomies such as environmental and other social costs (Roemer and Stern 1975).

The third stage of cost-benefit analysis is project implementation. This is the job of the project manager whose duty it is to monitor and supervise all the stages of the project. Project implementation involves considerable planning and the need to closely follow the details of an implementation chart. Risk and uncertainty play an important role during the implementation phase. Inflation may affect the values of benefits and costs and may lead to significant cost overruns. Problems also arise as a result of changes in the weather, which can delay the implementation or completion of the project.

EVALUATION OF COSTS AND BENEFITS

Concept of Shadow Prices

As noted previously, the shadow price reflects the opportunity cost between the alternative use of resources in a project. Under perfect competition, marginal cost reflects the shadow price which equals the market price. However, under imperfect competition, the market price does not reflect opportunity costs. In the goods and factor market, price diverges from marginal costs leading to an inefficient allocation of resources. Market prices are usually above opportunity costs because taxation and other distortions place a wedge between the cost of a resource and its selling price. In the case of public goods, the market price will not be a valid indicator of social benefits. Pareto optimal pricing would require prices which reflect each consumer's willingness to pay. This is usually difficult since consumers do not always reveal their preferences for public goods.

Shadow Wage Rate

In the implementation of projects, government must consider the impact of hiring labour on the rest of the economy. The shadow wage rate (SWR) reflects the social opportunity cost of labour, or the alternative product that could have been produced elsewhere in the economy, before the labour was drawn into the project. Labour is not homogeneous and it is important to examine the SWR in relation to the skill of the labourer, the region producing the labour, and the cost in terms of consumption of employing additional labour.

In a perfectly competitive market, the SWR corresponds to the value of the marginal product. That is, $SWR = MRP$, where MRP is the marginal revenue product of labour. All markets are cleared and the system achieves Pareto efficiency. The market wage therefore measures the opportunity cost of labour. In cost-benefit analysis, departures from perfect competition are assumed, so that the calculation of the SWR is more complicated.

Another limiting case is the existence of unskilled, unemployed labour. This means that when such labour is brought into the project, the alternative product foregone in the rest of the economy is zero, that is, $SWR = 0$ because $MRP = 0$. However, such labour has a cost in terms of its additional consumption of goods during the phase of the project.

The determination of the SWR under conditions of imperfect competition depends crucially on the sources from which the labour is drawn. Early discussions of the SWR paid attention to the creation of jobs in modern industry for which labour was supplied from traditional agriculture. The opportunity cost of employing labour in modern industry was related to the marginal productivity of labour in traditional agriculture (Ministry of Overseas Development 1977). However urban projects very often draw their labour from urban locations or from abroad. The calculation of the SWR is also likely to be complicated in relation to the improved productivity of previously underemployed workers.

The opportunity cost of bringing rural labour into an urban project depends on the indirect effects of rural urban migration, which include the social costs of migration, seasonal factors, the cost of training, and additional consumption costs. Additionally, the foregone output in the agricultural sector will have to be considered. The SWR for rural urban migrants will be equivalent to agricultural income foregone plus the real and "psychic" costs of migrating, plus the higher cost of living in urban areas (Lal 1974).

In highly open economies, labour is sometimes imported to carry out a project. This labour has a cost to the local economy in terms of foreign exchange. Imported labour will repatriate part of its income and there will be a loss of foreign exchange. Part of the income is spent on consumption in the domestic economy. However, because the economy is dependent on imports, increased consumption would also result in a foreign exchange loss. Therefore, the SWR of imported labour is the foreign exchange loss. Thus, following the Inter-American Development Bank (IDB 1981), the SWR of foreign labour equals expatriated wages plus domestic consumption by foreign labour in terms of foreign exchange.

The method used by Little and Mirrlees (1974: 270–73) assigns considerable importance to the role played by consumption in calculating the SWR. This approach measures the consumption of the wage-earner plus additional government resources devoted to consumption. Any surplus consumption accruing to others as a result of the worker moving into the new occupation is also considered. Thus, additional consumption, either in terms of transport costs or expenditure on nutrition, plays a very important role in the determination of the SWR.

Shadow Discount Rate

The benefits and costs of a project must be discounted by an appropriate discount rate, which is a rate which discounts the benefits back to the present. This rate allows the government to distinguish between projects to be done and those to be rejected. The shadow discount rate (SDR) either reflects the opportunity costs of the best alternative use of funds in the private sector, or the opportunity costs of using funds borrowed from the public sector. The latter is equivalent to the sacrifice of present consumption.

In cost-benefit there are two schools of thought in arriving at the appropriate rate of discount for public projects. The Social Rate of Time Preference (SRTP) School asserts that the SRTP is the rate that should be chosen whenever a project is financed from consumption. The SRTP is the compensation necessary to make consumers refrain from present consumption. The SRTP is close to the government's long-term bond rate which is an alternative rate to induce the public to forego present consumption.

The Social Opportunity Cost of Capital (SOCC) School asserts that the SOCC is a measure to society of the alternative use of resources elsewhere in the economy. The shadow price reflects the value of resources transferred from the private sector, or the rate the funds would earn in the private sector. This is based on the argument that private and public projects should have the same marginal yield. This implies that the shadow price of capital should be equated to the marginal product of capital. The difficulty of discounting at the SOCC is that the rate of return in the private sector must fully reflect the risks involved in investment. This rate might be quite high for use in government projects.

The Shadow Exchange Rate and Border Prices

According to Batra and Guisinger (1974), the shadow exchange rate (SER) should express the marginal social value of an additional unit of foreign exchange due to the implementation of a public project. The SER reflects foreign exchange scarcity and focuses on the balance of payments constraint in developing countries. In order to observe the SER, the official exchange rate must be adjusted for changes in tariffs on imports and subsidies on exports. The SER is therefore the product of the official exchange rate and a weighted average of tariffs and subsidies.

Little and Mirrlees (1974) have advocated an alternative method of evaluating the foreign exchange contribution of a project. They suggested that traded goods should be valued at border or world prices and non-traded inputs should be converted into their foreign exchange equivalent. This means that imports are valued at their cost, insurance and freight (CIF) value and exports at their free on board (FOB) value. The reason for valuing both traded and non-traded goods at world prices is that the world price provides the *numeraire* for evaluating the costs and benefit of the project. They argue that in developing countries foreign exchange is a better reflection of the relative social costs and benefits of the outputs of a project. Baldwin (1972) argues, however, that it is not easy to value the non-traded inputs. This involves an input/output analysis to identify the traded inputs which contribute to the creation of non-traded outputs such as power, transport, and construction.

Another method of valuing non-traded goods in terms of world prices is to use a conversion factor, which is the ratio of the border price to the domestic market price, less excise and sales taxes. The conversion factor is a short-cut method of eliminating the differences between the level of internal prices and border prices. These conversion factors will vary from sector to sector. For example, a conversion factor for any sector output (e.g., construction, transport, etc.) used as an input into a project, is a weighted average of the ratio of world prices to domestic prices of the inputs used to produce this sectoral output (Ministry of Overseas Development 1977: 13).

Ghatak (1978) has advanced a number of criticisms of the Little and Mirrlees method of border prices. First, border prices assume a highly open economy. They suggest that if a commodity has limited access to the world market, border prices should not be used. Second, the determination of border prices for heterogeneous goods is very difficult and time consuming. Third, Ghatak argues that Little and Mirrlees have not paid much attention to externalities which further complicates the derivation of border prices of non-traded goods.

FINANCIAL DECISION CRITERIA

Financial project appraisal deals with the decision rules for accepting or rejecting projects. We consider three criteria, namely, the Net Present Value of an investment (NPV), the Benefit/Cost ratio (BC), and the Internal Rate of Return (IRR). The first criterion is the NPV, which is based on discounting the net benefits of a project back to the present. The compound value of an investment over t years is

$$A = P_v(1+r)_t$$

where A = compound value
Pv = present value
r = discount rate.

Therefore, the present value of an investment is $P_v = \frac{A}{(1+r)^t}$. In order to evaluate the present value of money invested at the discount rate r, we multiply this sum A by the discount factor $\frac{1}{(1+r)}$. For example, the present value of $100.00 to be repaid one year from now at a 5 percent discount rate would be $Pv = \frac{100}{(1+r)} = \$95.24$.

Over n years, the discount factor would be $\frac{1}{(1+r)^n}$. To calculate the NPV of an investment, we subtract the costs of a project from its benefits overtime such that

$$NPV = \sum \frac{B_t - C_t}{(1+r)^t} = \frac{B_1 - C_1}{(1+r)} \quad \frac{B_2 - C_2}{(1+r)^2} + ... \frac{B_n - C_n}{(1+r)^n}$$

where B_t = Benefits in time t.

C_t = Costs in time t.

Table 9.1 shows hypothetical money values for a cement project with a discount rate of 5 percent over six years. The plant begins to record benefits in its third year even though the NPV is zero. The NPV of net benefits are highest in the sixth year. In the first two years capital outlays are high and NPV are negative.

TABLE 9.1: NPVs for cement project

Year	B_t $m	C_t $m	$(B_t - C_t)$ $m	Discount factor $(1 + 0.5)^t$	NPV $m
1	0	50	-50	.9524	-47.6
2	0	50	-50	.9070	-43.4
3	10	10	0	.8638	0.0
4	20	10	10	.8227	8.2
5	50	10	40	.7835	31.3
6	100	10	90	.7462	67.2
Total	180	140	40		15.7

The second criterion is the benefit/cost (B/C) ratio where B and C are the present values of benefits and costs, respectively. This measure requires that projects which have a B/C ratio greater than unity should be preferred. If the B/C ratio is used to rank alternative projects, then the project with the highest B/C ratio would be chosen.

The IRR is defined as the rate of discount that sets the NPV to zero. The IRR is then compared with the social discount rate. This approach requires that projects with the highest IRRs should be chosen. Further, projects which have IRRs less than the social discount rate should be rejected. The IRR is a solution to the polynomial

$$\frac{B_1}{(1+i)} + \frac{B_2}{(1+i)^2} + \ldots \frac{B_n}{(1+i)^n} = C_0$$

where B_n = cost benefit stream over n years

C_0 = initial costs.

We now discuss the ranking of projects using the above criteria. The budget constraint facing the government is very important in choosing projects. Consider three projects A, B and C, and the budget constraint is $300.0 million. If government spends this money on project A which is a fishing harbour, let us assume that the NPV is higher than if the money is spent on project B, a flour mill and project C, a school. However, government may decide to establish a flour mill which has a higher IRR, or a school with a higher B/C ratio. Government's decision will depend on its evaluation of social benefits and costs as well as its critical assessment of the decision criterion used.

We now outline a few criticisms of the IRR used for public investment decisions. First, it is argued that since the IRR is the solution to a polynomial equation, there can be more than one IRR because the polynomial will yield multiple roots. Second, IRRs with values less than zero are conceivable. Third, it is argued that the IRR gives a ranking to projects which bunch the benefits in the early economic life of the project relative to other projects. These weaknesses in the calculation of the IRR have led many decision makers to choose the NPV method. However, because of political and welfare considerations, it is difficult for government to rank projects on purely budgetary considerations. Equity considerations may sometimes be weighted heavier in the calculus of decision making.

ECOLOGICAL EXTERNALITIES, RISK AND UNCERTAINTY

One of the most difficult areas of cost-benefit analysis is the estimation of ecological externalities and various risks associated with projects. Damage to the environment can occur through the use of pesticides in agricultural projects, and the occurrence of pollution. Ecological externalities also generate uncertainties since the impact on the environment cannot always be predicted. It is necessary to identify the possible physical damages and impose some monetary value on the physical damage (see, for example, Dasgupta and Pearce 1978; Tietenberg 1996: 66–80 for a more detailed discussion).

Our discussion on the importance of risk and uncertainty in cost-benefit analysis borrows from Dasgupta and Pearce (1978) and the Ministry of Overseas Development (1977). The reasons why we need to consider risk and uncertainty stem from the difficulties of obtaining information for estimating future costs and benefits which may vary substantially from year to year. Some projects also have uncertain outcomes. Uncertainty may also arise from changes in technology and variations in individual tastes. These factors not only affect the costs of a project but may alter the demand for the output of a project.

The term risk usually refers to the assignment of a probability distribution to an outcome. In the case of cost-benefit analysis, the riskiness of a project is the estimation of the probability of different values of the NPV. According to Dasgupta and Pearce (1978: 177), if the decision maker knows exactly the outcome of each decision, given the "states of nature"or events which may occur repeatedly, then the probability distribution of these states of nature can be used to derive the probability distribution of outcomes for each decision. The calculation of expected values for the NPV depends on the alteration in the variables which determine the NPV such as interest rates, prices, and outputs.

Sensitivity analysis is an approach to analysing risks, by estimating the effect on NPV of variations in some of the assumptions made in the cost-benefit analysis. Sensitivity analysis helps to improve the understanding of the nature of the project and reduces risks by suggesting precautions to be taken. Sensitivity analysis is enhanced by market surveys or technical feasibility studies (Ministry of Overseas Development 1977: 48–50).

Decision theory is designed to deal with various attitudes to risks by decision makers. Attitudes to risks are complex, and the theory of games shows the decision maker the possible states of nature, possible pay-offs, and the results of his actions under each state of nature. One of these approaches known as the "maximin" pay-off criterion considers each strategy and its minimum pay-off. Under this principle the strategy with the highest minimum pay-off is chosen. The minimax regret criterion uses a different process of reasoning. For each entry in the pay-off matrix, the actual pay-off is subtracted from the potential pay-off. The difference is a measure of "regret". The maximum regret principle states that the decision maker should select the maximum regret it involves. He should then choose a strategy with the lowest maximum regret (Dasgupta and Pearce 1978).

SUMMARY

Social cost-benefit analysis is a very useful technique in appraising projects in both developed and developing countries. We have identified some of the major concepts used in this analysis, namely, shadow pricing, net present value, benefit/cost ratios, and the internal rate of return. The implementation of projects in developing countries is sometimes hampered by difficulties in the disbursement of funds. The progress of a project may also be slowed by weather and other risk factors which may lead to cost overruns. This implies that decision makers have to devise strategies to estimate the risks associated with various projects. Game theory provides a technical approach to achieve this.

Chapter Ten

The Budgetary Process and Budget Deficits

Ⓐll governments need to adopt an efficient system of budgeting in order to monitor and control public sector spending. It is important therefore to examine the budgetary process, and the causes and consequences of budget deficits in developing countries. I am concerned with the process of traditional budgeting which is the form of budgeting used most widely in developing countries. The discussion of deficit financing will be primarily theoretical. The reason for this approach is that deficit financing and the orthodox stabilization programmes required to correct budget and balance of payments deficits follow a similar theoretical approach. The next chapter will be partly devoted to the theoretical underpinnings of the IMF programmes which have been used extensively in developing countries. The budget deficit is defined here as the excess of total government expenditure over total government tax revenue. The term fiscal deficit will be used interchangeably with budget deficit.

THE TRADITIONAL BUDGETARY PROCESS

The budget can be described as a fiscal plan for allocating government expenditures. In chapter 1 a distinction was made between the current and capital budgets which form the accounting framework for traditional budgeting, which is a political as well as an economic activity. The process of traditional or incremental budgeting derives from established political power relations. The administrative agencies submit requests for funds to the executive or finance minister, whose proposals are approved or rejected by the legislature. In the Caribbean, these proposals are presented in the form of annual estimates, as well as a budget speech presented by the finance minister.

Alan Prest (1975: 33) identifies four stages in the budgetary process. These are budget formulation, budget authorization, budget implementation, and the postmortem. Budget formulation is an executive process comprising the estimates of revenues and expenditures. The considerations raised in the formulation stage would involve estimates of the costs of existing services and of outlays on continuing and new capital projects. Estimates of revenues are also prepared, and a consolidated statement of revenues and expenditures drawn up. Premchand (1983) has indicated that one of the main constraints in the formulation process is lack of information. If statistical data are not accurate or up-to-date, forecasting may underestimate the level of funding required. It may also be necessary to allow for the impact of price inflation on the estimates, because cost overruns often force governments to implement supplementary budgets, months after the annual budget has gained legislative approval.

Legislative authorization is the process whereby the budget proposals are presented in parliament and debated. In most countries this is usually a rubber-stamping exercise, but it allows opposition members to voice their criticisms of all the government's economic and social programmes. Parliamentary debate is therefore not solely confined to the budget itself.

Budget implementation depends on the system of tax collection and expenditure controls. In Barbados, for example, tax revenue is usually conservatively estimated, so that actual collections exceed budgetary projections. In some countries, significant lags in tax collection, resulting from tax evasion or inefficient administrative efforts, are constraints on the implementation process. Developing countries also need proper systems of expenditure controls. Intense competition for funds among various ministries can lead to expenditure levels which are too high relative to the country's resources and productivity levels.

The postmortem is the compilation of the auditor's report. The government's accounting systems should be consonant with the legal provisions. According to Prest (1975: 146), in some developing countries this final stage is perhaps the most inefficient and it may take months or even years to complete.

The type of budgeting outlined above rests on a behavioural model known as incrementalism. This theory stresses that decisions made about this year's budget are influenced by the budget of the year before. The budget examines those items for which increases or decreases over the previous year are requested. In this regard incrementalism is conservative, because there is very little examination of basic programmes. Wildavsky (1979) argues that this approach is cheaper on decision making resources. Further, incrementalism aids the process of securing agreement and reduces the burden of calculation. As Wildavsky (1979: 136) submits, "it is much easier to agree on a small addition or decrease than to compare the worth of one programme to that of all others".

Wildavsky's vision seems somewhat limited, however, and many writers have questioned this rigid adherence to incrementalism. Brown and Jackson (1990: 212) identify a number of disadvantages of incremental budgeting. The system may not be quick to change or adapt. Piecemeal changes may therefore characterize reforms of the social services. Incrementalism can also compound errors made in the past, simply because the system is not subject to in-depth revision. In short, incrementalism is a conservative system with a low level of political opportunity costs. It favours short-term political decision making.

Incrementalism has been highly criticized as inadequate in the context of developing countries. Simon Jones-Hendrickson (1985: 76–85) provides a long list of perceived deficiencies of budgeting in the Caribbean. First, he maintains that the budgets show inadequate attention to allocative efficiency. Incremental changes in tax rates and bases, without regard to efficiency, usually characterize Caribbean budgets. Second, expenditure decisions are made without due consideration to the financial consequences. In many cases, at the time of budget authorization, no indication is given of the manner in which the total budget deficit is to be financed, or of its perceived impact on the balance of payments. Third, he criticizes the line-item structure, which is not adequately linked to the development plan. Fourth, incrementalism gives excessive centralized control to the various ministers of finance and there is an absence of performance measurements and reviews.

ALTERNATIVE APPROACHES TO BUDGETING

The weaknesses of the traditional budget process led to three budgetary innovations in the post–World War II period. These are performance budgeting, programme budgeting, sometimes known as planning programme-budgeting system (PPBS), and zero-base budgeting. Premchand (1983: 319–47) reviews the development of these systems in the United States as well as other industrialized and developing countries.

Premchand notes that performance budgeting, which was introduced in the United States in the 1950s, was concerned with the efficiency aspects of achieving the objectives of various programmes. The performance budget consisted of three main elements: (1) programme and activity classification of government transactions, (2) performance measurements, and (3) performance reporting. The performance budget provided a work plan for each department. Performance measurement was used to increase productivity in terms of manpower and capital. This system was practised in the United States in the 1950s, but the measurement of productivity was elusive and the computation of costs was complex (Premchand 1983: 322).

The PPBS system was first introduced in the US Department of Defense in 1961 and extended throughout the US federal government in 1965. PPBS focuses on output and long-term planning. Programmes are classified by means of a programme structure and further subdivided into programme elements.

Cost-benefit analysis is used to estimate the total financial cost of accomplishing objectives. This system has been criticized on the grounds that a high degree of centralization is required to control the programme structure. Further, some analysts argue that it is difficult to measure the output of some government activities. The PPBS requires a high degree of administrative competence which might not be present in developing countries (see Goode 1984: 36 and Wildavsky 1979: 200).

Zero-base budgeting (ZBB) was introduced in the US federal government in 1977. Pyhrr (1973) is credited with the development of ZBB, and it was originally applied to the private sector in the United States in the early 1970s. ZBB requires the re-evaluation of ongoing programmes. In the ZBB system, last year's budget does not provide the basis for this year's budget. Each programme is analysed on its own merits. ZBB is decision-oriented, requiring all programmes to compete for scarce resources (see Wildavsky 1979; Schick 1978).

Pyhrr (1973: 5) suggests that there are two basic steps of ZBB, namely, the development of "decision packages" and the ranking of "decision packages". The first step is the analysis and description of each discrete activity in the decision packages. Ranking involves an evaluation of the importance of each package through cost-benefit analysis or subjective evaluation. A decision package identifies a discrete activity which includes the goals and objectives of the activity, the consequences of not performing the activity, measures of performance, alternative courses of action, and costs and benefits (Pyhrr 1973: 6). For ZBB to work, it must be properly managed and well designed to meet the needs of the organization.

Some developing countries have adopted some aspects of these systems, but the traditional system is still operational in most countries. It can be argued that these systems can add cosmetic changes, and can be adopted in some departments of government. It is quite difficult to apply them throughout the entire public sector, because developing countries lack the administrative capability to manage these systems. In any case, these approaches to budgeting have not been very successful in industrialized countries with more highly developed management systems (Wildavsky 1979).

STRUCTURAL CAUSES OF BUDGET DEFICITS

The traditional budgetary process discussed above enables government to determine whether there is a surplus or deficit on the current account and the size of the overall fiscal deficit. Why did many developing countries experience large and persistent budget deficits in the 1980s? Were these deficits due mainly to fiscal indiscipline or structural factors? This section attempts to answer these questions.

Government budget deficits in developing countries arise from two sets of causes. The first are structural factors determined by the type of economy and its relationship with the external world. The second set of causes stems from the implementation of government expansionary policies which may lead to sharp increases in expenditures. In some cases, governments may lack the necessary fiscal discipline to control public expenditures. In other situations government may have to increase spending to maintain levels of income and employment when the private sector goes into recession. We examine the reasons for fiscal deficits by looking briefly at the specific views of Morrison (1982) relating to the structural determinants of budget deficits in developing countries. This is followed by a closer examination of Tanzi's (1982a) concept of fiscal disequilibrium.

Morrison argues that there are five major structural factors which explain why some developing countries have larger budget deficits than others. These are as follows:

(a)   level of economic development,

(b)   growth of government revenues,

(c)   instability of government revenues,

(d)   government control over expenditures, and

(e)   extent of government participation in the economy (Morrison 1982: 468)

Morrison's first argument is that governments at relatively low levels of development may be unable to control their budgets because of "spending pressures" to improve education and infrastructure. Further, the existence of low private savings and low tax revenues leads to a situation where government feels justified in increasing public spending to satisfy public expectations. A hypothesis of Morrison's study is that "the political pressures to spend will outweigh the perceived inflationary costs of deficit financing" (Morrison 1982: 468). We believe that Morrison's "spending pressures" may apply to governments at any level of development in developing countries. His emphasis on the low level of development may not be required to support this argument.

The slow growth of revenues and the instability of revenues are two important structural causes of budget deficits. Slow revenue growth means that the budget requires deficit financing. Instability of revenues associated with export earnings means that an export shortfall will cause a decline in revenue from export taxes. As we argue later, this argument is highly applicable to petroleum export economies where corporation and export taxes are significant components of revenue.

Morrison's last two structural causes are closely related. Government may find it difficult to control expenditures because of inefficient budgetary systems. At the same time, government's heavy intervention in the economy increases the pressure on its budgetary system to provide subsidies and transfers to public enterprises. The administrative costs of government controls on prices and interest rates are also quite high.

Morrison's regression analysis employed to support his hypotheses reached the conclusion that the developing countries most likely to have larger budget deficits were those with a lower level of development, a higher degree of government participation in the economy, and less control exercised over government expenditures. Revenue instability and low revenues were not important. However, his use of per capita GDP to represent the level of development may not be adequate since it ignores the distribution of income.

Tanzi (1982a) attempted to explain the causes of budget deficits in developing countries by using the concepts of fiscal disequilibrium and

119

fiscal disequilibrium scenarios. Like Morrison, although he places some emphasis on the public expenditure variable, his work stresses the structural nature of budget deficits. Our analysis examines fiscal disequilibrium with reference to the Caribbean economies of Jamaica, Barbados, and Trinidad and Tobago.

Tanzi (1982a) has defined fiscal disequilibrium as the divergence between "permanent" government revenue and "permanent" government expenditure. For example, permanent (or maintainable) revenues are sustained over a period of time and do not include transitory, or windfall, components. Transitory revenue, for instance, might be from a petroleum or coffee export boom. Permanent expenditures are those which become internalized in the budget over time. Current expenditure has a tendency to be more permanent than capital expenditure. If government runs a large fiscal deficit year after year, fiscal disequilibrium will result.

Following Tanzi, a fiscal disequilibrium scenario can be described as a fiscal situation where a particular pattern of fiscal behaviour or causation predominates. In his analysis of developing countries, Tanzi identifies five dominant scenarios, which he calls export boom, public enterprise, inelastic tax system, terms of trade, and growth of public expenditure. The first and perhaps most important is the growth of public expenditure scenario, which is specific to Jamaica and Guyana but also has application to Barbados. The second, which applies to petroleum export-led economies like Trinidad and Tobago, is the petroleum export boom/slump scenario. Contributory, but weaker, is the tax inelasticity scenario. I believe that Tanzi's public expenditure and public enterprise scenarios are related, since public enterprises increase government expenditures. His terms of trade and export boom scenarios also cannot really be treated separately, because export price movements determine the terms of trade.

In Caribbean economies, for structural and political reasons, it is critically difficult to control public expenditures. This explains why government expenditure growth was a primary generator of large and persistent fiscal deficits in the Caribbean especially during the 1980s. Governments face significant pressure from their electorates to provide education, infrastructure, low-cost housing, welfare and health services. Heavy government expenditure, financed by money creation, was a principal cause of fiscal deficits and balance of payments pressures in Barbados and Jamaica between 1974 and 1984 (Howard 1989a). Strong public expenditure growth also characterized the fiscal systems of Jamaica, Barbados, and Guyana during the late 1980s.

Although it is desirable to curb the rate of growth of total expenditures, it is not always easy to achieve an absolute cut over a fiscal year. There has been a tendency in Barbados, for example, to overestimate current expenditure and underestimate revenue, so that the government's saving is sometimes much larger than projected. However, the recurrent costs of welfare services, foreign debt repayments, and salaries of civil servants create a built-in tendency for permanent expenditures to rise. An outcome below estimated levels may not necessarily indicate a genuine expenditure cut.

Premchand (1983) has suggested a number of ways in which expenditure control can be achieved. These include either across-the-board cuts or specific sector cuts in expenditure. Across-the-board cuts imply that all expenditures are treated equally. In the context of the severe disequilibrium in Jamaica and Trinidad and Tobago during the 1980s, there were severe cuts in the salaries of public servants, as well as a reduction in public service personnel. These issues of public expenditure control have already been examined in chapter 6.

Another factor responsible for the rapid growth of public expenditure and high fiscal deficits in Caribbean countries during the 1980s was the poor performance by public enterprises (see Howard 1992). Many of these enterprises were inefficient, and they became financial burdens for governments in small economies. Many were heavily subsidized. Although privatization has been advanced as a means to reduce government ownership and control, less developed countries sometimes encounter difficulties in selling these enterprises, especially when they are not considered profitable ventures. However, the privatization argument is highly plausible for industries which can function more efficiently under private enterprise. The heavy financial burden of public enterprises also forces governments to raise new taxes, which may have severe welfare costs.

Petroleum export-led economies can experience export slump fiscal disequilibrium. Oil price movements have an impact on the government's domestic budget deficit, that is, on the difference between domestic expenditure and domestic revenue. In the case of Trinidad and Tobago, the difference between foreign expenditure and foreign revenue represents the budget surplus on foreign exchange account. Oil revenues accrue in the form of foreign exchange, which is surrendered to the central bank, which credits the central government with the domestic currency equivalent in the form of deposits. The domestic budget may be in deficit during an oil export boom, even though the overall budget may be in surplus (see, for example, Morgan 1979 and Farrell 1981).

In petroleum export-led economies, fiscal policies cannot address the source of the fiscal disequilibrium. This is so because permanent or maintainable domestic revenues are determined by the effects of oil expansion on the non-oil sectors of the economy. In the long run, the economic problems which emerged in economies like Venezuela, Mexico, and Trinidad and Tobago can only be corrected by structural adjustment policies to diversify the non-oil sector, in terms of increased manufacturing output, food supplies, and output of services. In the short run, fiscal disequilibrium requires demand management policies, such as credit and wage controls and reductions in government expenditures.

The final scenario is the tax inelasticity scenario. Howard (1992) analysed the buoyancies of the tax system of Jamaica, Barbados, and Trinidad and Tobago. He found that the buoyancies of these systems were maintained only by heavy and sustained discretionary tax changes. The income tax systems of many developing countries are considered inelastic. Although we shall discuss tax issues in a later chapter, it is necessary to state the implications of an inelastic tax system for the fiscal deficit. A significant lag in tax collections means that a government has to rely more heavily on central bank financing. Over time, an inelastic tax system will sustain the level of the fiscal deficit.

The impact of worsening terms of trade on the overall budget deficit is difficult to quantify. The deterioration can be caused either by a sharp fall in export prices or by increases in import prices which help to generate domestic inflation. In the Caribbean, increasing oil prices in the 1970s played an important role in terms of trade deterioration. Imported inflation causes an increase in the nominal value of government revenues, especially when the indirect tax system is based on ad valorem rates. However, higher import and domestic prices also raise the nominal value of government expenditures. If the rate of change of government expenditures on public sector wages and capital projects exceeds the rate of change of the inflation tax, the government's deficit will worsen.

STATISTICAL EVIDENCE ON BUDGET DEFICITS AND SURPLUSES

The ratio of the fiscal deficit to GDP is perhaps the best statistic for comparing the relative size of the fiscal deficit of various developing countries. Of course, one serious problem with the use of this statistic is that the

TABLE 10.1: Budget deficit/surplus as a percentage of GDP for selected developing countries

Country	1990	1991	1992	1993	1994	1995
Bahamas	-6.8	-4.2	-6.9	-0.1	-3.2	-6.7
Barbados	-7.2	-1.6	-1.6	-2.1	-1.0	-0.8
Brazil	-6.1	-0.04	-3.9	-9.3	–	–
Chile	0.8	1.5	2.2	1.9	1.6	2.5
Ghana	0.2	1.6	-5.5	-2.6	–	–
India	-7.9	-8.1	-5.8	-7.4	-6.4	-5.3
Indonesia	0.4	0.4	-0.4	0.6	0.9	2.2
Jamaica	–	–	–	3.4	3.3	1.0
Kenya	-3.8	-2.6	-0.4	-3.4	-3.3	–
Korea	–	–	-0.7	0.3	0.5	0.4
Malaysia	-5.3	-4.3	-4.2	0.2	0.2	0.9
Mexico	-2.8	-0.2	1.5	0.3	-0.7	-0.5
Singapore	10.5	8.6	12.5	5.5	5.9	14.3
South Africa	–	-4.2	-8.0	-6.6	-5.7	-5.4
Thailand	0.4	4.7	2.8	2.1	1.8	2.4
Trinidad & Tobago	–	–	–	0.2	-0.3	0.2
Turkey	-3.0	-5.1	-4.2	-6.4	3.7	4.0

Source: IMF, *Economic Reviews*, no. 2, May–August 1998.

IMF, *International Financial Statistics Yearbook*, 1998.

GDP for many developing countries is very often computed with significant errors. This section looks at the size of the budget deficit or surplus for 17 developing countries chosen from Africa, Asia, Latin America and the Caribbean during the first half of the 1990s.

Many developing countries recorded high fiscal deficits in the early 1980s and high levels of external debt, partly due to excessive public expenditures, as well as external economic problems. In the Caribbean, for example, Howard (1992) has shown that Barbados and Trinidad and Tobago recorded budget deficits above 5 percent for most years of the 1980s, while Jamaica had deficits above 10 percent for most of the period between 1974 and 1990. The analysis in Table 10.1 reveals that stabilization and structural adjustment policies considerably reduced the fiscal deficits of these countries during the first half of the 1990s. Jamaica and Trinidad and Tobago recorded budget surpluses, while Barbados had much smaller deficits than in the 1990s. Fiscal deficits for the Bahamas were higher than for Barbados.

The Asian countries such as Singapore, Thailand, Malaysia, Korea, and Indonesia recorded budget surpluses for some years during the early 1990s. These countries are known for their high levels of national savings. Most of these economies, with the exception of Singapore, had budget deficits in the 1980s. Chapter 11 discusses the financial crisis of the Asian countries in 1997. However, there was no serious fiscal disequilibrium in the context of this crisis. The budget deficits for India and Turkey are much higher than other Asian countries.

Chile is the only Latin American country in our sample to record budget surpluses for each year for the period 1990–95. Mexico's budget deficits were relatively small. These countries have placed considerable emphasis on tax reform and structural adjustment after the difficult periods of the 1970s and 1980s. The deficits for South Africa are higher than for Ghana and Kenya. Overall, our analysis shows that most developing countries in our sample achieved some success in keeping down the level of the fiscal deficit during the early 1990s. This effort can be explained mainly by policies to downsize the public sectors in some of these countries in order to reduce the high levels of public expenditure.

FINANCING THE BUDGET DEFICIT

The crucial issue for fiscal policy in the Caribbean is the size of the fiscal deficit and how it is financed. This is because fiscal disequilibrium can also cause balance of payments disequilibrium. Much of the received theory on highly developed countries assume a closed economy, an emphasis on the distinction between bond financing and money creation, an IS/LM framework, a monetarist or Keynesian theory of demand inflation, and a highly developed money market. Many of the traditional macroeconomic textbooks also ignore the impact on the balance of payments when the government deficit is financed by borrowing from the central bank. Howard (1992) has shown that fiscal deficits financed by central bank money creation were the principal causes of balance of payments deterioration in Barbados, Guyana, and Jamaica during the 1970s and 1980s.

The government's deficit may be financed by the following methods:
1. Net foreign borrowing
2. Borrowing from the public
3. Borrowing from commercial banks
4. Borrowing from the central bank

5. Sale of public sector assets or distressed privatization
6. Inflationary finance

Foreign financing of the fiscal deficit comprises grants, concessionary loans, and commercial loans. Grants are mainly cash donations and project aid. Concessionary loans have a rate of interest which is lower than the market rate. There is also a substantial grace period and long maturity period for the repayment of the loan. Commercial loans have a high market rate of interest. The beneficial effect of foreign borrowing is that it makes foreign exchange available and has an initial expansionary effect on the economy. The disadvantage of foreign borrowing, especially if commercial loans are used is the impact on the external debt (see Tanzi 1990; Goode 1984).

The budget deficit can also be financed by the issue of government securities on the domestic market. In advanced economies, borrowing from citizens through the issue of bonds and treasury bills is a more feasible option given the sophistication of the money market. In small developing countries, borrowing from citizens is not a very reliable financing instrument partly because of the small money market and partly because citizens may show a preference for other types of savings such as savings and time deposits. Governments often resort to selling treasury bills to captive markets such as insurance companies, and national insurance and social security boards. These institutions are often required to invest a stipulated part of their funds in government bonds.

Borrowing from commercial banks is highly reliable in developing countries. In many countries, commercial banks are required to hold a stipulated percentage of their deposits in the form of government securities. When banks are highly liquid, they may prefer to hold securities in excess of the legal requirement. The private sector may at times compete with government for loans and advances. Governments match this competition by increasing interest rates on securities.

Government borrowing from the central bank is sometimes known as money creation or "printing money". The central bank lends money to government by holding government treasury bills or by way of "ways and means" advances. The term "printing money" is a misnomer because when a loan is made by the central bank to the government, there is no immediate physical transfer of cash to government or printing of new notes and coins. The central bank issues a cheque to government which is deposited in the banking system. When this money is spent, it contributes to the formation of new deposits in the banking system and new money is created in this manner.

Government can finance the budget deficit by selling assets to the private sector. This method is sometimes known as "distressed privatization". The consequences of such action do not always have long-term beneficial effects on the economy because the proceeds of the sales are often used to finance the current account. We have already considered privatization which serves other purposes than financing the fiscal deficit.

Governments can also finance fiscal deficits by generating inflation. This method is known as inflationary finance. Inflationary finance has significant welfare costs and may not be very effective in small developing countries. We outline the standard model of inflationary finance and the associated welfare costs.

The model of inflationary finance as outlined by Tanzi (1978) assumes an exogenously determined money stock. That is, government finances the fiscal deficit by money creation, and money supply changes are not dependent on other factors such as credit to the private sector. The model assumes a monetarist price transmission framework where the line of causation runs from an increase in the money stock to a rise in the price level. This line of causation is questionable, however, because in open economies inflation can lead to a rise in the money supply.

The theory of inflationary finance posits that the tax base is equivalent to real cash balances held (M/P). The inflation tax revenue R is a product of the inflation rate (n) and real cash balances (M/P). The inflation rate is generated by money creation to finance the fiscal deficit and the result is higher revenue from inflationary finance. In his empirical analysis, Tanzi (1978) found a positive relationship between money creation and inflation tax revenue for Argentina.

The welfare costs of inflationary finance are related to the effects of inflation on the income distribution and economic efficiency. The inflation tax causes a reduction in real money balances and penalizes fixed income groups. Continued high rates of inflation also lead to a distortion in resource allocation and therefore constitutes a welfare cost to the economy as a whole.

There are substantial reasons why the theory of inflationary finance may not apply to small, open, developing economies. These economies have a small domestic resource base, and an endogenously determined money supply. Most goods and services are imported and the domestic inflation rate is generated by external inflation. Increases in the money supply impact on the balance of payments to a greater extent than on the domestic price level. A caveat is necessary here. In petroleum export-led economies such as Trinidad and Tobago, money supply expansion can be highly inflationary. However, the source of money supply growth is usually an increase in foreign reserves as a result of a petroleum export boom, rather than central bank money creation. The inflation tax will also vary in some countries with the exchange rate and import prices, rather than with money creation. Furthermore, it is difficult to control the incidence of inflation which also increases nominal government expenditures. Inflationary finance is not practised in Caribbean economies. However, in many Latin American economies high levels of inflation have been experienced leading to stabilization crises. Chapter 11 examines some of these crises and the measures adopted to reduce the high rates of inflation.

BALANCE OF PAYMENTS IMPLICATIONS OF DEFICIT FINANCING

In advanced economies deficit financing is discussed in relation to its impact on income and price levels. An important line of inquiry in industrialized countries has been devoted to measuring the long-term multiplier effect on income of using either bonds or money creation to finance a deficit. This analysis is usually based on the underlying IS/LM theoretical framework. Further work has been conducted with regard to the "crowding out" impact of fiscal policy assuming wealth effects in the consumption function. Much of this theory makes assumptions about the behaviour of interest rates in closed systems. The analyses also depend on whether a Keynesian, monetarist, or rational expectations perspective is used.

In developing economies, however, it is more appropriate to assume that there exists a balance of payments constraint and that, because of small and inefficient money markets, fiscal policy plays a more active role than monetary policy. Further, it can be argued that the fiscal deficit is a fundamental mechanism disturbing money stock equilibrium. In developing countries, the relevant approach is to examine the consequence of the fiscal deficit for the balance of payments, assuming that the primary impact of the deficit is on domestic money and income levels.

It is useful to commence our analysis by defining the balance sheet of the central bank as follows:

$$H = C + R = NFA + D + u$$

where: H = High powered money or monetary base
          C = Currency with the public
          R = Reserves of commercial banks
          NFA = Net foreign assets of the Central Bank
          D = Central Bank credit to government
          u = Other items

The budget deficit can be financed by foreign borrowing which is a component of NFA. The other variables on the right-hand side constitute central bank assets and are strong determinants of new money creation. The reserves of commercial banks (R) also act as a fulcrum for credit expansion to the private sector and the government.

Central bank money creation expands the monetary base (H) and leads to balance of payments deficits through a reduction of the central bank's foreign assets. The effect may be particularly severe because money creation by the central bank does not reduce the resources of the private sector. When government borrows from the commercial banks this reduces bank reserves and leads to a transfer of financial resources from the private to the public sector. Commercial bank lending to the government leads to a smaller foreign exchange loss than money creation by the central bank. Borrowing from citizens by the government results in a direct transfer of resources to the government which implies that citizens have less money to spend on imports.

The extent to which deficit financing will affect a country's balance of payments also depends on citizens' demand for money. If the demand for money is stable, and the banking system creates money faster than the public's desire to accumulate money balances, these excess balances are off-loaded through a reduction of foreign assets, either by increasing imports or by exporting capital. This is a fundamental thesis of the monetary approach to the balance of payments (see Howard 1992; Kreinin and Officer 1978). Governments can therefore inflict great damage on a small economy through excessive expenditures which necessitate deficit financing by money creation.

DEFICIT FINANCING AND THE PUBLIC DEBT

The financing of the government's deficit by borrowing leads to a rise in the public debt. It is necessary to distinguish between the internal and external or foreign debt. An internal debt is incurred when government sells securities to citizens. This leads to a rearrangement of assets, whereby citizens surrender current purchasing power in return for government securities. An external debt comes about when government sells securities to foreign governments, foreign institutions or foreign individuals. External borrowing permits an inflow of foreign exchange as well as imports of real resources from abroad. Whereas taxation is levied compulsorily, the public debt reflects a voluntary exchange by citizens for the government's promise to repay interest on the debt in the future (see Buchanan and Flowers 1975: chap. 29).

Buchanan (1958) and Buchanan and Flowers (1975) have clarified the concept of the real burden of the debt. They argue that the real burden of public spending rests with taxpayers in the future when the debt requires servicing and amortization. Taxes have to be levied on future taxpayers to finance the interest changes. To the extent that payment of the external debt requires that taxes be paid to foreign citizens, the external debt may be regarded as being more burdensome. However, this view can be countered by the argument that the external debt permits a higher national income, by drawing resources from abroad rather than out of the national economy. In this sense the external debt has a more beneficial impact on the overall economy (Buchanan and Flowers 1975: 333). Further, if the external debt is a result of borrowing to increase the productive capacity of the economy rather than consumption, this component of the public debt can be regarded as desirable.

Many developing countries experienced considerable problems during the 1980s with the management of their external debt. The "debt crisis" was a result of specific crises facing the world economy since the 1970s as well as excessive expenditure policies by some developing countries, made possible by access to loans in the Eurodollar market. The second major oil shock of 1981 created large external debt burdens for many non-oil producing countries. The petroleum-exporting countries experienced massive current account surpluses on their balance of payments between 1979 and 1981, while the non-oil countries recorded counterpart deficits which reduced foreign reserve levels and raised their external debt burden. The problem was exacerbated by high interest rates in the Eurodollar market between 1979 and 1980 which increased the nominal burden of the external debt (see Weisner 1985 for a more extended discussion). Many developing countries had to rely on rescheduling of their debt as well as cancellation of some debts by industrialized countries. Howard (1992) gives a detailed analysis of the debt problems of Barbados, Guyana, Jamaica, and Trinidad and Tobago during the 1980s. Also, see Polanyi-Levitt (1991) for a detailed discussion of the origins and consequences of Jamaica's debt crisis between 1970 and 1990. By the mid 1990s many Latin American countries had adopted measures to manage their debt more efficiently, leading to a reduction in their debt service ratios.

BUDGET DEFICITS AND RICARDIAN EQUIVALENCE

In the previous section we observed that the external debt imposes a burden on future generations. This view is not universally accepted and some economists who subscribe to a principle attributed to David Ricardo argue that a budget deficit imposes a debt on current taxpayers. Our analysis here outlines the standard neoclassical view of the burden of debt on future generations, as well as the Ricardian principle. Our discussion looks at the main argument for and against Ricardian equivalence found in the literature.[1]

The neoclassical model of budget deficits as presented by Barro (1989: 38) and Bernheim (1989: 55) is as follows. An individual normally plans his or her consumption over a lifetime. Financing the current budget deficit increases aggregate lifetime consumption and reduces desired savings. If resources are fully employed this process leads to an increase in real interest rates and crowds out private sector investment in a closed economy. The public debt is shifted to subsequent generations through increased taxation. Barro suggests that in the open economy, the budget deficit has a negligible effect on the real interest rate in international capital markets. The budget deficit in the open economy is more likely to increase the current account on the balance of payments than raise the real interest rate.

The Ricardian approach to budget deficits, sometimes known as the Ricardian equivalence theorem, states that deficit finance and tax finance are equivalent. This means that borrowing to finance the budget deficit in the current period has the same effect as levying taxation on the current generation to finance government expenditure. This implies that the impact of the budget deficit would be borne by the current generation.

Browning (1994: 442) suggests that people perceive that their lifetime disposable incomes are reduced by the same amount, whether the deficit is financed by borrowing or taxation.

The Ricardian equivalence principle rests on the assumption supported by Barro (1989) that the present generation believes that its descendants will have to pay higher taxes. The present generation makes bequests to its descendants to offset these future taxes. Barro sees the family as a dynastic unit whose transfers are altruistic. Bernheim (1989: 63) also suggests that other assumptions of the Ricardian equivalence principle are the existence of perfect capital markets, rational and farsighted consumers, and non-distortionary taxation. Bernheim rejects the Ricardian equivalence on the basis of the unrealism of these assumptions. Capital markets are imperfect and a large section of the population neither makes nor receives transfers. It is also true that not everyone has children. Further, Browning's (1994: 443) view is correct that few persons know how much government spending is financed by borrowing or the implications of present borrowing for future taxation. In these cases the public perceives no burden of deficit financing, and the burden will fall on future generations.[2]

SUMMARY

The traditional government budget is a short-term fiscal plan. The budget can be used to achieve allocation, distribution or stabilization goals. Through its budget the government can project the size of its fiscal deficit. Alternative budgetary approaches, such as performance, programme and zero-based budgeting have been developed to overcome the weaknesses of traditional budgeting. These approaches have not been highly successful.

Chronic budget deficits in developing countries can be explained by structural factors as well as fiscal indiscipline by governments. Large budget deficits impact on the balance of payments especially when they are financed by central bank money creation. Inflationary finance is another method of financing the fiscal deficit. Although this method may be relevant to some large developing countries like Argentina, it has not been used in small economies in the Caribbean.

Chapter Eleven

Stabilization Policy

D
eveloping countries experienced turbulent economic circumstances during the 1970s and 1980s. The former period was characterized by the oil crisis of 1974 which produced stagflationary
conditions and severe balance of payments deficits in many countries.
World recession was a dominant theme of the early 1980s, and the term
"debt crisis" became a new slogan for policy makers in developing countries, as well as international lending agencies. Stabilization policies were
necessary to rescue fledgling economies from economic collapse. Although
the IMF was active in the 1950s and 1960s, the severity of the balance of
payments problems in the 1970s called for a higher level of intervention.
This chapter analyses the nature of IMF conditionality, the theory underlying the IMF stabilization model and the structuralist critique of this
model. We also look at selected stabilization experiences including the
"Asian crisis" of 1997/98.

THE ORTHODOX IMF STABILIZATION PROGRAMME

The stabilization programme of the IMF has been the subject of extensive
research and critique. Here I summarize the IMF lending arrangements, performance criteria, and the theoretical underpinnings of the IMF approach.[1]

The IMF stabilization programme utilizes predominantly the following three types of funding: stand-by arrangements, extended fund facilities and structural adjustment facilities. The last type of facility dates from the late 1980s, but stand-by arrangements have their origin in the 1950s. Compensatory financing facilities have also been used by countries experiencing export shortfalls.

The stand-by arrangement is negotiated between the IMF and the government of the country seeking to borrow funds from the IMF. The Letter of Intent sent by the country's government promises to adhere to the conditionalities established by the IMF. Stand-by arrangements are usually short-term, and governments requesting IMF credits must demonstrate that their countries have serious balance of payments difficulties. An IMF mission is sent to establish the causes of balance of payments deterioration. Killick (1984: 188) has shown that prior to 1980 the principal causes of balance of payments crises were expansionary demand policies, and cost and price distortions related to deteriorating terms of trade and overvalued exchange rates. External debt servicing problems assumed more significance from the 1970s. Generally speaking, financial, exchange rate and balance of payments crises provide the main rationale for IMF interventions in the present era.

The extended fund facility and the structural adjustment facilities are medium- to long-term programmes. The extended fund facility was established in 1974 to deal with the specialized needs of countries undergoing severe balance of payments problems requiring assistance for a longer period than guaranteed under the stand-by arrangement. Credits under the extended fund facility are drawn over a maximum period of three years, and are repayable over a maximum of ten years. Structural adjustment lending is available to support medium-term structural adjustments for countries experiencing prolonged balance of payments disequilibrium.

The IMF programme requires that a country observe certain "performance criteria" which determine its continued access to the drawing down of credits. These criteria can be expressed as quantitative targets over a short-time period. They include credit ceilings on total domestic credit, credit to the government and private sector, devaluation, reduction in current payment arrears, minimum levels for foreign exchange reserves, and restrictions on new external debt (see Killick 1984: 191–92). Payer (1974) has identified other components of a typical IMF programme. These are the abolition or liberalization of foreign exchange and import controls, deregulation including the removal of price controls and subsidies, and wage restraint or wage cuts in the public service.

133

Extensive research has been devoted to analysing the theoretical under-pinnings of the IMF programmes. It has been generally acknowledged that the Polak model and its elaboration by other IMF economists provide the cornerstone of the IMF's programmes (see Killick 1984: 217). The monetary approach to the balance of payments provides the rationale for credit control policies. This approach suggests that the balance of payments is a monetary phenomenon, and payments disequilibrium can be caused by excessive credit creation in the context of a stable demand for money.[2] The IMF has been heavily criticized for placing too much empha-sis on monetary variables and relegating other causes of payments disequi-librium to secondary importance.

But the IMF's approach is not purely monetarist. I agree with David (1985), that the IMF's analysis is eclectic, embracing the monetary app-roach to the balance of payments, Keynesian expenditure theory, and neoclassical free-market theory. The IMF is concerned with the reduction of aggregate spending, as well as intramarket price adjustment. This involves the correction of overvalued exchange rates by devaluation, inter-est rate and trade liberalization, and other market liberalization measures including price controls and the removal of subsidies.

The criticisms of the IMF programme are extensive (see Howard 1992: 73; Goode 1984: 275–78). These programmes are criticized for not paying sufficient attention to structural problems in the economy. This is the essence of the structuralist critique which will be discussed in more detail in the next section. IMF programmes also have the reputation of being too harsh, because they attempt to adjust the balance of payments deficit quickly and ignore the income distribution effects of instruments like devaluation. Many policy makers believe that the IMF is not really interested in growth and development in these countries. However, it should be noted that some of the balance of payments problems of these countries have been caused by governments who lack the fiscal discipline to control expenditure. The cost of adjustment is a contraction in economic growth and a worsening of the income distribution.

STRUCTURALIST CRITIQUE OF THE ORTHODOX IMF STABILIZATION MODEL

The structuralist critique of the IMF stabilization model is a body of thought originating in Latin America. We can distinguish between "old structuralism" and "neostructuralism". Old structuralism emerged in the 1950s and was associated with the economists of ECLA.[3] This school of thought focused on the causes of Latin America's structural problems and the diagnosis of inflation. The neostructuralists also stressed the structural determinants of economic performance, but they advanced more sophisticated models to explain the economic behaviour of developing economies. Lance Taylor is a leading advocate of neostructuralism and we shall discuss some of his views later. Both approaches to structuralism heavily criticized the IMF's emphasis on monetary contraction and devaluation as solutions to the stabilization problems of developing countries.

Sutton (1984) presents a summary of the old Latin American structuralist critique. The old structuralists argued that orthodox stabilization programmes fail to recognize the structural and institutional context of Latin America. First, the orthodox model could not curb the rate of inflation through monetary contraction because inflation was a structural problem caused by import substitution, inelastic supply, protectionism, and devaluation. Second, devaluation and demand management policies were regarded as recessionary. These policies slowed the rate of economic growth by restricting credit, restraining the growth of wages, and reducing the size of the government's budget deficit.

The old structuralists did not advance an appropriate alternative model to solve short-run stabilization problems. They emphasized long-term growth and development through structural reforms. These included land reform, tax reform and the stimulation of non-traditional exports. Income redistribution and the implementation of stabilization funds were also advocated. Old structuralism neglected short-run financial constraints (see Sutton 1984: 23–41).

The neostructuralists assumed the same structural characteristics of developing economies such as dependence on primary products, exogenously determined prices of imports and exports, underdeveloped money and capital markets and so forth. Listed below are the main arguments of neostructuralism as presented by Taylor (1987):

1. Both devaluation and monetary restriction can create stagflation in the short run. The term stagflation refers to output contraction and higher inflation.
2. "Both export subsidies and import quotas can be used in lieu of devaluation to avoid some of its unfavourable side effects. Quota liberalization, in contrast, can easily be stagflationary" (p. 1429).
3. Financial liberalization has a similar stagflationary effect. High

135

interest rates on deposits may not generate a desirable reallocation of resources into productive assets.

4. Given the effects of devaluation on capital flight, "a more slowly crawling peg reduces the relative return to holding foreign assets, and may lead to portfolio switches towards domestic assets with a consequent increase in bank reserves" (p. 1429).

5. Wage and price controls in addition to exchange rate control are proposed in a policy package called a "heterodox shock".

Jha (1994: 246) makes the point that although a mix of tariffs and controls may be necessary as noted by the neostructuralists, controls are hard to manage efficiently and may lead to distortions. Jha notes that there is validity in the structuralist arguments that some IMF policies are stagflationary in the short run. However, his point is well taken that the reduction of demand is easier to implement in short-term stabilization programmes, than altering aggregate supply which requires medium- to long-term structural adjustment measures.

IMPORTANCE OF FISCAL AND INCOMES POLICY

So far, we have looked at economic issues relating to the orthodox stabilization model. It seems that this model, though recognizing the importance of fiscal and wage variables, places considerable emphasis in practice on exchange rate adjustment and monetary contraction. My analysis here speaks to the important roles of fiscal and incomes policy in economic stabilization.

According to Premchand (1983: 3), "fiscal policy consists of the use of taxes, government spending, and public debt operations to influence the economic activities of the community in desired ways and is concerned with the allocation of resources between the public and private sectors and their use for stability and growth". Fiscal policy is dependable because its effects can be measured in areas such as employment, price stability, savings and investment, and the balance of payments.

Two major principles in the use of fiscal policy in economic stabilization is that budgetary instability should be reduced and budgets should be balanced (Premchand 1983: 28). Even though some governments find it difficult to achieve a balanced budget, I believe that an alternative approach is to reduce the budget deficit to between 1 and 5 percent of

GDP. In order to reduce the budget deficit through public expenditure control, Premchand (1983: 33) indicates that "government should aim at achieving a spending level that does not put undue constraint on the conduct of monetary policy nor limit work or investment incentives in the private sector". Therefore, the view is acceptable that in the conduct of its fiscal policy, government should avoid excessive borrowing from the central bank and policies which "crowd out" the private sector.

Worrell (1992) puts a strong case for employing fiscal policy as the main instrument of stabilization. "Adjustment policies may be improved upon by better articulation of fiscal policy. Fiscal policy must bear a much greater burden of responsibility for export promotion, economic stabilization and ensuring the provision of essential social and economic services" (Worrell 1992: 5). He further argues that fiscal policy has direct effects on growth, the balance of payments, inflation and social welfare and can address several targets. He opines that fiscal policy can be supported by monetary and exchange rate policy to secure a target rate of investment, basic services, and economic stabilization. I agree with Worrell that monetary policy is not as potent in developing countries partly because it is more limited in its objectives such as credit and interest rate control, and also because money markets in developing countries are shallow and underdeveloped. I, however, support the IMF view that monetary policy can have greater impact on the balance of payments through the control of credit creation by the central bank and commercial banks.

Even though government expenditure and tax policies may have more direct impact on output, there is a strong interdependence between fiscal and monetary policy. Khan and Knight (1982) make the point that this dependence occurs because the financing of the fiscal deficit by credit creation produces changes in the money supply. The diversion of credit to the government may also "crowd out" private sector spending. These factors limit the use of monetary and fiscal policy as independent instruments to achieve separate objectives. Pure fiscal policy is therefore rare (Premchand 1983: 4).

Incomes policy is a component of many stabilization programmes, and one of its aims is to reduce the budget deficit through public sector wage restraint. Incomes policy has also been used to control wage inflation. To the extent that high wages can also worsen the balance of payments deficit, incomes policy can be regarded as an appropriate stabilization instrument. Incomes policy takes a number of forms. These include wage freezes, wage cuts, minimum wage changes, flexible wage guidelines, and incentive-based incomes policy (Downes 1994: 69). These policies have been used in developing economies as part of their structural adjustment programmes.

There are a number of arguments for and against the use of incomes policy as a stabilization device in developing countries. Incomes policy, when combined with restrictive monetary and fiscal policies, can moderate the rate of inflation. Further, wage cuts and freezes reduce total absorption and relieve pressure on the balance of payments. Schemes which relate wages to productivity gains can improve the overall productivity of the labour force and enhance supply side efficiency.

Downes (1994: 79) has outlined some arguments against incomes policy. He argues that these policies are difficult to sustain for long-time periods, and wages and prices may increase suddenly after the controls are removed. Further, wage controls interfere with the market mechanism, distort resource allocation, and may also alter the income distribution. The costs of administering wage contracts and monitoring prices may be quite high.

SELECTED STABILIZATION EXPERIENCES

The Barbadian Crisis (1990–91)

The Barbadian experience with stabilization is interesting because it is the story of a small economy which has successfully applied a typical IMF stabilization programme in restoring fiscal and balance of payments equilibrium. This section draws on my previous work (Howard 1992) and Haynes (1997) in evaluating the Barbadian stabilization programme of 1991. I examine the nature of the IMF programme and its impact on the economy.

The Barbadian economy slumped into crisis in 1991, as a result of a sharp deterioration in the fiscal and balance of payments deficits. Howard (1992) reports that the fiscal deficit climbed to a record high of Bds$244.0 million in 1990, and was heavily financed by central bank money creation. The foreign reserves also fell by Bds$100.0 million in 1990. The heavy deficit financing occurred just before the general elections of 1991 in the context of a decline in the real sector in 1991. The reduction of the fiscal deficit was regarded as a principal objective of stabilization policy.

The IMF stabilization programme for Barbados in 1991 was designed to reduce public expenditure, increase tax revenues and restore balance of payments equilibrium. The Fund's programme emphasized fiscal policy and supportive monetary policies. Structural adjustment reforms were also recommended. Fiscal adjustment included an 8 percent cut in public sector wages and salaries, massive downsizing of the public sector, and the imposition of a wide range of indirect tax measures (see Haynes 1997 for details of the IMF programme). The programme also included some heterodox components such as the maintenance of a fixed exchange rate pegged to the US dollar, and a wages and incomes protocol agreed to by the "social partners" including government, the private sector and the trade unions. A national wage freeze was implemented for two years with the concurrence of the social partners (see Downes 1994; Haynes 1997).

Despite an initial decline in employment and a negative growth rate, the stabilization programme restored fiscal and balance of payments equilibrium. Analysis of the Barbadian recovery shows that positive growth was recorded after 1992. The real growth rate rose from −5.7 percent in 1992 to 5.2 percent in 1996. The net international reserves position improved substantially from Bds$35.0 million in 1991 to Bds$577.5 million in 1996. Current account surpluses on the balance of payments were recorded for five consecutive years between 1992 and 1996. The government budget deficits were smaller and more manageable after 1991. The period 1992 to 1996 was also characterized by increased commercial bank lending to the government in the context of higher bank liquidity and reductions in central bank money creation. This financing strategy helped to ease pressure on the balance of payments. The inflation rate generally remained low, falling from 6.3 percent in 1991 to 1.9 percent in 1995. Overall, the improvement in the Barbadian economy is the result of corrective fiscal measures, the restoration of investor confidence after 1991, and a recovery in the export sectors.[4]

Haynes (1997: 105–7) outlines a number of lessons to be learnt from the Barbadian stabilization experience including the fiscal crisis of 1991. I agree with his observations, some of which are noted below:

1. A fixed exchange rate is sustainable, but it requires disciplined fiscal and monetary policies. This is because aggressive fiscal policies place pressure on the foreign reserves and exchange rate. Monetary policy must accommodate fiscal policy, which requires substantial import reserve cover in the context of a fixed exchange rate.

2   "Macro adjustment should take place early, thereby reducing the severity of the problem and enabling the economy to cope in a coordinated non-traumatic way" (p. 106).

3. The government should not rely too heavily on the central bank

to finance the fiscal deficit. This often leads to foreign reserves depletion. This point has also been argued by Howard (1992).

4. Structural reform also helps to provide the foundation for long-term growth.

5. A successful incomes policy depends on cooperation between the government, private sector, and trade unions. In my view, the incomes protocol was very important in the Barbadian case. It should be noted that more emphasis was placed on the wage freeze than on monetary correction.

Heterodox Shock: Latin America and Israel (1985–86)

Rapid inflation presents a serious stabilization problem for many developing countries, especially those in Latin America. My analysis of Barbados showed that inflation was relatively low and stable and was not a problem. Two questions are important. What policy instruments should government use to stabilize an economy undergoing hyperinflation? Is monetary correction appropriate in these countries? Hyperinflation is the term given to persistent inflation exceeding 50 percent per month (Cagan 1956). My approach here briefly examines the nature of stabilization policy in Bolivia, Argentina, Brazil, and Israel which experienced hyperinflations in the mid 1980s. The stabilization approach used in these countries with the exception of Bolivia has been described as "heterodox shock" or "heterodox stabilization". This strategy deserves some attention and is discussed below.

Blejer and Cheasty (1988) and Kiguel and Liviatan (1992) discuss the nature and impact of heterodox stabilization policies. Kiguel and Liviatan suggest that heterodox programmes are those that include orthodox policies such as tight fiscal and financial policies and a fixed exchange rate combined with the initial temporary use of incomes policy and deindexation. The success of a heterodox strategy relies on maintaining orthodox fiscal policy throughout the programme. Further, orthodox demand management policies have a central role to play since inflation can be fuelled by excess absorption. Individuals expect a certain pattern or rate of inflation to continue. The heterodox elements of the shock programmes are intended to break the inertia associated with inflationary expectations. The argument is that orthodox programmes do not bring down inflation fast enough. Therefore, it is necessary to add heterodox elements such as wage and price freezes and deindexation to reduce inflation drastically (Blejer and Cheasty 1988: 868–71).

There are certain economic costs associated with the inclusion of these heterodox elements. First, price controls can have distortionary effects on the economy and generate black markets. Second, subsidy payments may worsen the budget deficit. Third, wages freezes, if continued for too long, could create pressures for much higher wage increases in the future. Further, these measures also entail the administrative costs of implementing and monitoring the controls.[5]

The Israeli stabilization programme has been described by Fischer (1987). He notes that inflation in Israel rose from about 2 percent in 1967 to 500 percent in 1984. Indexation was used to mitigate the negative effects of inflation on purchasing power. The Israeli government embarked on a programme in 1985 which included large cuts in the budget deficit, devaluation and the fixing of the exchange rate to the US dollar, suspension of wage contracts including indexation, and a freeze on prices. Fisher reports that these measures led to a fall in the inflation rate to 1 to 2 percent per month and the budget deficit remained low.

Similar disinflation measues were used in Argentina and Brazil in 1985. Heymann (1987) reports that whereas inflation in Argentina was around 700 percent in 1984, the inflation rate was cut to 3 percent per month. Cardoso and Dornbusch (1987: 288) also argue that the Brazilian stabilization demonstrated that "an incomes policy is an essential ingredient to non-recessionary stabilization". On the other hand, the evidence for Bolivia presented by Sachs (1987) shows that the hyperinflation was brought to an end by an orthodox stabilization policy which included a devaluation, a sharp reduction in the fiscal deficit, an IMF standby arrangement, and rescheduling of debt. Kiguel and Liviatan (1992) maintain that most of these studies evaluating the heterodox approach looked at the initial stage of the programmes, that is, the first or second year. However, Kiguel and Liviatan opine that after the initial phase the repeated use of incomes policy can have a destabilizing effect on the economy.

The Asian Crisis (1997–98)

My review of the Asian Crisis of 1997–98 is intended to show that serious weaknesses in financial and exchange rate systems can precipitate an economic crisis which requires stabilization policies. The strong economic development of Asian economies including Indonesia, Korea, Thailand and Malaysia had contributed to a rapid increase in capital inflows. Prior to the crisis of 1997–98, these economies had exercised fiscal prudence and had high rates of savings by world standards. The speed of the financial crisis which developed in mid-1997 was not anticipated by many observers.

What were the causes of the crisis? The IMF Staff (1998a), Lipsky (1998) and Martinez (1998) advance a number of reasons for the financial and capital account problems of the Asian economies, primarily Indonesia, Korea and Thailand. Our subsequent discussion draws heavily on these works.

The IMF Staff (1998a: 18) argue that the Asian economies were probably victims of their own success. First, large-scale financial inflows prior to 1997 caused "overheating pressures" in the economy leading to inflated property and stock market values. Second, the maintenance of pegged exchange rates with the US dollar had encouraged investors in the financial and corporate sectors to assume significant currency risks by way of unhedged foreign currency borrowing. Much of the new investment went to real estate, reflecting the region's lower export competitiveness, given the yen's weakness against the US dollar (Lipsky 1998: 11). Third, the financial systems of the Asian economies were weak showing inadequate regulation and supervision. Fourth, banks, industrial groups, and government had close ties with each other. Government-directed lending practices led to a deterioration in the quality of the banks' lending portfolios (IMF Staff 1998a; Martinez 1998).

According to Lipsky (1998: 10) the devaluation of the Thai bhat on July 2, 1997 led to speculation pressures in other countries in the region. Capital flight accelerated as increasing numbers of investors began to regard East Asia as a region of slowing export growth and weak banking systems. In the scenario, the authorities were slow to implement tough monetary policies to stem capital flight which contributed significantly to the spread of the crisis throughout the region.

The IMF intervened in the Asian crisis by providing US$36 billion to support reform programmes in the worst hit countries, Indonesia, Korea, and Thailand. This was part of an international support package totalling about US$100 billion (IMF Staff 1998a: 19). The IMF applied the orthodox monetary approach: high real interest rates, to halt currency depreciation, and fiscal restriction.[6] The Asian countries were also encouraged to open up their markets to foreign participants (Fischer 1998: 4). It has been suggested that the IMF's initial strategy for Asia was not a success. Although the strategy stopped the currencies from falling in early 1998, by May rising unemployment and further contraction led to more capital outflows and falls in currencies and stock markets. This led some countries to pursue fiscal expansion and reduce interest rates. This view is advanced by Wade and Veneroso (1998: 19).

Wade (1998: 1544) also suggests that the IMF strategy included the promotion of a more "Western-type" financial system in Asia, "with a huge reduction of corporate debt". He opines that the Fund had not "properly weighed the economic costs of doing this, nor even the question of whether it has any legitimate business in entering the field of structural and institutional reform". Wade believes that the IMF should not promote the idea of capital account liberalization in Asia, without government coordination. More freedom given to companies to borrow on international markets would make these countries more vulnerable to capital flight. Many of these views were expressed at the time of the Asian crisis. The most important lesson of this crisis is that capital account liberalization is not appropriate in countries with weak financial systems. Most developing countries have inefficient financial markets and any sudden significant outflow of financial resources could lead to a collapse of fragile financial systems.

Mathieson, Richards and Sharma (1998) and Martinez (1998) have examined the similarities between the Asian crisis and other financial crises in emerging markets. First, these authors argue that prior to the Asian crisis as well as the Mexican crisis of 1994–95, there was an upsurge in capital inflows just before the crises. These countries built up massive national and private debt denominated in foreign currencies. This led to unhedged currency and interest rate exposures which undermined the stability of the financial systems. Second, the financial systems were characterized by weak regulatory regimes. Third, the pegged exchange rate system was a weak defence against speculative capital account movements especially in the context of a weak financial system. Fourth, these crises triggered turbulence in other foreign exchange markets in the context of a globalized world economy. Mathieson, Richards and Sharma emphasize the need for strong macroeconomic policies and stronger prudential regulation limiting short-term capital inflows to avert such crises.

SUMMARY

We have covered a range of issues in this chapter relating to the need for stabilization policies in developing countries. The presentation noted that the orthodox stabilization model had a number of deficiencies. These included its heavy emphasis on demand management, sometimes to the exclusion of structural causes of balance of payments deficits. The structuralist critique of this model was summarized, although structuralism does not provide an appropriate alternative strategy for short-run stabilization.

We examined different types of stabilization experiences. The Barbadian experience reflected balance of payments problems and stable inflation. Orthodox fiscal restraint policies appeared to have provided a solution to fiscal and balance of payments disequilibrium. The experience of some Latin American countries in the 1980s was one of hyperinflation. In these countries a heterodox strategy was employed to bring down inflation. East Asia experienced a financial crisis which was treated with orthodox policies. It is still too early to evaluate the efficiency of these policies in Asia.

Chapter Twelve

Structural Adjustment

M any developing countries pursuing stabilization policies have also adopted structural adjustment programmes, which incorporate the neoliberal philosophies of the World Bank and the IMF. Structural adjustment is a medium- to long-term strategy which attempts to achieve two broad objectives:

1. Micro- or market-oriented reforms which alter relative prices in order to increase the efficiency of resource allocation.
2. Macro- or sector-oriented reforms to improve the productive capacity of the economy and thereby sustain, over the long run, levels of economic output. (See, for example, Rodrik 1990 and Weissman 1990 for similar definitions.)

Structural adjustment is not feasible if it is unsustainable. Rodrik (1990: 934) suggests that an economic policy environment is sustainable if it is perceived as stable by the private sector. Stability requires a small fiscal deficit, a realistic exchange rate policy, and a set of microeconomic incentives which can be operational into the future. Stability also demands the absence of sharp changes in the income distribution, which would create political pressures to reverse the adjustment process. The last consideration is perhaps the most difficult to achieve. According to Weissman (1990: 1632) the evidence for some African countries reveals that certain policies have worked against the poor. The impact of adjustment policies on the poor has implications for political stability and therefore the overall sustainability of structural adjustment programmes.

Given the definition above, structural adjustment programmes normally comprise the following policy initiatives:

1. The reduction in the cost of government, as well as the size of the fiscal deficit through:
   a. privatization and public sector reform
   b. tax reform
   c. wage restraint/incomes policy
   d. reductions in government expenditure.

2. Market liberalization by means of deregulation. Specifically, such policies include:
   a. removal of price controls and subsidies
   b. interest rate liberalization
   c. exchange rate adjustment or liberalization
   d. foreign trade liberalization, as sanctioned by the World Trade Organization (WTO), to increase allocative efficiency by reducing tariffs and eliminating import quotas
   e. capital account liberalization.

3. Outward-looking development policies including export promotion and the removal of barriers to foreign investment

4. Sectoral reforms to improve resource allocation, productivity, and overall levels of output

5. Social safety net policies to mitigate the social costs of adjustment, and to target social services for the poor. (For this element of structural adjustment, see Weissman 1990.)

Space constraints do not allow us to discuss all of these policies in detail. We confine our subsequent analysis to market liberalization. A previous chapter looked at some of the policy issues involved in privatization. Social safety net policies have already been discussed, while tax reforms will be analysed in chapter 15.

Market Liberalization

In developing countries, market liberalization has taken the form of removal of price controls and subsidies. In Latin America, Jamaica, Trinidad and Tobago, and Guyana, devaluation and exchange rate liberalization were the main instruments used in the late 1980s and 1990s. In the Caribbean, trade liberalization is more recent, and includes adjustment in Common External Tariff (CET) rates and the reduction of quantitative restrictions.

The objective of market liberalization is to improve the allocation of resources by correcting prices in the foreign exchange market, the markets for traded and non-traded goods, and credit markets. Failure to introduce appropriate prices could result in a number of negative consequences for the economy. The adverse consequences of an overvalued exchange rate include excess demand for foreign exchange and reserve losses; a bias in favour of import substitution; and foreign exchange rationing, which may lead to high bureaucratic costs and corruption. Negative real interest rates lead to a diversion of loanable funds to less efficient uses, credit rationing, and disincentive to save in domestic currency. Subsidies and price controls generally inhibit market efficiency.

The efficacy of market liberalization has been questioned in developing economies. Rodrik (1990) has argued that the efficiency benefits of liberalization are usually static, and theory is silent on the contribution of liberalization to the rate of growth of an economy. Theory is not conclusive on the distributional effects of liberalization. Such programmes in the short run have a cost in terms of increases in unemployment.

A significant free-market policy is the liberalization of exchange rates. The objective of exchange rate liberalization is to allow the exchange rate to find its own level, to reduce capital flight, and induce an inflow of foreign exchange. Also, exchange rate liberalization is intended to increase the flow of funds from the parallel market to the official market. Such a policy may not be efficacious in countries which experience seasonal inflows of foreign exchange. This consideration applies to most of the smaller eastern Caribbean countries.

Trade liberalization has taken the form of import liberalization in some Caribbean countries. In Trinidad and Tobago, most items on the negative list were removed by the end of 1992. Barbados abolished quantitative restrictions on imports in 1993, as well as lowered rates on external tariffs. Trinidad and Tobago and Barbados also lowered CET rates from 45 percent to 30 percent. The maximum CET was expected to be 20 percent in these countries by 1998.

Sufficient information is not available to assess the immediate benefits of import liberalization. In the real world, however, import liberalization may not necessarily lead to improved export performance. The experience of Turkey has shown that direct export subsidies may be necessary to supplement liberalization, in order to stimulate export growth (Aricanli and

147

Rodrik 1990). Further, changes in the organizational structure of manufacturing firms are important to achieve managerial and marketing economies.

Ramsaran (1994) has also identified certain conditions which must be satisfied for trade liberalization to be successful. First, he argues that trade liberalization requires the availability of foreign exchange during the adjustment period, which has to be long enough to allow resources in the domestic economy to shift from one activity to another. There is the fear that if foreign exchange is scarce, local industries may collapse during the adjustment process thereby generating unemployment. Like Rodrik, he believes that the adjustment process must be sustainable in the sense that social safety nets must be put in place because of increases in unemployment in the short run. Third, the success of trade liberalization depends on the macroeconomic framework. That is, appropriate exchange rate, wage and monetary policies must accompany trade liberalization. He seems to favour devaluation to support the trade liberalization strategy, although exchange rate adjustment has not been very successful in many developing countries.

An essential component of market reform is financial liberalization which comprises measures to free the market of financial controls such as interest rate ceilings and reserve requirements.[1] Economies characterized by strong financial controls and regulations are known as financially repressed economies. According to Fry (1988: 18), loan rate ceilings discourage risk-taking by banks and financial institutions and distort the economy in a number of ways. First, low interest rates produce a bias in favour of current consumption and against future consumption, and may reduce financial savings. Second, potential lenders invest in low-yielding assets. Generally, in a financially repressed economy, the theory of financial repression holds that funds will be allocated to inefficient investors. McKinnon (1973) advocates the abolition of interest rate ceilings and the raising of interest rates, to stimulate the growth of savings and investment, and improve the efficiency of the financial market. This approach is known as financial liberalization.

Wood (1994) investigated the financial liberalization thesis for Barbados and found that real deposit rates have a very small influence on investment in Barbados, and a policy of financial liberalization may not have the desired effect on the Barbadian economy, in the context of imperfect information and oligopolistic banks. In an analysis of Turkey, Aricanli and Rodrik (1990) found that financial liberalization had negative consequences for Turkey's economy, by increasing the fragility of the financial sector and raising interest rates on credit above reasonable levels.

Capital account liberalization is an element of financial liberalization. Many economists have recognized that though there are benefits associated with capital account liberalization, financial crises in emerging markets have shown that there are substantial risks of liberalizing the capital account, especially when financial markets are weak. Eichengreen and Mussa (1998) outline the benefits and risks of capital account liberalization. They argue that capital flows have become more important in the context of overall economic liberalization and deregulation, the increased multilaterilization of trade, and the growth of derivative markets such as swaps, options and futures. Capital mobility has enabled countries to diversify their financial asset portfolios. However, capital account liberalization was an important factor in the Mexican crisis of 1994–95 and the Asian crisis of 1997–98.

Johnston (1998) outlines the process of sequencing capital account liberalization. First, appropriate prudential regulations should be in place to minimize the risks of short-term capital flows. Prudential regulations comprise laws and procedures to ensure adequate risk management of financial institutions and protection of investors against fraud. Second, macroeconomic stability is a *sine qua non* for capital account liberalization.

Despite the arguments advanced in support of capital account liberalization, my view is that this policy is not recommended for many small developing countries like those in the Caribbean. I agree with Stiglitz's (1994) views that market failures in developing countries are more pervasive than in other markets and governments have a critical role to play in regulating financial institutions. This applies to regulation of the capital account of the balance of payments.

STRUCTURAL ADJUSTMENT EXPERIENCES

Latin America

Structural adjustment in Latin America was a response to the economic shocks of the early 1980s. This section presents an overview of the market liberalization measures, as well as the privatization strategies adopted. We do not provide an extensive statistical survey of each of these countries.

An important aspect of structural adjustment in Latin America was trade liberalization. Prior to the early 1980s, most countries in Latin America had numerous trade restrictions including high tariffs, foreign exchange restrictions, multiple exchange rates, and quantitative restrictions on imports. Alam and Rajapatirana (1993) present statistical data to show that most tariff rates in Latin American countries were above 30 percent in the pre-reform period but fell to under 20 percent in the post-reform period. According to the Organization for Economic Cooperation and Development (OECD) (1992), Mexico had some of the lowest tariff rates, falling from 24 percent in 1985 to 13 percent in 1990. Most of these reforms were designed to reduce protectionism which supported import substitution. One goal of trade liberalization is to reorient the economies towards export promotion.

Alam and Rajapatirana (1993) have suggested that trade liberalization in Latin America had a significant impact on the growth rates of imports. They argue that even though import levels were higher the rate of increase was not as strong as expected. This can be explained by the fact that the trade liberalization reforms were introduced at the same time as other stabilization and structural adjustment measures, which reduced domestic demand and constrained the rate of growth of imports. Further, strong currency devaluations raised import prices and suppressed import demand. Alam and Rajapatirana (1993) conclude that among the lessons to be learnt from trade liberalization in Latin American, is that successful reforms require a supportive macroeconomic environment, that is, tight fiscal and monetary policies, as well as exchange rate devaluations.

ECLAC (1996: 51) reports that by 1995 foreign trade liberalization in Latin America took a step backwards as tariffs increased and non-tariffs barriers were erected. Some countries like Argentina, Brazil and Mexico increased tariff rates to protect some sectors which were vulnerable to international competition. Mexico, for example, increased its tariffs on 65 products to between 25 percent and 260 percent in the case of imports from non-NAFTA (North American Free Trade Agreement) countries (see ECLAC 1996: 52).

Financial and capital market reform is also a feature of the Latin American structural adjustment process. According to ECLAC (1996: 54) these reforms included capital account liberalization, elimination of barriers to foreign investment, deregulation of interest rates, currency market liberalization, supervision and prudential regulation, and increased central bank autonomy. In Mexico, for example, the government had liberalized the foreign investment code in 1984, opening up new areas of the economy to investors from abroad, such as commercial banks, insurance companies, and petrochemical industries (OECD 1992).

Diaz-Alejandro (1985) makes the point that financial liberalization in the 1970s had a negative impact on the Latin American banking system. He argues that financial reforms "yielded by 1983 domestic financial sectors characterized by widespread bankruptcies, massive government interventions or nationalizations of private institutions, and low domestic savings" (Diaz-Alejandro 1985: 1). The negative impact of financial liberalization was particularly severe in Chile. He maintains that interest rate liberalization did not foster strong long-term intermediation. Short-term loans and deposits were a feature of intermediaries in many Southern Cone Latin American countries. Further, he asserts that total domestic savings did not increase as a result of financial liberalization in Latin America. Also, investment did not respond significantly to liberalization. He suggests, using Mexico and Uruguay as examples, that deposits denominated in foreign currencies, owned either by domestic or foreign residents, may increase the vulnerability of countries to crises. Overall, some regulation of financial systems and capital account movements seems to be required.[2]

Privatization was an essential component of structural adjustment programmes in Latin America. ECLAC (1996) notes that the privatization process accelerated in 1989 but the sell-off rate slackened after 1991. Argentina and Mexico were leaders in privatization in the second half of the 1980s when revenue from privatization equalled 8 percent of GDP.

Mexico is discussed here as an example of the privatization process in Latin America. We rely heavily on the OECD Economic Surveys, 1992 and 1995. Mexico ranked high among Latin American countries in the range of industries privatized. These included airlines, electricity, steel, banks, and telecommunications. The first phase of privatization occurred between 1982 and 1988 when mostly small and medium-sized enterprises were sold or liquidated. Major enterprises were privatized after 1988 following improvements in the economy. It is estimated that revenue from the sell-off of public enterprises totalled U.S.$23.7 billion in the 1988–94 period (OECD 1995). Most of the receipts were placed in a contingency fund and used to retire government debt. However, the privatizations were not successful in broadening share ownership among the population.

There are a number of lessons to be learnt from the Mexican privatization experience.[3] First, the process started with small enterprises to provide the government with valuable experience. Second, enterprises were carefully evaluated by professional accounting firms prior to sale. Third, enterprises were sold without prior physical restructuring, and modernization was left to the buyer. Fourth, markets in which the privatized enterprises operated were deregulated, and price subsidies abolished before privatization. Fifth, the actual privatization process was delegated to banks, and bidders for the purchase were carefully screened (OECD 1992: 90).

Jamaica

Jamaica is chosen here to illustrate the impact of structural adjustment in a Caribbean country. Handa and King (1997) report that the implementation of structural adjustment policies in Jamaica accelerated after 1989. Handa and King opine that prior to 1989, policies had centred around fiscal and monetary management rather than structural adjustment of the economy. As a result very little was achieved in terms of economic liberalization. Even though Handa and King see 1989 as the start of a phase of more drastic reforms in the liberalization of the economy, privatization and tax reforms had begun in Jamaica before 1989. Analyses by Anderson and Witter (1994) indicate that structural adjustment started before 1989, and was accompanied by stabilization policies.[4]

Trade liberalization in Jamaica was similar to the Latin American process. Handa and King (1997: 918) divide the Jamaican trade reform experience into three phases. The first period was 1983 to 1985 when quantitative restrictions (import licences) were abolished. These restrictions were designed to support the early policy of import substitution. In the second period 1987–91, tariffs were reduced and other quotas removed. The third stage started at the end of 1991 with the removal and reduction of stamp duties and tariff rates.

The early privatization process in Jamaica in the 1980s has been discussed by Howard (1992: 66–67). Handa and King (1997: 920) assert that the pace of privatization accelerated between 1989 and 1994, averaging eight companies per year. Privatization was combined with financial liberalization which took the form of relaxation of foreign exchange controls, removal of restrictions on foreign borrowing and deposit rate fixing by banks.

Research by Anderson and Witter (1994) evaluates the economic impact of Jamaica's structural adjustment programme in the 1980s. Handa and King (1997) analyse the implications of adjustment policies for the income distribution and poverty during the early 1990s. My presentation below reports the findings of these authors.

Anderson and Witter report that one of the achievements of the adjustment process in Jamaica was a reduction in the size of the public sector. This was also accompanied by an increase in the share of investment in the GDP at the expense of the share of consumption. The fiscal deficit declined as a percent of GDP from 29.6 percent in fiscal 1977–78 to 13.3 percent in fiscal 1988–89, primarily resulting from cuts in government expenditure.

I examined the evidence to gauge whether the trend in fiscal management continued into the 1990s. The fiscal budget recorded surpluses between fiscal 1991–92 and fiscal 1994–95. Thereafter, the fiscal budget went into deficit reaching 12.0 percent of GDP in fiscal 1997–98. These deficits resulted from debt service payments and increases in public sector wages and salaries.[5]

Structural adjustment should result in an expansion in exports as a ratio of GDP. Anderson and Witter showed that export growth was not buoyant during the 1980s because of the weakness in the aluminum market. Exports as a ratio of GDP actually fell from 36.0 percent in 1993 to 23.0 percent in 1997.[6]

Structural adjustment had significant negative effects on education, health and the social services. Education at all levels suffered because of cuts in the education budget. Anderson and Witter produce data to show that at the secondary education level there was a decline in performance levels. Health indicators were mixed with mortality levels showing an improvement. These authors regard the decline in the numbers of health care professionals as one of the significant features of the period. Overall, Anderson and Witter observe a deterioration in Jamaican living standards between 1977 and 1985.

The analysis by Handa and King (1997) shows that even though the Gini coefficient fell from 0.376 in 1989 to 0.335 in 1993, inequality actually rose in 1991 and 1992 when drastic market liberalization measures were taking place. Their analysis implies a fall in living standards in 1991 and 1992, but full recovery in 1993. During the early 1990s, the educational and health sectors continued to show similar levels of deterioration in real resources, and in the quality of service provided as previously observed by Anderson and Witter.

Turkey

My choice of Turkey in this section stems from the realization that Turkey is an example of a developing country that recovered from a debt crisis during the 1980s.[7] The structural adjustment policies applied had mixed results. Aricanli and Rodrik (1990) have shown that even though Turkey experienced success in mobilizing capital inflows and achieving a high measure of export-oriented development, liberalization policies had some negative consequences for the Turkish economy. A summary of the evaluation by Aricanli and Rodrik is presented below.

Turkey's structural adjustment policies were a response to a liquidity crisis caused by current account deficits around 1978. The structural adjustment reforms were introduced in 1980 and comprised devaluation, export subsidies, public enterprise reform and privatization, financial liberalization, import liberalization, and the promotion of direct foreign investment.

Aricanli and Rodrik (1990: 1347) assert that the increase in exports was the most significant achievement of the economic reforms, and this was primarily due to the export subsidies, repression of domestic demand, and the ability of Turkish exporters to penetrate the markets in the Middle East. They also argue that the rise in capital inflows was a response to the implementation of the reform package and not to the results.

The economic impact of liberalization was otherwise disappointing. Aricanli and Rodrik maintain that financial and trade liberalization had an inhibiting effect on private investment. Investment in manufacturing was discouraged by high interest rates, high inflation, and real currency depreciation. Housing and tourism were the only sectors experiencing an increase in private investment. Import liberalization had little impact on exports. The distribution of income remained highly unequal and structural problems persisted in the economy.

Sub-Saharan Africa with Special Reference to Ghana

Sub-Saharan Africa experienced intense structural adjustment programmes between the mid-1980s and early 1990s.[8] These programmes were supported by the IMF structural adjustment facility (SAF) and enhanced structural adjustment facility (ESAF). A detailed analysis of the various country programmes is beyond the scope of this book. However, evaluative work by Nsouli (1993) allows us to identify briefly broad results of structural adjustment. The results of Ghana's structural adjustment programme will also be examined.[9]

Structural adjustment in sub-Saharan Africa was largely a response to the recessionary conditions of the 1980s, declining terms of trade, and rising debt service burdens. Nsouli (1993: 21) writes that "between 1986 and 1992, 30 sub-Saharan African countries adopted adjustment programmes under the SAF and ESAF arrangements". These programmes were intended to remove severe structural and financial problems. The purpose of the adjustment programmes was to put the economies on a sustainable growth path, correct balance of payments disequilibrium, and reduce inflation. The programmes embodied measures to promote capital formation and increase productivity as well as mobilize savings. Further, social safety nets were designed to mitigate the costs of adjustment (see Nsouli 1993: 21). The measures had the same objectives as in other developing countries. These included market liberalization, exchange rate adjustment, reductions in government expenditure and overall fiscal deficits, and expenditure targeting to alleviate poverty.

Nsouli lists a number of broad achievements of the African programmes between 1986 and 1992 for the 30 countries. He writes that "there was an improvement in growth performance in nearly two-thirds of the cases, a reduction in inflation in about the same proportion, an improvement in the external account in nearly two-fifths of the countries, and an increase in international reserves in over two-thirds of the countries" (Nsouli 1993: 22). He indicates that the programmes were constrained by limited administrative and institutional infrastructure, data deficiencies, and shortfalls in financial assistance. Moreover, some countries suffered adversely from political instability, internal conflicts, and border problems which reduced the effectiveness of the structural adjustment measures.

Structural adjustment policies did not significantly increase the growth of domestic saving in sub-Saharan African. Domestic saving fluctuated between 1986 and 1993 and was well below the level of saving in other developing countries. Hadjimichael, Ghura and Muhleisen (1995: 2) have provided IMF data to show that the average savings/GDP ratio was 11.8 percent in sub-Saharan Africa for the period 1986–92 compared with 24.5 percent for all developing countries, 30.0 percent for Asia, 19.1 percent for Latin America, and 18.9 percent for the whole of Africa. The sustainability of structural adjustment in sub-Saharan Africa was seriously constrained by the low level of domestic saving.

Our summary evaluation of Ghana's experience with structural adjustment between 1983 and 1991 is based on the work of Nowak, Basanti and Horvath (1996). Their analysis is an incisive critique of the strengths and weaknesses of Ghana's programme, which was one of the most successful in sub-Saharan Africa. Ghana's economic recovery programme took place during the period 1983 to 1991. The main achievements of this programme was the restoration of fiscal discipline, liberalization of trade and exchange rates, and a significant decline in inflation. The recovery in real growth was achieved without a contraction in domestic demand (see Nowak, Basanti and Horvath 1996: 22). However, one of the weaknesses of the programme was the sluggish response of private savings and investment. The reform effort attracted a high level of capital inflows which helped to sustain domestic absorption.

It suffices to comment briefly on the structural constraints on the growth of investment during the period of the economic recovery programme. Nowak, Basanti and Horvath argue that the private sector never played a dominant role in the process of structural adjustment in Ghana. Government regulation remained strong and parastatal monopolies continued to operate in cocoa marketing, banking, insurance and the utilities such as energy and communications. Privatization and parastatal reform was a slow process, and there was limited direct foreign investment.

Financial markets in Ghana also remained underdeveloped and dominated by the public sector. Financial liberalization did not achieve much success in generating medium-term and development finance (Nowak, Basanti and Horvath 1996: 39).

Ghana's economic recovery programme included social safety net policies. Nowak, Basanti and Horvath report a reduction in poverty from 37 percent of the population to 32 percent. There was considerable emphasis on government expenditure on education and health. Enrolment in primary and secondary schools increased, mortality rates declined, malnutrition fell among children, and average life expectancy increased over the economic recovery programme period. However, Ghana still lagged behind other developing countries in terms of primary school enrolment (see Nowak, Basanti and Horvath 1996: 45).

SUMMARY

The foregoing analysis covered a range of issues in this chapter relating to the need for structural adjustment in developing countries. The presentation looked at structural adjustment policies which incorporate neoliberal views related to market liberalization and deregulation of the economy. We noted that in the case of many Latin American countries, Jamaica, and Turkey, market liberalization did not have the success predicted by the theory. This phenomenon can be explained by the structuralist critique. In developing economies where markets do not function well, the liberalization of inefficient markets may pose widespread problems. My view is that markets in developing countries should be subject to a prudent degree of regulation, which will vary according to the economic circumstances of each country.

Chapter Thirteen

Introduction
to Taxation

G overnments cannot function without levying taxes on citizens. The principal purpose of taxation is to finance public expenditure. Taxation constitutes an involuntary saving by taxpayers which is diverted to government for use in resource allocation. This chapter discusses the equity and efficiency principles of taxation, as well as other criteria for evaluating the tax system. I am also concerned with the relationship between taxes and growth, taxation and stabilization as well as administrative aspects of taxation. These principles apply to developed as well as developing countries. The chapter highlights broad theoretical issues rather than detailed empirical analyses.

THE EQUITY PRINCIPLE

The equity principle states that the tax burden should be equitable. This means that a taxpayer should not pay more than a fair share of taxes. According to this criterion, a person is asked to contribute to the general revenue according to the benefits received from the payment of taxes, or according to ability to pay. Under the first aspect of the equity criterion known as the benefit principle, taxes are the prices citizens pay for the goods and services they buy through their government. Such prices are assessed on each citizen according to the benefits directly or indirectly received. The benefit principle can be applied to certain forms of taxation where the beneficiaries are easily identifiable. These forms of taxation include fuel levies, highway tolls, and other user charges. However, the benefit principle has limitations as a general principle of taxation, because most citizens do not reveal their true preferences for public goods.

The benefit principle also helps to facilitate the earmarking of revenue. Earmarking is a budgetary instrument whereby the government allocates a specific amount of revenue, or a percentage of revenue, to special funds. Earmarking is normally achieved through legislation. For example, a special fund can be established to finance rural transport or training. Premchand (1983: 159) has outlined some significant advantages of earmarking. First, it brings about greater managerial efficiency. Second, earmarking provides a link between the costs of taxation and the benefits of expenditures. In this way, expenditures can be targeted to individuals or various sectors of the economy. Third, earmarking can lead to greater accountability from a legislative point of view, because policy makers can identify the sources and uses of funds. On the other hand, when taxes are placed into a consolidated fund, it is possible to misallocate tax revenues to low priority areas. Fourth, earmarking reduces uncertainty in annual budget allocations. However, because earmarking ties expenditures to specific levies, it is sometimes argued that earmarking introduces rigidity into the allocation of funds (Musgrave and Musgrave 1973).

The other aspect of the equity principle is the ability to pay principle. Under this criterion a tax is not linked directly to the benefit received. The government fixes a revenue target, and the citizens are asked to contribute according to their ability to pay. In many systems, such revenues are paid into a single consolidated fund. Under this principle, income or wealth is usually regarded as an index of a person's fiscal capacity.

The ability to pay principle rests on the concept of equal sacrifice introduced by John Stuart Mill (Musgrave 1985: 18). According to Mill, taxes should be levied according to the equal sacrifice made by taxpayers. Musgrave (1985) distinguishes between three concepts of equal sacrifice found in the literature. The equal marginal sacrifice principle means that the marginal utility of income for each individual should be equal following the imposition of a tax. The equal absolute sacrifice doctrine states that each taxpayer suffers the same loss in total utility as a result of the tax. Proportional sacrifice occurs when a tax causes the same percentage loss in total utility to taxpayers. These concepts assumed that utility was measurable in cardinal units; the marginal utility of income was known with certainty; marginal utility declines as income increases, and interpersonal comparisons of utility are allowed. The last two conditions have been criticized in the literature and overtaken by the new welfare economics of Pareto optimality (Musgrave 1985: 20). Further, some economists argue that consumption is a better measure of ability to pay than income, and that taxation should be based on consumption.

The ability to pay criterion can be divided into two further principles, those of horizontal and vertical equity. The principle of horizontal equity means that people in equal positions, or enjoying equal levels of welfare, should be treated equally, and they should contribute the same amount of tax. The vertical equity principle asserts that people in unequal positions should be treated unequally. This principle is sometimes interpreted as requiring progressive taxation. The main problems in applying the equity principles relate to the difficulty of defining equals. This calls for an interpersonal comparison of welfare levels, which is difficult in practice. In levying taxes, the equity principle is one of the most important considerations facing the governments of small developing countries, because most of the people are poor (see Goode 1984).

THE ROLE OF THE TAX SYSTEM

The tax system should have efficiency objectives. The government should be able to collect enough revenue to carry out its welfare and development programmes, without significantly disturbing the efficiency of the market system. Excess-burden analysis deals with the efficiency costs of taxation. An excess burden or deadweight loss is said to result when a tax causes a distortion in resource allocation or expenditure patterns leading to a fall in welfare. Excess-burden analysis will be pursued in more detail in a subsequent chapter. The principle of efficiency often conflicts with the equity criterion. For example, a non-distortionary tax, like a general retail sales tax, may be preferable on efficiency grounds, but may be burdensome on the poor. Certain types of trade tariffs in open economies may lead to consumer excess burden, but should be used judiciously to discourage the consumption of specified imports.

There are other criteria for evaluating the tax system. We now discuss the differences between a progressive tax, a regressive tax and a proportional tax. A progressive tax is defined as a tax whereby the ratio of tax to income increases as income increases. Traditionally, this has been a feature of the income tax, although modern tax reform has reduced the importance of the progressivity principle. A regressive tax is one whereby the ratio of tax to income rises as income falls. For example, a poll tax or head tax, where everyone pays the same amount, is said to be regressive in its incidence. Regressivity is considered to be inequitable because a regressive tax affects the poor more than the rich. A proportional tax is characterized by a constant ratio of tax to income. A proportional tax is sometimes known as a flat tax.

A neutral tax is a tax which does not lead to a change in relative prices. Neutral taxes are therefore not distortionary and are considered to be efficient. For example, VAT is a neutral tax, because it raised the absolute level of prices rather than relative prices. On the other hand, an excise tax on a commodity raises the price of the taxed commodity, and distorts consumer choices. Therefore, an excise tax is non-neutral. Policy makers may sometimes impose non-neutral taxes to raise revenue, for equity considerations, or to achieve other goals besides resource allocation.

There are other requirements for a good tax structure. Taxation should be efficiently administered, and the taxation procedure should be understandable to the taxpayers. Further, the taxes should have low administrative and compliance costs. The concepts of administrative and compliance costs are defined in chapter 20. Administrative tax reform aims at a reduction of these costs to improve efficiency and reduce tax evasion. Chapter 20 also examines tax evasion and the principles of efficient tax administration.

Taxation also has a distributive purpose. All governments must be conscious of the unequal distribution of real income. Taxation can aid income redistribution by facilitating certain transfers to those persons who are most disadvantaged. These transfers include pensions, social security, national insurance, and unemployment benefits. Taxation also aids in income redistribution when government spends money on education and low-cost housing, thereby making it possible for citizens to improve their standard of living. Some of these issues have been dealt with earlier in chapter 7.

The major contribution of Musgrave on the distributive role of the tax system was the distinction between specific tax incidence, differential tax incidence, and balanced budget or expenditure incidence. Differential tax incidence, which refers to the distributional changes that result when one tax is substituted for another, is particularly important in assessing the impact of tax reform. Budget incidence examines the effects of all aspects of government activity on private real incomes. Empirical incidence studies have focused more on tax incidence than on budget incidence. Tax incidence will be dealt with in greater detail in a subsequent chapter.

The tax system also has a stabilization role. This is very important in small open economies which suffer from cyclical instability as a result of crop failures and falling export prices. These factors reduce government revenues, and policy makers are forced to impose new taxes or increase tax rates. The use of taxation as a stabilization device should not be pursued for too long, because taxation curtails consumer demand and dampens investment.

Howard (1992) demonstrated the use of taxation as a stabilization instrument during the 1980s in the Caribbean. He argued that heavy indirect taxation was designed principally to suppress aggregate demand in order to restore equilibrium to the balance of payments of Jamaica and Barbados. The early 1980s was a period of recession in the world economy marked by the intervention of the IMF in Jamaica and Barbados. There are many reasons why some Caribbean governments resort to heavy indirect taxation in times of recession. These taxes are easy to collect and easy to manipulate through the budget. Further, indirect taxation affects all income groups. However, the use of indirect taxation as a stabilization device can lead to a deterioration in the income distribution. This is so because such taxes are regressive. Further, indirect taxes during the 1980s were not good built-in stabilizers. This is why governments had to change tax rates and bases year after year. Contractionary indirect taxes can also reduce the rate of growth of the economy.

In developing countries the tax system should be growth oriented. Our analysis draws on Marsden (1990) and Shoup (1990) who dealt with the relationship between taxes and economic growth. According to Marsden (1990), countries with lower taxes have experienced higher rates of economic growth. Marsden draws on regression analysis for a number of non-oil developing countries to show that an increase of one percent in the tax/GDP ratio was associated with a decrease in the rate of economic growth of 0.36 percent (Marsden 1990: 30). He advanced the view that the stronger effects of lower taxes on growth in the lower income countries occur because modern technology and improvement in skills implied greater scope for productivity growth. He argued that gross investment grew at higher rates in low-tax countries averaging 8.9 percent annually (Marsden 1990: 31). Further, the regression analysis of the growth of exports found that taxes on foreign trade had a negative effect on that sector. Marsden's analysis can be criticized on the ground that it ignored other factors influencing growth by focussing exclusively on the tax/GDP ratio. However, his analysis indicates that high taxes have some influence on the slower rates of growth of some developing countries.

Shoup (1990) identified the economic and non-economic characteristics of a growth-oriented tax system. First, in order to stimulate entrepreneurship, profits should be taxed at a low rate. A low rate of tax could be achieved with accelerated depreciation over a period of years. In many developed countries, this approach has been followed but has been biased towards foreign investment. Second, the tax system should avoid reducing what Shoup described as gainful consumption. According to Shoup (1990: 37), gainful consumption is defined as "consumption that pays for itself in part or in whole through increased production". To achieve this, Shoup advocated that taxation should not be levied on families at very low income levels. The non-economic characteristics of the tax system would include improving administrative efficiency, increasing taxpayer compliance, and reducing tax evasion.

TAXABLE CAPACITY AND TAX EFFORT

In the 1960s and early 1970s, considerable research was devoted to measuring the taxable capacity and tax effort of developing countries. This research was led by economists in the IMF in an effort to assist aid donors and international lending agencies in their evaluation of the fiscal performance of the government (Goode 1984: 84–87). Much of this analysis was conducted by economists such as Lotz and Morss (1967) and Chelliah (1971). Our discussion of taxable capacity leans heavily on Prest (1978). According to Prest, taxable capacity can be interpreted as the amount of tax which could be justly or fairly imposed on a country. However, there are considerable difficulties in measuring the maximum feasible tax. Economists attempted to assess taxable capacity by using international comparisons of tax levels. Following Prest (1978), cross-section econometric studies defined taxable capacity on the basis of what two or more countries may be expected to achieve in their levels of taxation given the same economic characteristics.

Many of the early studies were devoted to determining the determinants of the tax ratio (T/Y). Lotz and Morss (1967) made an important contribution to this analysis by including the "openness" of a country as a better estimator of taxable capacity in poor countries than the per capita income measure of development. In the analysis of Lotz and Morss, the tax ratio is regressed on per capita income and openness, where the latter is measured by imports plus exports as a ratio of GDP. The predicted tax ratio as given by the regression equation is equivalent to the taxable capacity of a country. Tax effort is obtained by dividing the actual tax ratio by the predicted ratio. If the ratio of the actual share to the predicted share is less than one, the country has a low tax effort. Ratios greater than one indicate a high tax effort. A country can have a high tax effort and high capacity, or low capacity and low effort. Many of the quantitative studies on tax levels in developing countries also focused on factors such as the share of agriculture or mining in the GDP, the degree of urbanization, the degree of monetization, and country size as determinants of taxable capacity (Tanzi 1991: 117 and Musgrave 1969b).

In more recent times Leuthold (1991), recognizing the shortcomings of using cross-country data in tax effort studies, used a panel of cross-country and time series data to derive tax effort indices for eight relatively homogenous African countries, namely, Ivory Coast, Senegal, Mali, Cameroon, Kenya, Nigeria, Ghana, and Tanzania. He calculated tax effort indices for both direct and indirect taxes. He regressed the tax share T/Y on the share of agriculture in income, the ratio of exports plus imports to income, the share of mining in income, and the share of foreign grants in GDP. He found that only the foreign trade variable had the expected sign and was significantly different from zero, implying the importance of foreign trade as a determinant of tax ratios. Tanzania and Kenya were identified as high tax effort countries, and Cameroon and Mali as low tax effort countries. The other four countries had tax effort indices statistically equal to one.

Although Leuthold attempted to improve the technique for calculating tax effort, interest in this research seems to have declined during the 1980s and 1990s. More emphasis came to be placed on the efficiency of taxation and tax administration reform rather than on tax effort as a criterion. Howard (1992: 11) has argued that high tax ratios may not show that the tax system is elastic, but may indicate that a country is able to increase discretionary tax rates year after year. Further, a high tax effort may not necessarily be good for development, but may suppress private sector savings and initiative.

Despite the foregoing observations, one reason for low tax ratios in some developing countries is the design of the tax system. Some systems contain a large number of taxes and many nuisance taxes which lead to considerable collection lags. Tanzi (1991) has suggested a number of indices to gauge the effectiveness of these systems in raising tax revenue. Two of these criteria are the concentration index and the dispersion index. The concentration index measures "the proportion of total tax revenue generated by, say, the three or four major taxes or tax rates" (Tanzi 1991: 158). The tax system should have relatively few tax rates. Simplification of the tax system therefore improves its effectiveness.

Tanzi's dispersion index measures the average share of total tax revenue accruing from minor taxes. The aim of tax policy would be to reduce the use of minor taxes with small yields. Countries should therefore attempt to achieve a high concentration index and a low dispersion index in their tax system. Tanzi's indices are useful as a guide to tax system design in developing countries.

TAX ELASTICITY AND TAX BUOYANCY

The tax elasticity and tax buoyancy concepts measure the response of tax revenue to changes in income. These concepts are important in developing countries where considerable lags exist in tax collection and where it is possible for many individuals to evade taxes. The distinction between tax elasticity and tax buoyancy was developed by Mansfield (1972). Tax elasticity measures the automatic response of tax revenue to income changes. Revenue increases under the elasticity concept exclude the effects of discretionary or legal changes in tax rates or in the tax base, as well as the introduction of new taxes. Tax buoyancy measures the total response of revenue changes (including discretionary adjustments) to changes in income. High tax elasticities are considered good for a country since government can pursue expenditure policies without the need for increasing tax rates and bases frequently.

The elasticity of total tax revenue is given by

$$E_T = \frac{\Delta T}{\Delta Y} \frac{Y}{T}$$

where T = adjusted total tax revenue
Y = income.

Separate elasticities can also be devised for individual taxes. E_T can also be measured for a time series by the double log equation

$$log\ T = log\ a + b\ log\ Y$$

where b = coefficient of tax elasticity
T = tax revenue adjusted for discretionary changes.

The same equations are used for tax buoyancy, but T is not adjusted for policy changes. Work by Howard (1992) has shown that indirect taxes in Barbados before 1990 were buoyant, but this reflected frequent changes in tax rates and bases to counter the effects of recession in the 1980s. The moderate tax buoyancies for income taxes in Jamaica and Trinidad and Tobago were due to the operation of structural and administrative factors which are discussed below.

Structural and administrative factors reduced the size of the buoyancy coefficients in Caribbean economies. In the first place, the operation of the industrialization model by way of foreign investment produced a "revenue deprivation effect" on the public sector. The growth of import replacement industries as well as enclave export industries was associated with a tax incentive strategy which exempted a large proportion of capital imports and raw materials from customs duties. Income tax concessions were also granted to such industries. Even though these industries contributed to output and value added, these measures appear to have deprived the governments of revenue, leading to low tax buoyancy. Another structural argument, which is difficult to support by concrete evidence, is that the growth of an "underground" economy in Jamaica, and to a much lesser extent in Barbados, may have reduced significantly the revenue productivity of the tax base (Howard 1992).

The administrative factors reducing tax buoyancy include tax evasion and tax collection lags. Boyd (1984) argued that tax evasion was signifi-cant in Jamaica although it was difficult to gauge the extent of evasion. In Barbados and Trinidad and Tobago a similar argument is possible. It is also well known that MNCs reduce their tax liability through transfer pricing. Although it is not possible to estimate the magnitude of the taxes lost through transfer pricing, they are probably substantial in relation to the value added by these firms. The problems of tax evasion and transfer pricing are not easy to deal with administratively, and they impact negatively on the buoyancy of the tax system.

SUMMARY

The principles of taxation apply to all market economies. These are the benefit principle and the ability to pay principle. Taxation can enable government to stabilize the economy and adjust the income distribution. We also argued that taxation should be efficient and contribute to economic growth. The chapter also discussed a number of concepts relevant for developing countries, such as elasticity, buoyancy, tax effort, and taxable capacity. We noted that the emphasis on tax effort and taxable capacity has declined, and public finance economists became more concerned in the 1980s and 1990s with reforming the tax system to make it more efficient. The next chapter outlines the conceptual framework for understanding the process of tax reform.

Chapter Fourteen

Incidence and Efficiency Costs of Taxation

G overnments in market economies are concerned with the negative economic effects of taxation on consumers and producers. The incidence of a tax is its impact on the distribution of real income and that some forms of taxation may be burdensome for the poor. The efficiency cost of a tax or its excess burden is the loss in consumer or producer welfare as a result of the imposition of a new tax or increase in taxation. My analysis summarizes and clarifies the major aspects of the received theory on these concepts.[1] First, the partial and general equilibrium approaches to tax incidence is outlined. This is followed by a conceptual analysis of excess burden and the rules of optimal tax theory. These concepts are relevant for tax policy and tax reform in both developed and developing countries.

METHODS OF INCIDENCE ANALYSIS

It is necessary to distinguish between the statutory and economic incidence of taxation. The statutory incidence of a tax indicates who is legally responsible for paying the tax. For example, a 40 percent corporation tax levied on a business means that the corporation has a tax liability to government of 40 percent of its net profits. The economic incidence of a tax refers to the individuals who bear the taxes. Thus, a corporation tax can be shifted to consumers through higher prices or borne by the owners of the corporation. The economic incidence is equivalent to the alteration in real income due to the tax.

Musgrave (1959), Break (1974) and others have also made a distinction between the sources-of-income side of the household budget and the uses-of-income side in analysing tax incidence. Incidence effects on the uses-of-income side stem from the alteration in relative prices as a result of taxes. The sources-of-income side of the budget considers the impact of a tax on incomes such as wages, interest, profits, and dividends. Generally speaking, incidence analyses looks at both sides of the consumer budget.

Another distinction in the tax incidence literature is that between partial and general equilibrium incidence analysis. Partial equilibrium analysis is the traditional approach which focuses on the incidence of a tax in a single market. According to Rosen (1992) this type of analysis is appropriate when the market for the commodity being taxed is small, relative to the economy as a whole. This approach is not acceptable for measuring how a tax affects the distribution of real income throughout the economy.

The general equilibrium analysis is a multi-sector, multi-equation approach which looks at the interaction between markets and sectors. Harberger (1962) presented a general equilibrium model of the incidence of the corporation tax which set the stage for the development of highly technical approaches to tax incidence, as exemplified by the work of McLure (1975), Mieszkowski (1967) and Shoven and Whalley (1972). We now look briefly at the partial equilibrium approach.

PARTIAL EQUILIBRIUM ANALYSIS

Partial equilibrium analysis utilizes the method of comparative statistics to show how a tax may be shifted from producer to consumer. The economic incidence of a tax in a single market will depend on the elasticities of supply and demand: the more elastic the supply curve, the less the tax borne by producers. The producer can attempt to escape the tax, if he can vary his supply in response to the new price. Conversely, if supply is perfectly inelastic the producer will bear all the tax. When the demand curve is perfectly inelastic, the entire burden of the tax will fall on consumers. This means that the same amount of the good will be purchased by consumers regardless of the tax. A highly elastic demand curve means that the consumer will bear less of the tax.

Further, tax incidence is independent of whether the tax is levied on producers or consumers. That is, the allocation of the burden is not dependent on the statutory incidence of the tax. If the tax is levied on the producer, he is legally liable for paying the tax, but demand and supply elasticities will determine the division of the burden between producers and consumers.

SPECIFIC, DIFFERENTIAL AND BALANCED BUDGET INCIDENCE

A very important contribution by Musgrave (1959) is the distinction between specific, differential and balanced budget incidence. Musgrave discusses the concept of incidence within the context of budget policy. The most important aspects of budget policy are resource transfer, incidence, and output effects (Musgrave 1959: 207). Resource transfer is the reduction in resources available to the private sector as taxes are paid to government. Incidence is the change in the distribution of real income attributable to budget policy. Output effects occur as a result of government expenditures which cause changes in employment and production levels. According to Musgrave, the balanced budget approach combines tax and expenditure effects, and it is difficult to reach conclusions about incidence on the basis of tax changes alone.

Specific tax incidence is not very helpful for policy making since it deals with the effects on the income distribution resulting from a specific tax change, without analysing changes in other markets, other tax changes, or movements in factors of production between sectors. Specific tax incidence is best analysed in the partial equilibrium framework.

Differential tax incidence is the distributional effects which occur when one tax is substituted for another of equal yield. The differential tax incidence is important in tax reform programmes. For example, government may want to determine the incidence of substituting a VAT for another type of consumption tax regime. Break (1974: 12) identifies some of the difficulties of the differential incidence approach which ignores the side effects of redistributional tax policies. For example, one tax may affect aggregate demand on a greater scale, or raise prices to undesirable levels. Further, the differential tax incidence approach ignores the interdependence between the tax and expenditure sides of the budget.

Balanced budget incidence refers to the effects of government expenditure on the income distribution, when an increase in government tax revenues is balanced by an equal increase in expenditures. However, it is the allocation of expenditures rather than its quantity which determines the incidence. For example, a proportion of tax revenues will finance transfer payments such as pensions. Part of the taxes will go towards the expansion of health care and education. As we have seen in chapter 7, these expenditures contribute significantly to changes in the income distribution. It is sometimes argued that expenditure policies are more effective than tax changes per se in bringing about a desirable distribution of income.

GENERAL EQUILIBRIUM ANALYSIS

The Harberger Model

The Harberger (1962) model is the first general equilibrium model of tax incidence. It is based on the following assumptions:

1. Fixed factor supplies
2. Perfect factor mobility. The movement of factors tends to equalize after tax rates of return in the long run
3. Perfect competition in factor and product markets
4. A closed economic system
5. Production functions are linearly homogeneous with constant returns to scale
6. Homogeneous marginal propensities to consume among consumers
7. No fixed assets in money terms.

Harberger conducted his analysis in terms of two factors and two products. Most of his assumptions are unrealistic, especially those relating to perfect competition and perfect factor mobility. However, using these assumptions we can trace the effects of the imposition of a corporation tax on the corporate sector in the context of the Harberger model. In the language of general equilibrium analysis, a corporation tax can be regarded as a partial factor tax (TXK), that is, a tax (T) on the use of one factor capital (K) in the production of one product (X) (see Break 1974). The corporation tax will lead to the following consequences:

1. The corporation tax induces a flow of capital from the corporate to the non-corporate sector.
2. The flow of capital from the corporate to the non-corporate sector will lead to a rise in the rate of return in the corporate sector as

the supply of capital contracts, and a fall in the rate of return in the non-corporate sector. In the process of time, rates of return would be equalized in both sectors.

3. Output in the non-corporate sector will expand and that in the corporate sector will fall. Further, prices in the corporate sector will rise relative to the non-corporate sector.

4. Workers will shift from the corporate to the non-corporate sector.

5. The corporate tax burden will be shifted to workers if the corporate sector is highly labour intensive and if the elasticity of substitution between labour and capital is low in either sector.

6. Harberger asserts that if the elasticities of substitution between labour and capital is the same in the two sectors, and is equal to the elasticity of substitution in consumption of the products of the two sectors, the owners of capital will bear the full burden of the corporation tax.

Harberger has argued that the corporation tax tends to fall on the owners of capital (Harberger 1974). Given the unrealism of its assumptions, his model can only be regarded as a guide to tax incidence. Imperfect factor mobility and imperfect competition will lead to a pattern of shifting of the tax burden not in keeping with the Harberger model. Break (1974: 146–52) discusses these limitations of the Harberger model. Chapter 16 examines the possible incidence effects in developing countries when one drops Harberger's assumption of a closed economy.

The Harberger model can also be criticized on the grounds that it ignores provisions in the tax code related to tax deductions. Harberger assumed that the corporation was financed by equity capital. In the real world, interest expense is deductible in determining the tax base. The corporation can use debt financing to finance the cost of capital. In this case, the corporation tax does not change the cost of capital (Krelove 1995). This implies that the incidence of the tax might not necessarily fall on the owners of capital. Further, Stiglitz (1973) and King (1974) have indicated that the Harberger model does not consider the treatment of investment tax credits and tax allowances which may alter the incidence of the corporation tax. Depreciation allowances should also be considered before evaluating the incidence of the corporation tax, as well as other provisions in the tax code which reduce the cost of capital (Brown and Jackson 1990: 532–33).

Tax Equivalence Relations

The basic Harberger model has been extended by Mieszkowski (1967) and McLure (1975). Break (1974) has described these extensions as the Harberger-McLure-Mieszkowski (HMM) model. The basic contribution of the HMM approach is that it helps to determine the equivalence of certain taxes in the determination of tax incidence. Following Krelove (1995: 40), one can argue that excise taxes on a basket of goods are equivalent to a broad-based sales tax at the same rate. Similarly, a broad-based sales tax, such as the VAT, is equivalent to a personal income tax, if it is assumed that consumption equals income, factor supplies are fixed, and the sales tax has no effect on relative prices. Therefore, knowledge of one commodity tax may help determine the incidence of another commodity tax and the operation of one factor tax may help determine the incidence of another factor tax.

The same reasoning applies to partial factor taxes. Let us assume two goods X and Y, and two factors labour (L) and capital (K), then a partial factor tax on capital (TXK) may help to determine the incidence of TXL and TYK. Factor taxes on both factors at the same rate, that is, $TXL = TYK$ can be used to derive an income tax at the same rate.

Following Mieszkowski (1967), the imposition of a partial factor tax or a corporation tax TXK has two effects, namely, the output effect and the substitution effect. First, the price of the good in the taxed sector tends to rise and quantity declines. The output effect is therefore equivalent to an excise tax on the product X. The output effect will be greatest if the elasticity of substituting labour for capital is zero. Following Atkinson and Stiglitz (1980: 173), the nature of the substitution effect is determined by the extent of substituting labour for capital in the corporate sector. If X is capital intensive, the tax reduces the demand for capital and reinforces the substitution effect.

General Equilibrium Analysis of Tax Incidence in India

General equilibrium analysis of tax incidence has been confined predominantly to the developed countries. One departure from this trend is the work of Shome (1978), who applied the general approach to the incidence of the corporation tax in India. Shome retained the same neoclassical assumptions of the Harberger model such as perfect markets, full employment, inelastic supply of all factors, and perfect intersectoral mobility of factors. Further, he divides the entire Indian economy into two sectors following the Harberger model, and he assumes two factors of production, labour and capital. Shome's analysis examines the effects of a marginal change in the existing corporation tax rather than the introduction of a new corporation tax. He presents a different theoretical model from Harberger and estimates empirically the incidence of the corporation tax for India in the fiscal year 1971–72. Shome (1978) found that the entire burden of tax was not borne by capital but was shared by non-capital factor earners as well. This is in contrast to Harberger's finding of a 100 percent burden in the United States. The assumptions of Shome's model are unrealistic for a country like India with underdeveloped capital and labour markets, and high unemployment. These assumptions are subject to the same criticisms as those of Harberger. It is entirely possible, however, that the corporate tax is shifted to workers in developing countries in the long run under conditions of imperfect competition.

METHODOLOGY OF TAX INCIDENCE MEASUREMENT

Public finance economists have carried out extensive studies in both developed and developing countries to measure the incidence of specific taxes. Major studies on developed countries include Pechman and Okner (1974), and Musgrave, Case and Leonard (1974) for the United States; Gillespie (1976) and Whalley (1984) for Canada. There exists a large number of studies for developing countries which have been reviewed by Bird and De Wulf (1973), De Wulf (1975) and Shah and Whalley (1991). This section considers the methodology of tax incidence measurement especially the shifting assumptions used in most of these studies.

Tax incidence studies are generally conducted along the following procedures:

1. Annual family income is divided into income ranges usually into decile shares of income.
2. Tax revenues are then allocated to each income group on the basis of the shifting assumptions made for each tax.
3. Taxes are also allocated on the basis of expenditure patterns of each income group.
4. Effective tax rates are then computed for each income group. The effective tax rate is the tax revenue from a particular tax allocated to an income group, divided by the total income attributable to the group.
5. An analysis of the effective tax rates from the lowest to the highest

decile income group gives an idea of the regressivity, proportionality or progressivity of the tax system.

6. Judgements about regressivity and progressivity will depend on the shifting assumptions used in the study.

Perhaps the most controversial aspects of tax incidence analysis are the shifting assumptions used in the studies. Different shifting assumptions are used for the major taxes such as personal income taxes, corporation taxes, sales and excise taxes, property and payroll taxes. According to Shah and Whalley (1991), most studies in developed countries agree that the personal income tax is borne by income recipients and is progressive because of increasing average tax rates. Less agreement exists in relation to other taxes.

The tax shifting assumptions about the corporation tax are controversial. The tax can be regressive if it is assumed to be shifted to consumers. The corporation tax is assumed to be progressive if it is shifted backwards to shareholders who are in the upper deciles of the income distribution.

Property taxes are also subject to various shifting assumptions. Property taxes on land are assumed to fall on landowners or on capital owners and are therefore progressive in their incidence. Property taxes on commercial structures and housing would be allocated to rent-payers and owner-occupiers. In this case, the incidence will be regressive. The property tax assumptions vary depending on whether one assumes an old view or new view of the property tax discussed in this chapter.

Sales and excise taxes are assumed to be regressive if borne by consumers, and progressive if borne by the recipients of factor incomes (Krelove 1995; Shah and Whalley 1991). Payroll taxes are sometimes assumed to be shifted to labour.

One of the most comprehensive incidence studies in developed countries is the Pechman and Okner (1974) study. It is useful to state briefly the results of this work, since it is representative of the shifting assumptions used in studies in the developing countries. The Pechman and Okner study used eight sets of incidence assumptions and was based on a representative sample of 72,000 families and income data for 1966. They calculated effective tax rates for the least progressive and most progressive sets of incidence assumptions. The study found that the United States tax system was essentially proportional for the majority of families. The rich paid higher effective rates than lower income families, and this is explained by the assumption that the corporation and property taxes were borne by the owner of capital.

INCIDENCE STUDIES IN DEVELOPING COUNTRIES

Incidence studies in Latin America, based on the shifting assumptions discussed earlier, have been reviewed in some detail by Bird and De Wulf (1973). Space constraints do not permit a detailed description of these various studies which are now somewhat outdated. An article by De Wulf (1975) also discussed the pattern of incidence in India and other developing countries. De Wulf (1975) distinguishes between the "formal incidence" of the Indian tax system and the "effective incidence" of those tax systems reviewed by Bird and De Wulf (1974). Formal tax incidence attempts to indicate the burden of taxation as intended by the legislator. Effective incidence is an estimate of the tax burden after allowing for explicit tax shifting assumptions. According to De Wulf (1975: 65), the formal incidence is "a quantification of the presumed intentions of the fiscal authorities". The formal incidence approach classifies all taxes as direct or indirect and these are merely allocated to the income classes, implicitly assuming that indirect taxes are shifted and direct taxes are not. The studies in India also make an urban/rural classification to shed greater light on tax incidence.

In the Caribbean, studies on tax incidence in Jamaica have been reviewed by Alleyne (1991) and Howard (1992). The results of these studies are as follows:

1. Lovejoy (1963), on the basis of 1958 data, found that the tax burden in Jamaica was proportional for indirect taxes and progressive for direct taxes.

2. McLure (1977) estimated that the burden of indirect taxes in Jamaica in 1972 was regressive in the lower income groups, progressive in the middle income groups and regressive in the highest income groups. Personal income taxes were progressive.

3. Wasylenko (1986) found that indirect taxes were progressive in the lower income groups, slightly regressive for the third to seventh deciles and progressive in the highest income groups. Direct taxes were progressive up to the eighth decile and regressive thereafter as a result of tax evasion.

4. Alleyne (1991) reported that payroll property and food taxes were regressive. Income taxes followed the same pattern as that observed by Wasylenko (1986). Overall, indirect taxes were roughly proportional.

175

The studies of tax incidence in developing countries were plagued by methodological and data problems. The results are sensitive to the shifting assumptions which can cause the burden of taxes to appear either regressive or progressive (Whalley 1984). This is especially true for assumptions about property and corporation taxes.

Another problem in these studies is the measurement of income. Krelove (1995) and Meerman and Shome (1980) have indicated that these studies are based on income earned in a particular year, which ignores the income distribution through the lifecycle of the household. This implies that a given household could belong to a different income class at different times. Therefore, lifetime incidence should be examined. This approach is much more difficult than the traditional approach, and it is doubtful whether it is useful in developing countries with deficient data bases.

The critique by Shah and Whalley (1991) of incidence studies in developing countries places emphasis on the non-tax policy elements which should be included in the analyses. Tax incidence will vary from economy to economy depending on these non-tax institutional features. These include "informal or black markets, urban rural migration, credit rationing, industry concentration, product market competition, price controls, import licensing regulations, exchange controls, and quantitative restrictions, cartels, and the extent of unionization" (Shah and Whalley 1991: 540). These non-tax features may alter the conventional incidence assumption derived for developed countries. Shah and Whalley discuss how these features may alter shifting assumptions, arguing that the possible incidence effects of such a package would imply regressivity of the tax burden. Institutional features are sometimes difficult to capture in the context of quantitative analysis. The consideration of these features may, however, lead to qualitative comments on the partial tax incidence results.

CONCEPT OF EXCESS BURDEN

Excess burden analysis deals with the efficiency costs of taxation. The gross burden of a tax is the revenue collected. However, the total burden may exceed revenue collected because an excess burden or deadweight loss results. An excess burden is said to result when the tax interferes with consumer choices and decisions by production units. This distortion in resource allocation or expenditure patterns leads to a fall in welfare. Excess burden can therefore be viewed as a loss of consumer surplus due to a tax increase in excess of revenue paid to the government.

The only tax without an excess burden is a lump sum tax or poll tax. A lump sum tax is a fixed sum that a person pays yearly which is independent of his income level. A lump sum tax has an income effect only but there are no substitution effects. This means that it does not distort consumer preferences for goods and services. Further, lump sum taxes do not affect relative prices. However, poll taxes are regressive with respect to income. Despite their efficiency poll, taxes are not generally used as an instrument of tax policy.

The partial equilibrium approach to measuring the loss in consumer surplus on excess burden may be adequate for illustrating excess burden in a single market. The excess burden will vary directly with the elasticity of demand for the tax good. This means that the more inelastic the demand for the good, the consumer finds it more difficult to substitute and the less the loss in welfare. Given the elasticity of demand, excess burden varies inversely with tax yield. That is, the lower the excess burden when demand is inelastic the greater is the tax yield. Auerbach (1985) and Rosen (1992) give a more detailed treatment of excess burden analysis. Our subsequent analysis will be confined to optimal taxation which is based on the need for policy makers to minimize excess burden.

OPTIMAL TAXATION

The literature on optimal taxation is highly technical. Contributions have been made by Ramsey (1927), Mirrlees (1971) and Auerbach (1985). Good introductions to the literature are Stern (1984) and Sandmo (1976). No attempt is made here to review this literature or present formal proofs of optimal tax theory. This section outlines the optimal tax rules derived from optimal tax theory. The relevance of optimal taxation for developing countries is then discussed.

The basic problem of optimal taxation is to choose tax rates to minimize the loss of an individual's utility, that is, minimize excess burden, subject to a required amount of tax revenue to be raised by the government. The theory derives rules of efficient taxation providing a solution to this problem. These rules are the Ramsey rule, the inverse elasticity rule, and the Corlett-Hague rule.

The Ramsey rule states that in order to minimize excess burden "the proportional reduction in compensated demand as a result of the imposition of the set of taxes should be the same for all goods" (Stern 1984: 350). There are two important aspects of the Ramsey rule (Zee 1995: 72). The first is that it is stated in quantity terms and not prices. This is so because it is the reduction in quantity which leads to a loss in excess burden. Changes in relative prices merely induce quantity changes. Second, it is the compensated or Hicksian demand change that matters. The Hicksian demand curve depends only on the substitution effect. This is important because excess burden relates to the distortion in consumer preferences due to the substitution effect.

The second rule is the inverse elasticity rule which states that tax rates should be inversely related to elasticities of demand. The rule implies that since excess burden varies directly with elasticities, this means that high tax rates should be imposed on inelastic goods, a policy which would lead to less distortion in consumer preferences. According to Stern (1984: 351) the inverse elasticity rule appears to be inegalitarian. To the extent that Ramsey formulated the problem in terms of one consumer the rule ignores distributional questions.

The third rule has been advanced by Corlett and Hague (1953). This rule states that given two commodities, the commodity which is complementary to leisure should be taxed at a heavier rate. Even though leisure is a non-taxable commodity, it can be taxed indirectly by taxing a complementary commodity. If leisure were taxable, revenues would be raised with no excess burden. Thus taxing leisure would be an efficient form of taxation (Rosen 1992: 335).

Mirrlees (1971) is credited with originating optimal income taxation. Most researchers distinguish between linear income taxation which is equivalent to a flat tax or tax with one marginal rate, and non-linear taxation where the marginal rates differ. The conclusions of the Mirrlees non-linear model, as stated by Stern (1984: 356) are that "(1) The marginal tax rate should be between zero and one. (2) The marginal rate for the person with the highest income should be zero. (3) If the person with the lowest wage is working at the optimum, then the marginal rate he faces should be zero."

Mirrlees' conclusions are significant for optimal tax theory. A zero marginal rate of tax ensures no excess burden. A zero marginal rate on the rich, however, implies less equality in the income tax system. Optimal tax theory argues that lower marginal rates on high income groups would lead to an increase in work effort. A zero marginal rate at the bottom also ensures that the income effect would outweigh the substitution effect leading to increased work effort. The optimal tax theory therefore suggests that the tax schedule, with marginal tax rates on the vertical axis and taxable income on the horizontal axis, should be an inverted U-shaped graph. The income tax schedules for most countries do not follow this pattern. In most cases, the marginal tax rate is zero at the bottom, followed by a few marginal rates related to the taxable income band. In 1999, for example, Jamaica had a zero marginal rate at the bottom and a single flat rate of twenty-five percent for higher incomes. The optimal tax theory, however, suggests that marginal rates on the highest incomes should be reduced wherever possible to guarantee efficiency.

We can now summarize the main applications of optimal tax theory for tax design as suggested by Stern (1984: 368) and Burgess and Stern (1993: 789–90). First, wherever possible, lump sum taxes should be used to raise revenue. This is based on the view that lump sum taxes have no excess burden. Second, tax revenue is raised most efficiently by imposing taxes on goods and services with inelastic demands. This is the well-known inverse elasticity rule for efficient taxation. Third, the optimum policy for any one tax is sensitive to assumptions about other taxes. Therefore, the implementation of any particular policy tool depends on how it affects other objectives including the income distribution. Fourth, taxation concerned with distribution and externalities or market failure should focus on the source of the problem and concentrate taxation there. Fifth, there is no presumption in favour of uniform indirect taxation. Stern suggests that uniformity is a poor guide for developing countries. The optimal tax theory appears therefore to favour taxation with differential rates. The next section briefly evaluates the application of optimal tax theory to developing countries.

RELEVANCE OF OPTIMAL TAXATION FOR DEVELOPING COUNTRIES

The rules of optimal taxation discussed above can probably apply to an economy where lump sum taxes are available, and detailed information about resource allocation is available to the planner. However, the theory of optimal taxation appears to relegate the importance of distributional considerations, and therefore poses a number of problems in developing countries where most of the people are poor. Musgrave (1976) argues that the optimal tax theory disregards horizontal equity. According to McLure

(1989: 350), "both difficulties of implementation and perceptions about inequity cast considerable doubt on the practical utility of optimal taxation". Difficulties of implementation include lack of knowledge about elasticities of factor supply and product demand.

Further, optimal tax theory assumes that the cost of tax administration and compliance costs are nil. As a result "the theory furnishes few workable guidelines for the reform of tax systems" (Gillis 1989: 501). Given administrative considerations, Diamond (1987: 644) has argued that rather than tax each commodity at a separate rate, it may be better to lump together large categories of commodities and impose uniform *ad valorem* taxes. However, this does not solve the problem of inefficient administrative systems in developing countries. Modern tax reform has placed more emphasis on neutral taxation to reduce the complexities of tax systems in developing countries.

Gillis (1989: 515) maintains that the above reasons explain why optimal tax theory has not achieved much success in tax reform in developing countries. Additionally, the literature has been highly technical and not understandable to many fiscal policy makers. Gillis contends that neutrality may be a better guide to policy making, even though the concept of optimality is more intellectually appealing.

SUMMARY

Most public finance texts spend considerable time outlining the theory of incidence and excess burden. Other technical articles discuss these concepts in great detail with the use of copious algebra and diagrams. Our objective in this chapter was not to duplicate these approaches. The chapter focused on defining and clarifying the concepts for use in the application of tax policy. We differentiated between partial and general equilibrium tax incidence, and examined the approaches used in tax incidence studies. We noted that the optimal tax theory may be difficult to apply in developing countries. This chapter as well as the previous one provide a foundation for understanding the theoretical and practical issues involved in tax reform, and the economic impact of various types of taxes. The most important concepts reviewed were neutrality, incidence, excess burden, and efficiency.

Chapter Fifteen

Supply-Side Tax Policy and Tax Reform

T he emphasis on market liberalization in the 1980s was reflected in the application of supply-side tax policies to enhance the efficiency of the tax system. Some of the principles of tax reform in the 1980s and early 1990s were derived from supply-side tax policy. The worldwide tax reform movement embraced a number of characteristics. Tax reform led to a sharp fall in maximum income tax rates and a reduction in the number of progressive tax bands. At the same time, the income tax base in most countries was broadened by reducing various exemptions, deductions, and concessions in the tax code. Corporate tax rates were also reduced, and the top marginal personal income tax rate was fixed at the same level as the corporate tax rate in many countries. Finally, a VAT was introduced in a large number of developing countries to complement the income tax reforms. The worldwide tax reform movement was also influenced by the US tax reform of 1986. This reform reduced considerably the overall progressivity and complexity in the tax scale (see Auerbach and Slemrod 1997).

This chapter also presents the salient features of tax reform in the United States, Indonesia, Latin America, and Barbados. The study on Barbados is more detailed and builds on the work of Howard (1992) and Howard and Mascoll (1994). Barbados represents the case of a small developing country which carried out massive tax reforms. Space constraints do not allow us to present an in-depth discussion of tax reforms in other developing countries. Most reforms followed similar principles. An edited work by Bahl (1992) provides extensive analyses of the Jamaican tax reforms of 1986. Howard (1992) evaluates the principles which guided tax reforms in Jamaica, Barbados, and Trinidad and Tobago before 1992. Discussions of the Mexican tax reforms can be found in the OECD Economic Survey (1992: 124–29). Gillis (1989a) presents articles evaluating tax reforms in Indonesia, Colombia, Jamaica, Uruguay, and Chile, while summary treatments of tax reforms in some developing countries are given by Burgess and Stern (1993: 804–18).

SUPPLY-SIDE TAX POLICY

Supply-side tax policy is concerned with the negative substitution effects of high income tax rates. Following Gandhi (1987a), we make the distinction between the traditional or "basic" supply-side tax policy and the new or "popular" approach. Supply-side policy is an aspect of supply-side economics which analyses broader issues such as the efficiency of free markets, deregulation of government activity, and the need to stimulate the economy on the supply-side through tax incentives to enhance economic growth.

According to Gandhi (1987a: 5–8), "basic" supply-side economics is an application of classical and neoclassical theory to government decision making, with particular emphasis on the efficiency of the aggregate supply schedule. Supply-side efficiency can be improved by policies which reduce tax distortions. "Basic" supply-side economists therefore recommend tax reforms which eliminate loopholes in the tax code and lower nominal progressivity. "Popular" supply-side tax policy is characterized by a preoccupation with tax cuts particularly in the "top marginal tax rates rather than on reform of the tax system in all its aspects" (Gandhi 1987a: 9).

The "popular" supply-side approach to tax cut analysis is based on the neoclassical specification of the first-order price effects of a tax change (Ture 1982). This approach is concerned with the cost of work effort vis-à-vis leisure and with the price of saving relative to current consumption. The theory posits that taxes on income reduce work effort, enterprise, and saving. Reductions in personal income taxes increase the propensity to save and invest, and they also increase work effort. Decreases in corporate taxes raise the net of tax rates of return, leading to re-investment in new enterprises.

Robert Keleher (1982) supports the view that it is changes in marginal tax rates, rather than changes in average tax rates, that are important to "popular" supply-side tax policy. Marginal tax rate changes are equivalent to relative price changes which affect allocation. Further, marginal tax rate changes should not be seen as revenue or income changes. Proponents of supply-side tax policy do not see tax cuts as injections of purchasing power or spending. In an open economy, it is impossible to ignore the purchasing power effects of massive tax cuts on the balance of payments.

Most research on the impact of "popular" supply-side economics has been done in the free market economy of the United States. According to Keleher (1982), the bulk of the evidence reveals that income tax reductions have only a limited effect on the overall supply of labour. The author is not aware of any previous empirical studies to show the extent to which tax cuts increase work effort, saving, and investment in small open economies like those of the Caribbean. Tax cuts seem to have more potency in stimulating aggregate supply, via their effects on increasing the capital stock (Keleher 1982).

It is generally recognized in the literature that the Laffer curve concept is the centerpiece of "popular" supply-side tax policy. As tax rates increase, tax revenues expand, but after a certain point, increases in tax rates become unproductive and tax revenues decline. The precise empirical point where tax rates become unproductive will vary for different economies. There is, however, little evidence in small countries relating to the Laffer curve. Tax cuts aimed at specific sectors (e.g. investment) may be self financing. That is, tax cuts may lead to an increase in tax revenue through expansion of profits. The Laffer effect (or self-financing tax cuts) is more likely to exist for narrowly based taxes than broadly based taxes (Keleher 1982).

Further, although supply siders may argue that an across-the-board cut in tax rates would produce an increase in tax revenues, there is no real guarantee that the fiscal deficit would fall. There is the view that a tax cut would produce an increase in the deficit, at least in the short run. However, if we assume that supply-side economics relates to the long run rather than the short, the first-round increase in the deficit might not be viewed as a problem. Lester Thurow (1984) posits the alternative view of the supply siders who believe that the free market would adjust quickly in the short run and that the incentive effects would be large and positive.

Supply siders accept the monetarist view of the relationship between inflation and the money supply in closed systems. According to William Orzechowski (1982), monetary restraint is advocated to curb inflation, which erodes the incentive impact of a tax cut. This last consideration is not as important in the small open system, because the money supply is endogenously determined and inflation is largely imported. Further, the principal impact of money creation by the banking system in open economies is on the balance of payments rather than on price levels (Howard 1989a).

Supply siders have identified developing countries that have benefited significantly from low tax regimes (Bartlett 1987). These include the so-called "four tigers" of Southeast Asia: Hong Kong, Taiwan, Singapore, and South Korea. Much of this evidence has been highly selective, and it sometimes ignores the large number of other sociopolitical, national, and international economic factors influencing economic growth in Southeast Asia. These countries provide evidence of the effects of supply-side tax policy, imposed there long before it became popularized in the United States. Hong Kong represents a model of a low-rate, neutral tax system, while countries like Taiwan and South Korea demonstrate the widespread use of tax incentives to lower effective tax rates to stimulate development. These cases are special, and the successful policies followed there may not be applicable to Caribbean countries, which have different labour regimes and sociocultural systems.

Winston Griffith (1987) has discussed the view that the effective lowering of the profit tax rate through the widening and deepening of fiscal incentives was an important factor in the export-led growth of Singapore. According to Griffith, this policy cannot be considered in isolation from other variables enhancing development in Singapore which are not present in the Caribbean. Particularly, he argues that the Singapore government was able to control the trade unions, thereby depressing wages and enhancing foreign investment and economic growth. In the Caribbean, on the other hand, there are conflicts between the distributional objectives of the trade unions and the state's objective of economic growth. This factor partly explains the lack of international competitiveness of the Caribbean traded-goods sector, even in the context of efforts to lower the effective rate of profit tax through fiscal incentives.

I agree with Gandhi (1987a: 13) that supply-side economics has significant limitations in developing countries. Many of these countries suffer from market inefficiencies, missing markets, and a highly skewed resource base characterized by dependence on one or two crops. Further, in many low income developing countries income taxation is not a significant revenue earner. Supply-side tax policies, with the emphasis on reductions in marginal income tax rates, may not lead to sharp increases in tax revenues and rapid economic growth as predicted by supply-side economics. Despite these limitations, many developing countries have adopted comprehensive tax reforms in keeping with the recommendations of supply-side economics. These reforms have improved the performance of their tax systems. However, we argue that other structural and institutional changes must be considered along with fiscal policies in explaining any improvements in the growth performance of some developing countries.

PRINCIPLES OF TAX REFORM

Although supply-side tax policy provides a broad rationale for tax reform, there are a number of complex issues in any comprehensive tax reform exercise. Gandhi (1987a) has identified the following: efficiency, equity, simplicity, and revenue maintenance. Two other principles are cost-effectiveness and base broadening. A comprehensive tax reform should be evaluated on the extent to which it achieves a balance of the above objectives.

Supply siders place great emphasis on the efficiency aspects of taxation. They consider efficiency and neutrality as the most desirable objectives of a tax system (Gandhi 1987b). Supply siders are less concerned about the equity objective of taxation. According to the efficiency criterion discussed in chapter 14, different taxes impose welfare costs or excess burdens on the economy by distorting resource allocation. One goal of taxation is to minimize the welfare costs, thereby increasing the efficiency of resource allocation. Neutral taxes do not interfere with relative prices and are believed to be more efficient than non-neutral taxes. Thus, a broad-based VAT is considered a neutral tax, whereas an excise tax levied on a specific commodity is considered non-neutral to the extent that it can lead to a change in the price and consumption of the taxed good relative to some other good. The efficiency criterion has also been discussed in textbooks under the caption of optimal tax theory. Chapter 14 contains a discussion of optimal tax theory.

An efficiency-oriented tax system will attempt to reduce the level of differentiation in tax rates. Extensive rate differentiation may lead to greater equity in the distribution of the tax burden, but it can be counterproductive from an efficiency point of view. However, if the tax system emphasizes efficiency, tax rates on various goods and services should be inversely related to the price elasticity of demand. This is the Ramsey rule of efficient commodity taxation. The rule can be generalized for many consumers, although Ramsey (1927) assumed a one-consumer economy (Stern 1984: 350). We have already noted in chapter 14 that the Ramsey rule is inegalitarian, since necessities are insensitive to prices.

The equity criterion has already been discussed in chapter 13. Horizontal and vertical equity have always been regarded as primary objectives of taxation. In this regard, income redistribution is a central issue in any tax reform analysis. Massive income tax cuts may alter the income distribution in favour of higher-income groups. However, this is an empirical issue. Equity has been achieved in many tax reform by raising the standard deduction thereby eliminating many persons from the tax net. Income redistribution becomes a more serious problem if the tax cuts are accompanied by a reduction in the area of government expenditure related to the provision of basic social services.

Despite the importance of the equity criterion, I share the view of Stern (1984) that the tax system should not be regarded as a major instrument of redistribution. First, certain types of indirect taxes are known to be regressive. These include the VAT, sumptuary excises, and import duties. Commodity taxes generally fall on a broad range of goods used by the poorest sections of the community. Second, highly progressive direct taxation was regarded in the past as a vehicle of income distribution. As Gandhi (1987a) notes, this applies to nominal progressivity, but if one allows for tax avoidance and evasion, relief from corporation tax, and exclusions, nominal progressivity will not reflect the effective progressivity of direct taxes. Modern tax reform has therefore concentrated on lowering nominal progressive tax rates and instituting higher basic exemption levels, in an attempt to balance equity and efficiency. Given these limitations of the tax system, more emphasis will have to be placed on expenditure policy to redistribute income in poor countries.

A primary consideration in tax reform is revenue maintenance. In the context of severe fiscal disequilibrium, governments of small countries like those in the Caribbean cannot afford to lose too much revenue, particularly by way of massive income tax cuts. Caribbean governments in the 1980s attempted to recoup revenue losses resulting from income tax reform by increasing distortionary indirect tax rates or, as in the cases of Jamaica and Trinidad and Tobago, levying a broad-based VAT. Tax revenue insufficiency can be a constraint on income tax reform that is designed to balance equity and efficiency. Base broadening is the policy designed to ensure revenue maintenance. Base broadening also increases efficiency, because the tax system does not differentiate between individuals on grounds of political patronage and preferences. In most cases, base broadening is achieved by including fringe benefits in the tax base and reducing allowances and deductions.

Another consideration is simplicity. Flat-rate taxation, despite its bias against equity, is more simple to administer than a system of highly differentiated rates. Modern tax reform has emphasized simplicity, which further enhances taxpayer compliance. Joseph Pechman (1989) notes, however, that in developed countries little progress has been made in simplifying the tax laws on tax returns. In some countries, the VAT has been complicated as a result of the adoption of multiple rates, zero-rating, and exemptions. The next section examines the Barbadian tax reforms of 1992 to gauge the extent to which they were designed to achieve a balance of equity, efficiency, and simplicity.

Because of the complexity of the issues involved in tax reform it appears that the latter should be tailored to suit the specific economic circumstances and administrative capacities of poor countries. It makes no sense to implement a VAT in a country which has few intersectoral linkages, or in an economy based on high levels of informal activity. If the reforms reduce administrative costs through the principles outlined above, then the reforms can be regarded as being cost-effective.

SELECTED TAX REFORM EXPERIENCES OUTSIDE THE CARIBBEAN

The United States Tax Reform of 1986

The United States tax reform of 1986 was a landmark tax reform which influenced tax reform worldwide. Our overview looks at the provisions and economic effects of the United States Tax Reform Act of 1986, hereafter referred to as TRA86. This reform was intended to simplify the tax system, as well as bring about greater equity and efficiency of taxation. The broad provisions of TRA86 can be summarized as follows:[1]

1. The most significant feature of TRA86 was the reduction in marginal tax rates for individuals. Actual marginal tax rates were 0, 15, 28, 33 percent, with the average tax rate reaching a maximum of 28 percent of taxable income. This schedule replaced the former 14 rate structure.

2. TRA86 established a standard deduction of US$5,000 in 1988

and phased in a personal exemption level of US$2,000 by 1989. These levels were indexed to inflation. These measures substantially reduced income taxes for low income individuals.

3. The corporate tax rate was lowered from 46 to 34 percent. The 10 percent tax credit for machinery and equipment was repealed.

4. TRA86 repealed the individual dividend exclusion, whereby a taxpayer could shield up to US$200 in dividends from tax each year.

5. Sixty percent exclusion for long-term capital gains was repealed. All realized capital gains became fully taxable as income. This implied that long-term capital gains were taxable at 28 percent instead of 20 percent.

6. The Act reduced opportunities for individuals to use tax shelters to reduce their tax liability. Losses from passive tax shelters were made non-deductible. Passive investments were defined as investments in real estate and other business ventures in which the taxpayer does not participate beyond the supply of funds.

Auerbach and Slemrod (1997) have evaluated research done on the quantitative economic impact of TRA86, and the extent to which it achieved the goals of fairness, simplicity, and efficiency. They argue that the extensiveness of the changes introduced by TRA86 complicates the analysis of the response of various groups to the tax reform. The survey by Auerbach and Slemrod reached a number of conclusions. First, labour supply and saving were not significantly affected by the reforms. On the other hand, investment in equipment seems to have a significant elasticity to after-tax cost. Second, most analyses concluded that "TRA86 improved the efficiency of the tax system, although the magnitude of the improvement was disputed" (Auerbach and Slemrod 1997: 620). Third, although it is reasonable to argue qualitatively that horizontal equity improved, the evidence on this is not definitive. Fourth, the evidence suggests that the tax reform achieved some simplification at the personal level but introduced other complications to the tax system.[2]

The Indonesian Tax Reform (1983)

My analysis of the Indonesian tax reform draws on the work of Gillis (1985) and Asher (1997). Indonesia is an example of an Asian petroleum exporting economy which pursued a successful comprehension tax reform, as part of a structural adjustment programme. Indonesia's tax system before reform was a highly complex system characterized by inequities between taxpayers. During the 1970s a low tax ratio characterized taxes from the non-oil sector. Gillis (1985) reports that by 1982 the non-oil tax ratio was 6.6 percent of GDP. By 1981 Indonesia was very dependent on taxes from the oil sector, and non-oil taxes provided only 29 percent of total tax revenues. Despite buoyant oil revenues in the 1970s, the non-oil sectors continued to stagnate. There was therefore a case for tax reform to raise the contribution of non-oil taxes (Gillis 1985: 225–26).

The objectives of the Indonesian tax reform in 1983 were the increase in non-oil revenues, more effective income distribution, reduction of inefficiency, and a reduction in the costs of transferring resources to the public sector (Gillis 1985: 231). The goals reflect the principles of equity, efficiency and neutrality. The reform also stressed the simplification of the tax structure. Simplification required the dismantling of incentives.

The reformed income tax law applied to both individuals and businesses. It replaced separate taxes on individuals, businesses, dividends, royalties, and withholding tax. An identical rate structure was adopted for personal and company taxes. The new system was based on the principal of a broad base and low rate. The tax rate was lowered from 50 percent for individuals and 45 percent for firms to a maximum inaugural rate of 35 percent. The reformed system relied heavily on withholding mechanisms to improve simplification and enforcement. Institutions were required to withhold tax from payments of dividends, interest, rents and royalties at a rate of 15 percent.[3]

The other significant aspect of the Indonesian tax reform was the introduction of a VAT. The new VAT was levied at a flat rate of 10 percent with exports zero-rated. Luxury goods were taxed by an additional sales tax at rates between 10 and 20 percent.[4]

Asher (1997: 150–60) presents a comprehensive evaluation of the Indonesian tax reform. We summarize briefly his main arguments. First, the tax reform increased the ratio of non-oil tax revenue to total tax revenue from 31.6 percent in 1983 to 57.8 percent in 1989, fulfilling the revenue objective. Second, income tax revenue was not buoyant initially but rose to 3.15 percent of GDP in 1989–90 which was higher than 2.42 percent of GDP in 1983. Third, the VAT was a substantive contributor to revenue. Fourth, a definitive quantitative analysis of the distributional impact of the tax reform was not available, but the base-broadening initiatives and tax rate reductions would have resulted in a positive impact on equity. Asher concludes that it is possible to reform a tax system in a short space of time, but the achievement of neutrality and efficiency is an extremely difficult task.

Tax Reform in Latin America

The objectives of tax reform in Latin America were the pursuit of neutrality, the streamlining of both tax policy and tax administration, and reducing the importance of vertical equity. Revenue maintenance in the context of stabilization policy was also an objective of reform.[5] The goal of neutrality was important to reduce distortions created by preferential tax treatment to sectors and individuals. Neutrality was achieved by base broadening and flatter rate schedules. Attempts were made to modernize tax administration by streamlining certain functions such as collection, auditing, and taxpayer service. Withholding taxes were extended to increase compliance.

The most important tax changes introduced by the reform in Latin America are listed by Shome (1995a: 15–16) as follows:

1. The number of income tax rates were reduced and the marginal rates fell. The burden of tax on lower income groups was reduced by raising the level of exemptions.

2. "Between 1986 and 1992 the rate dispersion of the corporate income tax was reduced and tax rates were scaled back from a maximum of 42 percent to 35 percent."

3. The introduction of the VAT was a very important aspect of reform. Countries also reformed their VATs by reducing the number of rates and improving tax administration. There is, however, some concern about widespread evasion of VAT in the region.[6]

4. Tariff rates were reduced under the trade liberalization programme. The declining emphasis on import taxes was associated with a rise in the share of consumption taxes in total tax revenue.

5. The experience of Latin America suggests a common philosophy on tax reform even though the emphasis on different taxes varied from country to country. For example, Colombia and Mexico focused to a greater extent on income taxes, while Argentina and Bolivia concentrated on the VAT. Chile paid attention to both areas. The countries developing faster were more concerned with equity, international compatibility, and modernization of the tax administration.

Colombia provides a good example of tax reform in Latin America. The Colombian tax system has undergone numerous changes since the 1960s. McLure and Zodrow (1997) report that reforms were often dramatic reversing earlier fundamental decisions. Further, reforms were often in response to the conventional wisdom of the day as well as changing economic conditions. Our discussion looks at some of the more recent changes.

Haindl, Dunn and Schenone (1995) outline the Colombian tax reforms of 1986, 1990 and 1992. They argue that these reforms were designed to prevent double taxation of enterprises and individuals and promote investment. Neutrality and simplification were also objectives of tax reform. The 1986 reforms unified the profit tax rate of corporations and limited companies at 30 percent, which was equal to the highest marginal rate of income tax and capital gains tax. In 1991 the capital gains tax on shares traded on the stock exchange was eliminated. The 1986 reforms also exempted dividends received by individuals from taxation. The 1992 reform introduced a method for adjusting taxes for inflation.

What are the lessons of the Colombian experience? First, the Colombian case showed a gradualist or incremental approach to tax reform, reversing past policies and introducing new initiatives. McLure and Zodrow (1997) suggest that there is some virtue in patient reform. Second, the Colombian approach also shows that tax reform must synchronize with prevailing economic conditions. The introduction of inflation adjustment to deal with inflation is an example of this. Third, the Colombian reform underlines the importance of good tax administration.[7] Fourth, Haindl, Dunn and Schenone (1995) have argued that the 1986 tax reform had a positive effect on the investment rate. This implies that tax neutrality may be good for development.

THE BARBADIAN TAX REFORM

This section analyses and evaluates the Barbadian income tax reform introduced in July 1992 and compares it with the pre-1992 system. These reforms were a modified version of original proposals put forward by the IMF in a mission to Barbados in 1992. My analysis is based on the work of Howard (1992), and Howard and Mascoll (1994).

First, my approach compares the effective tax rates of the old income tax system (1986–92) with the effective rates of the reformed system (post-

July 1992). Second, I evaluate the extent to which the Barbadian tax reform of 1992 reflected modernist principles discussed previously including cost-effectiveness, efficiency, revenue elasticity, simplicity, base broadening, and fairness.

The methodology employed here assumes a representative married individual who has two children and whose spouse has income. Further, our representative individual is assumed to claim the standard deduction of Bds$15,000 under the old system (1986–92), and Bds$13,000 in the reformed system. The currency unit used is the Barbadian dollar (Bds$2.00 = US$1.00). Effective tax rates are calculated by dividing income tax payable by total assessable income.

The Old Income Tax System (1986–1992)

Barbados experienced two major tax reforms in 1986 and 1992. The most important features of the 1986 tax reform were the introduction of a standard deduction of Bds$15,000 and the abolition of income tax for individuals earning Bds$15,000 or less (Howard 1992). This reform reduced tax payable for the entire set of taxpayers at a cost of almost Bds$80 million over a two-year period. The 1986 tax reform can be considered a massive income tax cut, but it did not achieve many of the principles of tax reform discussed earlier.

The old tax system became highly complicated for two reasons. First, a complex system of itemized allowances and deductions emerged, enabling certain individuals to claim allowances well in excess of Bds$15,000. These numerous tax breaks and shelters introduced an element of discrimination into the old tax system, which considerably reduced tax neutrality. Further, the types of itemized deductions were not related to the need for horizontal equity. High-income individuals were in a better position to take advantage of these opportunities, particularly the unlimited mortgage interest deduction, because lower income individuals were less able to satisfy borrowing criteria. The 1986 reform therefore failed to simplify the tax system.

Second, the old income tax system became overburdened with levies in the form of payroll taxes. These levies were really surtaxes on income and were earmarked for specific purposes. The money value of levies, including the transport, health, training and employment levies was increased after 1986, in response to severe recession in the Barbadian economy. Additionally, an individual stabilization tax (or surtax) was imposed on incomes. This tax rose from 1.5 percent on assessable income below Bds$15,000 to 4.0 percent on the part of income exceeding Bds$15,000.

The IMF mission to Barbados (1992) reported that at income levels of Bds$30,000, the effective rate of income tax, including PAYE, levies, national insurance contributions and stabilization tax reached 55 percent of assessable income.

Mascoll (1991) found that the 1986 tax measures benefited mostly upper income individuals who experienced a fall in their effective income tax rate from 28.3 percent in 1985 to 19.2 percent in 1987. The average effective tax rate for middle income taxpayers fell from 12.9 percent in 1985 to 12.8 percent in 1987. For low income taxpayers, the effective tax rate decreased from 9.6 percent in 1985 to 8.8 percent in 1987. The levies and stabilization tax mentioned above were particularly burdensome on middle and low income individuals.

The Reformed Tax System (Post-July 1992)

The 1992 income tax reform in Barbados was implemented using a phased approach in order to minimize revenue losses. Measures effective from July 1992 were as follows:

1. Reduction of the maximum tax rate for year 1992 from 50 percent to 40 percent
2. Elimination of most itemized deductions and allowances
3. Withdrawal of exemptions for pension income, but taxpayers over 60 years may claim a deduction of Bds$20,000
4. Imposition of a 12.5 percent withholding tax on interest, along with a 12.5 percent final tax on dividends
5. Increase in the corporation tax rate from 35 percent to 40 percent
6. A general property tax rate of 0.95 percent of land value was introduced, but a lower rate of 0.35 percent for owner-occupied houses remained on the first Bds$100,000.

Measures effective from 1 January 1993 were as follows:

7. Elimination of individual stabilization tax
8. Reduction of the standard deduction from Bds$15,000 to Bds$13,000 with allowances of Bds$500 each for a maximum of two children in 1993 and Bds$1,000 per child in 1994
9. Introduction of two rates of income tax – on income between Bds$13,000 and Bds$37,000 per annum, the rate was 25 percent and 40 percent above that level
10. Elimination of earmarked levies in two stages: 1 January 1993 and 1 January 1994

193

11. The introduction of a dependent spouse allowances of Bds$3,000 per annum effective from 1 January 1995.

This phased approach meant that the benefits of tax reform varied over time for different individuals as shown by the variation in effective tax rates between 1993 and 1994 (Tables 15.1 and 15.2).

Table 15.1: PAYE effective tax rates under reformed system compared to old system

Assessable Income*	Effective Tax Rates (%)		
$	Old System	1993	1994
13,000	0	0	0
15,000	0	1.7	0
30,000	10	13.3	12.5
50,000	20	21.5	20.7
70,000	27.1	26.8	26.2
100,000	34	30.8	30.4

Source: * Calculated from data provided by Ernst and Young, *Barbados Budget*, 1992, Bridgetown, Barbados.
  * Analysis assumes individual is married, has two children and spouse has income.

Table 15.2: Total effective tax rates under reformed system compared with old system

Assessable Income*	Effective Tax Rates (%)		
$	Old System	1993	1994
13,000	14.0	10.9	8.2
15,000	14.0	12.6	8.2
30,000	25.3	24.2	20.8
50,000	32.6	29.7	26.9
70,000	37.2	32.8	32.0
100,000	42.3	34.8	33.4

Source: * Calculated from data provided by Ernst and Young, *Barbados Budget*, 1992, Bridgetown, Barbados.
  * Analysis assumes individual is married, has two children and spouse has income.

The 1992 reforms caused a decline in overall effective tax rates. Table 15.2 shows that total effective tax rates for persons earning Bds$13,000 declined from 14.0 percent in 1992 to 10.9 percent in 1993. By 1994, total tax rates fell to 8.2 percent for the two lowest assessable income groups. The steepest decline in total effective tax rates were for the income group earning Bds$100,000. The tax reform, therefore, significantly benefited individuals in this group.

The analysis reveals an increase in PAYE effective tax rates in 1993 for income groups earnings Bds$30,000 and Bds$50,000. The expected effective tax rates for these two groups in 1994 were higher than in 1992. It can be argued, therefore, that the middle income groups were losers as a result of the PAYE tax reform. The only group to register a significant fall in PAYE effective tax rates was the Bds$100,000 income group. This was primarily a result of the fall in the top marginal rate from 50 percent to 40 percent. This reduction in PAYE effective tax rates for the highest income groups followed the pattern observed by Mascoll (1991) for the 1986 tax reforms. Overall, the PAYE system lost some of its progressivity as a result of the two marginal rates of 25 percent and 40 percent.

Evaluation of the 1992 Barbadian Tax Reform

The 1992 tax reform in Barbados was part of the worldwide tax reform movement, as well as an essential component of the country's structural adjustment programme initiated in 1991. The principal goals of tax reform were to increase the efficiency, equity, and simplicity of the tax system. Over the years, the Barbadian tax system had become unfair, highly complex and contained a large number of concessions and preferences which favoured the rich and propertied interests.

Under a programme of structural adjustment, a uniform tax system is best for resource allocation. A less discriminatory tax regime makes for simplicity and reduces political patronage in the form of tax shelters. A highly progressive system places pressure on government to discriminate by way of preferential treatment of high income individuals. Highly progressive systems also encourage tax evasion.

The 1992 Barbadian tax reform embodied some of the modernist principles of the worldwide tax reform movement discussed in earlier sections. These are simplicity, efficiency, revenue maintenance, equity, cost effectiveness, and base broadening.

The first feature of the 1992 reform was the simplification of the tax system. The elimination of stabilization taxes and various levies eased the burden on lower income groups and improved the simplicity of administering the tax system. Simplicity was also achieved by the flat rate of 40 percent on incomes above Bds$37,200 and the new standard deduction of Bds$13,000.

Simplification meant the elimination of itemized deductions. Tax authorities were no longer required to scrutinize numerous documents submitted by tax payers to support claims for deductions. Simplification also guaranteed the removal of incentives for tax avoidance by highly paid individuals, by reducing their ability to exploit loopholes in the tax code.

Tax systems with less progressivity favour efficiency. The 1992 tax reform by lowering the top marginal rate, improved the system's ability for reducing the negative substitution effects of taxes on income thereby promoting efficiency, that is, lowering the welfare loss associated with high marginal rates.

The 1992 reform was more revenue-efficient than the previous system. Revenue efficiency was achieved by broadening the tax base, the abolition of itemized deductions, and the lower Bds$13,000 standard deduction.

Although the 1992 reform was primarily efficiency-oriented, a large section of the labour force continued to be exempt from PAYE taxation. Under the new system, persons earning less than Bds$13,000 were exempt from PAYE. Our analysis also showed that overall effective tax rates fell for this group from 14.0 percent in 1992 to 8.2 percent in 1993 (see Table 15.2).

Was the 1992 reform cost-effective? Under the old system (1986–92), the cost of tax administration was high. There were the administrative costs of collecting about seven direct taxes (including levies), when two or three taxes would have served the same purpose because all revenue were placed in a single consolidated fund. Although we have found no estimates of the administrative costs of both systems, a less complex system should certainly be more cost-effective.

The 1992 reform broadened the tax base and, therefore, allowed fewer taxes and lower tax rates on a broader range of incomes. This improved efficiency. Tax systems which are highly discriminatory, like the 1986–92 system, channel resources into undesirable areas. Further, the broadening of the tax base to include pensions affected pensioners with incomes below Bds$20,000. Only pensioners with above-average income received benefits from the exclusion of income under the old system. The previous exclusion of high income pensioners placed a higher burden of tax on workers with dependents, than on high income retired individuals.

SUMMARY

The tax reform movement of the 1980s and 1990s was a worldwide movement embracing a large number of developing countries. Supply-side tax policy was an influence on this movement. Supply-side tax policy emphasized efficiency and neutrality, two principles which characterized most tax reforms. These goals could be achieved by simplifying the tax systems and broadening the tax base.

The US tax reform had considerable influence on tax reforms throughout the world. We briefly summarized this reform, noting that the nature of its impact on the economy had been researched, but there were no definitive conclusions. The tax reforms in Latin America, Indonesia, and Barbados were also reviewed.

Chapter Sixteen

Taxes on Income and Wealth

I t is now appropriate to examine the general principles of direct taxes on personal incomes, profits of corporations, property, wealth, and payroll taxes. The main focus is on the rationale for these taxes and their probable economic impact. Some emphasis will be placed on the institutional aspects of direct taxation in developing countries. Table 16.1 shows the contribution of taxes on income to revenue in developed and developing countries. The contribution of personal income taxes is highest in the developed countries with the United Sates showing a ratio of 40.9 percent. The ratio of personal income taxes to revenue is very low in the sample of developing countries.

PERSONAL INCOME TAX

A widely debated issue in public finance is whether the tax system should be an income-based system or a consumption-based system. In the past an income-based tax system was considered superior to a consumption-based system because it was believed that progressivity guaranteed equity. Some modern theorists have argued that, to the extent that income taxes are progressive, their relative effect in curtailing saving is likely to be greater than the relative effect of indirect taxes. Other theorists have pointed to the negative effects of progressive income tax systems on people's desire to

TABLE 16.1: Taxes on income as a percent of total revenue in developed and developing countries

Developed Countries	Personal Income Tax	Corporate Income Tax	Property Tax	Social Security Taxes
United States (1995)	40.9	10.9	1.0	33.2
Canada (1994)	40.0	7.5	–	18.2
Japan (1993)	3.7	12.4	4.0	26.5
Belgium (1994)	28.7	5.4	2.7	33.8
France (1995)	13.4	4.0	2.1	43.5
Germany (1993)	14.7	1.2	0.03	47.9
Italy (1994)	29.0	5.6	1.4	29.0
Spain (1993)	24.3	5.7	0.4	38.9
Sweden (1995)	5.8	8.1	3.6	35.4
Switzerland (1993)	12.3	9.1	2.9	55.4
United Kingdom (1995)	26.6	9.2	6.4	17.2
Developing Countries				
Botswana (1993)	3.9	21.3	0.1	–
Ghana (1993)	6.4	8.2		–
Zaire (1995)	7.9	22.8	–	–
India (1995)	9.3	10.7	0.08	–
Indonesia (1994)	8.1	40.0	0.6	2.0
Sri Lanka (1995)	5.4	7.2	3.8	–
Argentina (1992)	0.2	–	2.3	43.9
Grenada (1995)	9.0	11.14	2.2	–
St Kitts and Nevis (1994)	4.0	10.26	1.5	10.7
St Vincent (1995)	9.7	11.48	0.6	5.0
*Barbados (1995)	18.3	11.44	4.6	–

Source: IMF, *Government Finance Statistics Yearbook*, 1996.
　　*Central Bank of Barbados, *Annual Statistical Digest*, 1996.

work and invest. These analysts also believe that steeply progressive taxation fosters capital flight from open economies. Negative attitudes associated with progressive income taxation have lessened as a result of the tax reform movement with its emphasis on flatter tax systems.

Conditions for Success of the Income Tax

Income taxes have moderately increased their importance in some higher income developing countries (Tanzi 1990). Goode has advanced a list of conditions which he first proposed in 1951, for the successful operation of an income tax. These conditions are "(1) the existence of a predominantly money economy; (2) a high standard of literacy; (3) prevalence of honest and reliable accounting; (4) a large degree of voluntary compliance on the part of taxpayers; (5) a political system not dominated by wealthy groups acting in their self-interest; and (6) honest, reasonably efficient administration" (Goode 1984: 102).

Goode's conditions for the operation of an income tax have some merit for developing countries. First, in many developing countries it is difficult to gauge the income of subsistence producers even in a monetized economy. Second, literacy is also highly important. Taxpayers must be able to file claims by completing tax return forms. This means that standards of literacy must be relatively high. In many countries in Africa and Latin America literacy levels are low thereby restricting the coverage of the income tax. Third, deficient accounting and administrative systems in some developing countries may also lead to considerable lags in tax collection and underreporting. Administrative deficiencies are compounded by the problems of applying PAYE systems to shopkeepers, primary producers, and self-employed persons. Tax evasion and avoidance are likely to be high in tax systems which are poorly administered.

Goode's list of conditions omits the underground economy. In chapter 1 we observed that the underground economy was a constraint on overall fiscal policy and development planning. Growth of underground economies in many developing countries also reduces the yield of the income tax. The underground economy is a haven for both legal and illegal activities, moonlighting, currency substitution, and so forth. These activities do not enter the official estimates of the GDP, and they provide no income tax to the government. Income tax revenues in Jamaica and Guyana, for example, may have been significantly constrained by the existence of large underground economies especially during the recessionary years of the 1980s.

Definition of Income

A comprehensive definition of income is necessary to operate an income tax system. Legislation identifies the components of income subject to income tax, and these components vary from jurisdiction to jurisdiction. There is therefore no universal legal definition of income. Economists have attempted to provide an economic definition, and the one which is widely cited as an ideal income concept for tax purposes is the Schanz-Haig-Simmons (SHS) definition. This is a comprehensive definition of income which states that income is equal to consumption plus the change in the value of wealth over the relevant income period, which for tax purposes is usually one year.[1]

The SHS definition of income, though it provides a guide for estimating the income tax base, is difficult to apply wholesale in practice. Goode (1977) raises some conceptual questions relating to the meaning and acceptability of the SHS definition. First, the SHS definition includes unrealized capital gains. It is difficult to tax unrealized capital gains which can pose valuation problems due to price fluctuations. Capital gains should be included in taxable income only when they are realized. Second, Goode argues that though it is correct to include consumption as a part of the SHS definition, it is impossible to make allowance for leisure, which is sometimes classified as consumption, in assessing income for taxation. Third, the SHS definition indicates that life insurance death benefits as well as gifts and inheritances should be included in the income of beneficiaries. Goode asserts that death benefits, bequests and gifts should be excluded from taxable income. In many jurisdictions, these items are subject to special taxes and not included in the income tax base. Goode concludes, however, that the SHS definition provides guidance in estimating the income tax base.

Taxable Income, Allowances, and Deductions

The legal approach to the composition of income diverges from the SHS definition. Of course, the legal definition of income for income tax purposes varies from country to country. My approach identifies the method of computing income tax payable, the various components of income, as well as allowances and deductions.

The standard computation of individual income tax liability is as follows. First, the taxpayer estimates his assessable income which is the aggregate of factor income payments. An alternative concept known as adjusted gross income is used in the United States. Second, assessable income is reduced by allowances and itemized deductions to arrive at taxable income. Income tax rates are then applied to taxable income to yield income tax payable. Normally, the taxpayer submits an income tax return which records PAYE income tax deductions and other prepaid taxes. If these tax deductions are greater than tax payable computed on his taxable income, he is entitled to a refund. Conversely, if previous tax deductions are less than tax payable, the individual pays net taxes to the government. Table 16.2 shows the maximum personal income tax rates chargeable on taxable income in developing countries. Most rates are

TABLE 16.2: Maximum income tax rates in developing countries

Country	Personal Income Tax Rate (%) 1997	Capital GainsTax Rate (%) 1997	Corporate Tax Rate (%) 1995
Argentina	30	30	30
Bahamas	0	0	0
Barbados	40	0	40
Bolivia	13	0	25
Botswana	25	25	35
Brazil	25	15	25
Cayman Islands	0	0	0
Chile	45	45	15
Colombia	35	35	30
Hong Kong	20	0	15**
India	30	20	40
Indonesia	30	30	30
Kenya	32.5	0	35
Korea	40	50	30
Malaysia	30	30*	30
Mexico	35	35	34
Nigeria	25	20	35
Singapore	28	0	27
South Africa	45	0	35
Uganda	30	0	30

Note: *Applies only to real property gains. **Rate for 1997.
Sources: Compiled from Ernst and Young, *Worldwide Corporate Tax Guide and Directory*, 1995; and Ernst and Young, 1998 *Worldwide Executive Tax Guide*, 1997, published by Ernst and Young International Ltd.

lower than 35 percent, which reflects the success of income tax reforms in lowering high personal marginal tax rates.

Normally, assessable income for tax purposes includes both local and foreign sources of income. In some countries, dividends from ordinary shares and interest from bank deposits are included in assessable income. In other countries, these incomes are subject to withholding taxes. Other types of income include annuities, royalties and interest from bonds, and business and property income. The treatment of pension income varies widely. In Barbados, pensioners benefit from a deduction which considerably reduces their net tax payable. It should be noted that realized capital gains are not included in assessable income in a large number of developing countries where capital gains are not taxable.

Prior to the tax reforms of the 1980s and early 1990s, the tax systems of many developing countries were overburdened by a large number of deductions including medical, life insurance, and unlimited mortgage interest deductions. The grant of allowances and deductions is to ensure some horizontal equity in the system, and enable government to achieve goals such as investment and savings mobilization. Allowances for children, pensioners and personal allowances help to achieve the equity objective. We have seen in chapter 15 that the simplification of tax systems led to a reduction in the number of deductions and allowances thereby enhancing tax neutrality.[2]

Income Taxes and Labour Supply

Many economists have argued that the personal income tax provides a disincentive to work, save and invest. Further, a progressive income tax combined with inflation erode the real value of an individual's earnings and thereby his standard of living. This section examines the disincentive effect of the income tax on work effort, a thesis which has provided a rationale for income tax reform. Most of the empirical work on this issue has been carried out for developed countries. I am aware of two recent quantitative studies for developing countries by Rochjadi and Leuthold (1994) and Alleyne (1997). The theory is quite relevant for developing countries.

Our first discussion concerns the so-called work/leisure choice which can be distorted by the income tax. The basic neoclassical model postulated in the literature is that the labour supply of an individual is a function of his or her after-tax income. The individual maximizes his utility function subject to a budget constraint which is reduced by the income tax rate. Further, the individual has a choice between work and leisure, where leisure is the total hours available to him or her minus hours of work.

The income tax leads to a substitution and income effect on the taxpayer. The substitution effect decreases work effort and causes the taxpayer to demand more leisure. The substitution effect therefore leads to a decline in productivity and a loss in output. When the substitution effect is stronger than the income effect throughout the economy, there is a general loss in welfare resulting in an inefficient allocation of resources.

The income effect of personal taxation is favourable to work effort. The income tax reduces income and causes the worker to work harder to recoup his loss of income. The overall impact of the tax on collective productivity depends on the relative strength of the substitution and

203

income effect for the economy as a whole. Some individuals will work harder and some will demand more leisure. The neoclassical theory is, therefore, indeterminate with respect to the entire economy. However, some theorists argue that in some economies, a backward-bending supply curve of labour exists partly determined by this type of analysis.

Institutional factors have an impact on the actual labour supply curve. Atkinson and Stiglitz (1980: 40) argue that the labour supply curve may be discontinuous with a cluster of persons at the kinks in the tax schedule. At lower levels of income, there may be less opportunities for the worker to substitute work for leisure. At higher levels of income, perquisites and various allowances add to the income of individuals who may not necessarily reduce their work effort.

Early survey research on 306 solicitors and accountants by Break (1957) suggested that income tax was of secondary importance in determining their hours of work. It is difficult to report the extensive early work on this area. For a good survey of early studies see Break (1974: 180–91). A later study by Hausman (1981) presented estimates of changes in labour supply for heads of households in the United States using econometric methods. Hausman's work showed that husbands work about 8 percent less than they would in the absence of taxes. He also found that a "proportional tax with exemptions causes less reduction in labour supply than the current system – 1 percent instead of 8 percent" (Hausman 1981: 29).

Rochjadi and Leuthold (1994) found that Indonesian workers respond to increases in taxation by reducing labour supply. The response was, however, small, especially for male workers. Female workers were more responsive to tax changes. This was one of the first econometric studies on taxation and labour supply in a developing country. Alleyne (1997), using the same methodology of Rochjadi and Leuthold, reported that the labour supply response to taxation in Jamaica is larger than that found by Rochjadi and Leuthold for Indonesia. Further, females reduce their labour supply in response to taxation less than males. The labour supply response was larger at higher income groups across gender.

Income Taxes and Savings Behaviour

A progressive income tax will have a greater disincentive effect on savings than a proportional or regressive tax. This is based on the theory that high income families have a greater marginal propensity to save than low income families. The literature has investigated the impact of the after-tax rate of return on the elasticity of saving. Early studies for the United States concluded that taxes did not have a significant effect on saving. Work by Blinder (1975) and Evans (1983) found a low interest elasticity of savings. See reviews by Boskin (1978) and Jackson (1993). Studies by Boskin (1978) and Summers (1983) found that elasticities ranged from 0.20 to 0.60. These studies suggested that lowering the tax rate on income from savings would increase the rate of growth of saving. Inflation also reduces the real rate of return to savings as well as the real value of savings. Indexation has been used in some countries to tie exemptions and deductions to the rate of inflation.

The Income Tax in Hong Kong and Singapore

Hong Kong and Singapore are chosen to illustrate the operation of the income tax. These countries have successfully employed a low rate income tax system to accelerate the development process. Our observations rely heavily on tax information compiled by Ernst and Young (1997). In the case of Hong Kong, the information is relevant for the income year ending 31 March 1998. For Singapore, the income assessment year is 1997.

Hong Kong has three separate income taxes. First, the profits tax is levied at a flat rate of 15 percent on business or trade income. Second, there is a property tax levied on 80 percent of rental income at a standard rate of 15 percent. Third, a "salaries tax" is levied on taxable incomes at four progressive rates ranging from 2 percent to a maximum of 20 percent. Ernst and Young reports that most income is taxed at a rate of 15 percent which is low compared with other developing countries (see Table 16.2).

Hong Kong's system of personal deductions and allowances is restricted to allowances for children and dependent relatives. Child allowances can be claimed for up to nine children. There are also dependent parent and grandparent allowances as well as separate disabled dependent allowances, dependent sibling allowances and single parent allowances (Ernst and Young 1997: 210). The system of allowances underlines the importance of the family unit.

The property tax on rental income in Hong Kong plays an important role in a society where retail office space is among the most expensive in the world. Sharply rising rents on office space and residential properties were a characteristic of Hong Kong society in the early 1990s (see Kogan Page 1995). Hong Kong does not have a capital gains tax nor social security taxes. Interest income not derived from business and dividend income are exempt from taxation.

Although Singapore also has a low-rate income tax system, the structure of tax rates and allowances is remarkably different from that of Hong

Kong. In 1997, Singapore had 10 marginal tax rates ranging from 2 percent to a maximum of 28 percent. The large number of tax rates counteracts the neutrality characteristic of the tax reform movement.

The system of deductions and allowances is also much broader than Hong Kong's. Considerable importance is attached to child and dependent relative allowances. Deductions are also granted for life insurance premiums and pension fund contributions.

There are no capital gain taxes in Singapore. For the income assessment year 1997, tax on dividend income was a withholding tax of 26 percent, unless the dividend was declared from profits that were exempt from tax. Dividends declared from exempt profits are tax-free. Most forms of interest are taxed with other incomes at the personal income tax rates (see Ernst and Young 1997: 452).

CORPORATION TAX

Corporation tax is a tax on the net income of corporations. Table 16.1 shows that generally the ratio of corporate taxes to total revenue tends to be higher in developing than in developed countries. Most developing countries in our sample collect more revenue from corporate taxes than from personal income taxes. This is partly explained by the high level of corporate tax revenues from the mineral sectors of these economies. Table 16.2 shows in part corporate tax rates for selected developing countries. It should be noted that most corporate rates were below 35 percent. The Bahamas and Cayman Islands are tax haven destinations where no income tax is charged.

Public finance economists have identified a number of reasons for taxing corporations. First, the corporation is a legal entity with limited liability of its owners. This implies that the corporation should be taxed separately. Second, shareholders are able to pool their capital thereby promoting the interests of the corporation. This means that the corporation should be taxed as a result of the benefits they gain from incorporation. Third, the corporation tax is one way by which the state can appropriate part of the economic surplus of a country. This view holds that the corporation benefits from the provision of government infrastructure and other services, and, therefore, should not be allowed to retain all of its profits.

Arguments have also been advanced against the corporation tax. Corporation taxes which are too high can retard the development of the corporate sector. Such taxes increase the risks involved in investment thereby deterring firms from becoming incorporated. In developing countries, a high corporation tax may force foreign firms to invest elsewhere. The corporation tax may therefore act as a disincentive to further inflows of capital. Corporation taxes may also affect savings. Lewis (1955) asserted that economic development can only occur if the level of savings increases, and if there is a rise in the share of profits in the national income. The corporation tax can therefore reduce the rate of capital accumulation.

Corporation tax systems can be classified according to the extent to which corporate income taxes and personal income taxes on shareholders are integrated. The primary concern here is that corporate profits are taxed under the corporation tax, and dividends paid to shareholders are taxed under the income tax. This introduces an element of double taxation. The arguments for integration are designed to reduce double taxation. We examine the case for and against integration by analysing the various systems under which corporation taxes are levied. These are the classical, full integration, split-rate, dividend deduction, and the imputation system. Other tax credit and schedular systems have also been implemented.

The classical system

The classical system is practised in some countries including the United States and Jamaica. This system is sometimes known as the separate entity system, whereby the corporation is regarded as a separate legal entity distinct from its shareholders. The corporation tax on net profits and the income tax on dividends are levied separately. In this scenario, dividends are subject to double taxation. The mechanics of the classical system are shown in Table 16.3.[3]

TABLE 16.3: The classical system

Category	$
(1) Profits before corporation tax	500.00
(2) Corporation tax at 40%	200.00
(3) Net dividend income (1) – (2)	300.00
(4) Personal income tax at 40% (or (3) x 0.4)	120.00
(5) Total Tax (2) + (4)	320.00

Cnossen (1993) and King (1995a) argue that the classical system has serious distortionary effects on the economy. The system discourages businesses from incorporating, especially those new businesses financed by equity capital. Companies are therefore encouraged to finance their business by using debt which increases the risk of bankruptcy (King 1995a: 150). The discrimination against new equity also contributes to the concentration of market power (Cnossen 1993: 49).

According to King (1995a), there are valid arguments against integration. A switch to an integrated system leads to a revenue loss, compared with the revenue generated by the classical system. This revenue deficiency has to be made up by raising taxes in other areas of economic activity. The classical system is also easier to administer than an integrated system such as the imputation system discussed below. Systems which are based on tax credits introduce biases into corporation tax assessments, especially when distinctions are made between dividends generated by local and foreign investments. Sometimes the tax system may give preferential treatment to foreign over local investment or vice versa, thereby creating economic distortions.

The Jamaican tax reform of 1986 introduced a classical system. The corporate income tax rate in 1986 was fixed at 33⅓ percent, and a final withholding tax of 33⅓ percent was levied separately on dividends, interest, royalties, management fees, and branch remittances to both residents and nonresidents. The 33⅓ percent tax rate was levied on all income derived from countries without a treaty withholding tax rate. Otherwise the corporate tax was the treaty rate applicable to the investor. A tax incentive programme was established to offset the negative impact of investment as a result of the classical system. Tax incentive programmes in Jamaica offer tax exemptions to companies registered under the Export Encouragement Act or Hotel Incentive Act as well as the Jamaica Freezone Act (Ernst and Young 1995). By 1997, a flat-rate tax of 25 percent replaced the 33⅓ percent rate on all incomes (Ernst and Young 1997).

The Full Integration System

The full integration system is the polar opposite of the classical system. In the full integration system, there is no distinction for corporation tax purposes between profits and wage incomes and other forms of income. Full integration eliminates the economic distortions of the classical system, and also completely eliminates overtaxation. Proponents of a full integration system argue that the corporation tax should be abolished, and shareholders taxed under the personal income tax on their share of imputed corporate profits, which would be equivalent to a tax on distributed and undistributed profits (see Brown and Jackson 1990: 526). Cnossen (1993: 51) points out that full integration is impractical because of its high costs. Further, delays in completing corporate tax assessments would impact on the filing of shareholders income tax returns. Also, the determination of equity for various income taxpayers would be neglected under full integration.

The Split-Rate and Dividend Deduction System

Under the split-rate system dividends are taxed at a lower rate than undistributed profits or retained earnings. The split-rate system approximates the classical system if the tax rate differential is small (King 1995a).

Under the dividend deduction system, in order to provide dividend relief for shareholders, a proportion of profits for distribution are deductible before taxable profits are determined. The corporation tax is then applied to profits after deduction. Shareholders are then taxed under the personal income tax on dividend income which is the difference between profits before corporation tax and the amount of corporation tax charged (Cnossen 1993). These systems still contain a measure of overtaxation but not to the same extent as the classical system.

The Imputation System

The imputation system is practised in many European countries. This system offers more dividend relief for shareholders than the other systems. According to King (1995a), the personal income tax base of the shareholder is the sum of dividends received plus a tax credit for taxes paid by the company. The net dividend is therefore grossed-up by the value of the tax credit. The personal income tax is then applied to the grossed-up dividend. The value of the tax credit is subtracted from the income tax paid to give net income tax payable (see Cnossen 1993: 77). In some countries, a tax credit system is utilized where a tax credit is applied to dividends received, but the net dividend is not grossed up.

We follow the methodology used by Cnossen (1993: 57) and King (1995a: 154) to illustrate the imputation system in Table 16.4. The table shows the level of relief given to shareholders who have already been taxed under the corporate tax rate of 40 percent. This is indicated by the imputed corporation tax to shareholders of $100.00 which is equivalent to a tax credit of 50 percent. This implies that the grossed-up factor is one-

TABLE 16.4: The imputation system

Category	$
(1) Profits before corporation tax	500.00
(2) Corporation tax at 40%	200.00
(3) Net dividend income (1) – (2)	300.00
(4) Imputed corporation tax (½) × (3)	100.00
(5) Grossed-up income (3) + (4)	400.00
(6) Personal income tax at 40% or (5) × (0.4)	160.00
(7) Tax credit (4)	100.00
(8) Net income tax (6) – (7)	60.00
(9) Total Tax (2) + (8)	260.00

third. His grossed-up income is therefore $400.00 indicated in line 5. The personal income tax at 40 percent is applied to his grossed-up income, resulting in gross income tax payable of $160.00 minus the $100.00 tax credit or $60.00. Total tax payable by the corporation and shareholder is $260.00.

It is useful to compare the level of taxation in the imputation system with that of the classical system shown in Table 16.3. Under the classical system the shareholder pays $60.00 more than under the imputation system. The classical system is clearly a more punitive system.

Depreciation

A very important variable determining the base of the corporation tax is depreciation. The faster the rate of depreciation of a firm's assets, the lower is its net income subject to tax. This implies that taxes on net income would decline. Companies therefore prefer depreciation rules which allow their assets to depreciate at an accelerated rate. The two methods of depreciation discussed here are the straight-line method and the declining balance method. The use of these methods vary from country to country.

Under the straight-line method, the firm deducts the same amount from the historic cost of the asset over the asset's life. That is, the historic cost (c) of the asset is divided by the asset life (n) to arrive at the annual amount of depreciation. For example, for an asset with a historic cost of $10,000 and a life of five years, $2,000 will be written off each year. The straight-line method is the simplest depreciation method.

Accelerated depreciation permits companies to deduct larger amounts in calculating their taxable profits in the early years of the life of the asset.

Some countries allow firms to deduct the full cost of the asset in its year of purchase. This practice is known as expensing, and allows the firm to increase its net income over the life of the asset, if it can invest the amount of tax saved.

The double declining balance method permits larger deductions in the early years in contrast to the straight-line method. Under the double declining balance method, twice the straight-line percentage is deducted from historic cost in the first year, and the same depreciation rate is applied to the book value which remains in subsequent years. For example, consider an asset with a historic cost of $100,000 to be depreciated over ten years. In the first year, the amount of depreciation is $20,000. In the second year, the firm writes off $16,000 or 0.20 x $80,000. A different method and rate of depreciation may be applied to different classes of assets.

Economic Effects of the Corporation Tax in Developing Countries

In chapter 14, we discussed the incidence of the corporation tax in the context of the Harberger model. Harberger (1962) concluded that in the long run, assuming a closed economy, the incidence of the corporation tax is borne by the corporation. Shoven and Whalley (1972) have supported Harberger's findings. Our discussion on developing countries is limited by the realization that not much econometric work has been done on the impact of the corporation tax in developing countries. Our limited comments will therefore be highly qualitative.

There is wide consensus in the literature that a corporation tax is borne by the owners of capital in the short run in both developed and developing economies. The controversial Krzyzaniak and Musgrave study (1963) was the first serious econometric approach to examine the impact of the corporation tax in the short run. They found that businessmen were able to pass on fully the corporation tax by increasing prices, and the tax did not reduce the after-tax income of corporations. The tax was therefore fully shifted to customers in the short run.

Lent (1977) has observed that in developing countries there are not many opportunities for shifting the corporation tax in the short run. Companies selling their products to export markets are circumscribed in their pricing policies by world prices. However, it is difficult to generalize for developing countries. Further, later in this chapter we discuss the difficulties posed by transfer pricing in taxing multinational corporations. These prices arise because it is not always possible to identify the nature of transfers between MNCs. It is, therefore, not easy to assess the impact of the corporation tax in developing countries. According to Lent (1977), the wide variety of socioeconomic conditions call for a separate evaluation of the equity, efficiency, and administrative implication of the corporation tax in each developing country.

In the long run the corporation tax may be shifted to domestic consumers in developing countries through higher prices. However, as in the short run, many firms are price takers in the world market and are unable to shift taxes to foreign consumers. The corporation tax may restrict capital inflows into developing countries (Goode 1984). To overcome this, many developing countries have offered generous investment tax credits and allowances to foreign firms.

CAPITAL GAINS TAX

Capital gains taxes exist predominantly in industrialized countries. However, some of the large developing countries have capital gains taxes or tax capital gains as part of ordinary income. These countries include Brazil, Chile, Colombia, Argentina, India, Indonesia, Turkey, Morocco, Nigeria, and Puerto Rico (Ernst and Young 1997). In some countries capital gains are taxed at the same rate as personal income tax. In other countries they are taxed at a lower rate (see Table 16.2). Capital gains are increases in the value of capital assets such as financial instruments, land and buildings, and stocks and shares. The main reasons for taxing capital gains is the equity criterion. Capital gains contribute to income, especially of high income earners and should, therefore, be taxed under the vertical equity principle.

An important issue in the taxing of capital gains is the so-called realization criterion (Muten 1995). Under the SHS definition of income discussed earlier, both unrealized and realized capital gains should be included in income. A capital gain is realized when the asset is sold. Unrealized capital gains occur when the price of a capital asset rises and it is not sold. Muten (1995) identifies the difficulties in taxing unrealized gains. First, it is sometimes difficult to value many capital assets. These include shares, real property, and pieces of art. Second, an unrealized gain may not last for too long in volatile markets. It is not administratively feasible to tax unrealized gains because of their shifting character. Current practice is to tax only realized gains.

A second issue in the taxing of capital gains is the impact of taxation on the real value of capital assets. Some countries have instituted inflation adjustments such as indexation to protect the real value of capital gains. One method is to index the acquisition cost of the capital asset to the rate of inflation (King 1995b). Indexation methods introduce complexities into the tax system especially in times of rapid inflation. Indexation is practised in England where only gains in excess of the rate of inflation are taxed. There is validity to the argument that when indexation is extended to capital gains, but not other forms of income which are affected by inflation, distortions and horizontal inequities can arise in the tax system (King 1995b: 158).

Much of the debate on the capital gains tax in the United States centres on the advantages and disadvantages of capital gains tax cuts. This type of debate is not important in developing countries because of the insignificance of the capital gains tax. Capital gains tax cuts became a prominent feature of tax policy in the United States since the 1980s. The argument for reducing the tax rate is that lower tax rates on capital gains increase investment activity. The critics of tax cuts argue that most capital gains accrue to wealthy individuals and tax cuts, therefore, benefit the rich. There is an argument for reducing the capital gains tax rate for persons who hold stocks for long periods thereby rewarding productive investment (Lowenstein 1995).

PROPERTY TAX

The contribution of property taxes to revenue is low in both developed and developing countries (Table 16.1). Our discussion here focuses on the traditional and new view of the incidence of the property tax and draws on the work of Aaron (1975), Break (1974), Mieszkowski (1972), and Pechman and Okner (1974). Chapter 18 is devoted to analysis of different types of land tax systems in developing countries. Under the traditional view, the property tax is regarded as a regressive excise tax. This view distinguishes between land fixed in supply, owner-occupied housing, rental housing, and other business property. The traditional view uses partial equilibrium analysis.

A tax on land fixed in supply is borne by the landowner, that is, the tax cannot be shifted in terms of higher land prices. The tax is said to be capitalized into the value of the land when its burden is concentrated on the current owner of the property. The tax reduces the capital value of the land on its announcement. This leads to a fall in the net income from the land and the current owners will suffer a capital loss.

In the case of owner-occupied housing the owner pays the full amount of the property tax. He cannot shift the tax which tends to be regressive since rich owners may pay a smaller percentage of their incomes than lower income owners. This is especially the case if the tax is a flat levy. According to Aaron (1975), the theory of tax incidence suggests that owners of residential property bear property taxes in proportion to their consumption and housing expenditures. This view posits that because the ratio of consumption to income falls as income increases, the ratio of property tax also falls as income rises. This view regards the property tax as a regressive levy.

According to the traditional view, the property tax on rental housing will be shifted forward to tenants or borne by the owner. The tax reduces the supply of rental housing and raises its price. Empirical analysis in the United States (Pechman and Okner 1974) found that the burden of the tax on both owner-occupiers and tenants was highly regressive.

The traditional view is more complicated when applied to business properties. The incidence of the tax will depend on the elasticities of demand and supply for the products of the business. If the demand for the product is elastic, some firms may find difficulty shifting the full burden of the tax to customers.

The new view of the property tax was originally advanced by Mieszkowski (1972) and elaborated by Aaron (1975). The new view assumes a general equilibrium framework and holds that all owners of capital bear the property tax. According to Mieszkowski (1972: 74), the "basic effect of the imposition of property taxes by thousands of local governments is to decrease the yield on reproducible capital". The property tax is fundamentally a tax on capital.

Mieszkowski (1972: 75) assumes that the supply of land is fixed. The total supplies of capital and labour are assumed to be fixed. Product and factor markets are perfectly competitive and capital is perfectly mobile between industries and cities. Given the absence of risks, the after-tax rates of return on all capital are equalized. These assumptions lead to the view that a uniform tax on the value of all land and capital would be borne by the owners of capital. Further, because the proportion of income from capital rises with income a tax on capital tends to be progressive (Rosen 1992: 550).

Aaron (1975) discusses the excise tax effects of the property tax. If we assume that the property tax is not levied at a uniform rate, as is the practice in the United States where property tax rates vary widely between regions, the property tax can be regarded as an excise tax on capital. There is a tendency for capital to move from high-tax to low-tax jurisdictions thereby reducing the before-tax rate of return. The before-tax rate of return increases in high-tax jurisdictions as capital leaves. According to Aaron (1975: 40), the process continues "until after-tax rates of return are equal – until differences in before-tax rates of return exactly offset differentials in tax rates". Rosen (1992) maintains that these excise tax effects lead to a complicated adjustment process and not much is known about their effects on the progressivity of the property tax.

The new view of the property tax was developed in the United States where property tax rates vary widely and capital mobility is on a larger scale compared with the situation in small developing countries. In the latter countries, there is not a wide variation in tax rates to cause extensive excise tax effects. In developing countries, the property tax is levied predominantly on land and structures and the traditional view may have more relevance.

Taxes on Wealth, Transfers, and Assets

Wealth taxes are predominantly found in European countries. They are direct taxes levied on individuals and are sometimes known as net worth taxes or annual wealth taxes (AWT). Taxes on property transfers, gifts, and inheritance are found in both developed and developing countries. Some developing countries have taxes on the assets of companies. For example, Mexico has a minimum tax of 1.8 percent on net assets levied on resident and nonresident corporations permanently established in Mexico. Other developing countries with asset taxes on companies include Jamaica, India, and Pakistan. Uruguay has a net worth tax on corporate net worth (Ernst and Young 1995). Barbados has a tax on the assets of commercial banks. Our discussion focuses on the rationale for these taxes as well as the problems they pose for tax administration.

Annual Wealth Tax
Our analysis of the AWT draws on the work of Due (1960) and Sandford (1995b). The AWT is a tax on net wealth which includes the stock of financial and personal assets, land and real property, and so forth. Only the net worth of the asset is included for valuation. The arguments for the

AWT are derived from the general principles of taxation. The principle of horizontal equity states that persons with the same taxable capacity should be taxed equally. Wealth increases an individual's taxable capacity. In this respect, the AWT supplements the income tax for rich individuals. In terms of vertical equity, the AWT can be regarded as a substitute for the top rates of a progressive income tax (Sandford 1995b: 51).

Another advantage of an AWT is that it may promote efficiency. A wealth tax has a tendency to push investments out of cash and low income securities into higher yielding assets (Due 1960). This means that liquidity preference is reduced and the taxpayer has an incentive to diversify his portfolio. Another efficiency argument is that the AWT is likely to have a less disincentive effect on work and investment incentives than an income tax of equal yield. This is because the AWT is based on past effort whereas the income tax is related to present effort. If an individual is taxed on past effort, he is less likely to be discouraged from working (Sandford 1995b). The disincentive to work can also mean a disincentive to save.

Perhaps the main difficulty of wealth taxation is the valuation of net wealth. Certain types of assets are easier to value than others. Cash, deposits, and real estate present no serious problems. However, other assets like works of art, antiques, and so forth may be difficult to value. Some individuals have ways of concealing their wealth by investing in other countries. This implies that underreporting can provide a serious problem for the authorities. Most developing countries do not have the administrative tax structures capable of managing a wealth tax.

Taxes on Transfers, Inheritance, and Assets

According to Yucelik (1995: 188), there are basically three types of transfer taxes at death. There are: (1) the estate tax imposed on the entire estate left by the testator without reference to inheritors; (2) an inheritance tax imposed on the individual shares of inheritors; and (3) an accessions tax on the donee with progressive rates on the value of bequests received during the lifetime. The first two types of taxes are sometimes known as death duties. The arguments for these taxes are the same as for annual wealth taxes, that is, vertical and horizontal equity.

Estate taxes are usually easier to administer than annual wealth taxes. Estate taxes require a valuation of the estate of the testator. The main problem is that the estate can be deliberately undervalued thereby reducing tax liability. Inheritance taxes on shares are more difficult to value because shares can be subject to price fluctuations. Another type of transfer tax is the property or real estate transfer tax. This tax is usually payable by the purchaser of real estate. Barbados, for example, has a property transfer tax with a higher rate on the purchaser than on the seller. Developing countries with inheritance and gift taxes include Bolivia, Brazil, Chile, Colombia, Hong Kong, Korea, Morocco, Philippines, Singapore, South Africa, Taiwan, and Turkey (see Ernst and Young 1997 for tax rates on estates and gifts.)

As indicated earlier, some developing countries levy a tax on the gross value of a business' assets or on the business' net worth. The tax is usually a small percentage of business assets. Krelove and Stotsky (1995) have suggested that the main reasons for asset taxes is to add an element of progressivity to the corporate income tax. An asset tax spread over a wide range of companies including multinationals may pose serious valuation problems. These problems include estimating market values of assets, determining the ownership of the assets, and inflation adjustments (Krelove and Stotsky 1995: 182).

PAYROLL TAXES

Payroll taxes are found in almost all developing countries with social security schemes. The payroll tax is a flat levy imposed on wage incomes up to a legally defined ceiling. A proportion of the tax is paid by employers and a proportion by employees. The relative contributions of employees and employers vary from country to country. Payroll taxes are used not only to finance social security, but also other government projects. Sometimes such taxes are used in developing countries to finance the budget deficit. The introduction of payroll tax funded security systems has been a recent development in some Latin American countries like Argentina, Mexico, Uruguay, and Peru (ECLAC 1996: 50). Social security payroll taxes constitute a fairly high proportion of revenue in developed countries (see Table 16.1).

Some attention has been focused on the incidence of the payroll tax. Employers' ability to increase prices as well as the elasticity of the supply of labour determine the payroll tax burden. If labour supply is inelastic, the tax will be borne by labour through a reduction in net wages. Early work by Brittain (1957) came to the conclusion that the incidence of the payroll tax falls on labour. Since the payroll tax is a flat levy, it is also regressive on lower incomes beneath the income ceiling for the application of the payroll tax rate.

SUMMARY

This chapter has traversed a wide range of issues on income taxation. We acknowledge that the application of these tax systems varies from country to country. The use of capital gains taxes has increased in developing countries. Corporate taxation comprises a larger proportion of revenue in developing countries than in the developed countries. The chapter also showed the overall importance of the income tax in developing countries.

Chapter Seventeen

Indirect Taxation in Developing Countries

O ur analysis is now concerned with the theory and potential impact of taxes on goods and services in developing countries. The term indirect tax will be used in this chapter in our discussion of this category of taxes. There are three main types of indirect taxes: excise duties, sales taxes, and taxes on international trade. Excise taxes are levies on specific goods and services. They are usually imposed either at specific or *ad valorem* rates. We can also include environmental taxes as a form of excise tax. There are two types of sales taxes: single-stage taxes like the retail sales tax and multistage taxes like the VAT. Sales taxes are general levies over a wide range of goods and services. Sometimes they are levied at a single rate or multiple rates. Trade taxes comprise customs or import duties, sometimes known as tariffs, and export duties. Chapter 18 discusses export duties.

QUANTITATIVE ASPECTS OF INDIRECT TAXATION IN DEVELOPING COUNTRIES

Our discussion here draws on the detailed work of Burgess and Stern (1993). Tanzi (1990) and Bird (1987) have also presented information on trends in taxation in developing countries. The quantitative features of indirect taxation in developing countries are as follows:

1. Taxes on goods and services were more important than income taxes in developing countries. Bird (1987) found that indirect taxes provided over half of central government revenues in 56 of 96 non-oil developing countries.

2. There was an increased tendency to general sales taxes in developing countries. Sales taxes were 2.5 percent of GDP and 13.8 percent of tax revenue, slightly higher than individual income taxes at 2.08 percent of GDP and 10.57 percent of tax revenues, respectively (Burgess and Stern 1993).

3. The VAT is the most important new addition to sales taxes in these countries.

4. Import duties are the most important single sources of revenue in developing countries. However, the level of import duties appears to be negatively related to per capita income, positively related to the degree of openness, and negatively related to the country's raising of revenue from domestic taxes on goods and services (Burgess and Stern 1993: 780).

5. Total trade taxes were 5.1 percent of GDP and 29.37 percent of tax revenue in developing countries. They are similar in importance to total income taxes which were 5.21 percent of GDP and 30.37 percent of tax revenue (Burgess and Stern 1993). High income developing countries have lower proportions of trade taxes than low income developing countries.

6. Export duties have declined in importance contributing 0.62 percent to GDP and 4.12 percent to tax revenue (Burgess and Stern 1993). The reasons for this are explained in chapter 18.

7. Excises are about as important as general sales taxes in developing countries, contributing 2.1 percent of GDP and 12.6 percent of tax revenue (Burgess and Stern 1993). The increased importance of excises is associated with the fall in customs revenue. Excises are also more simple to administer and have greater revenue buoyancy.

8. There was a correlation between rising per capita income, falling customs revenues, and the growing importance of income taxes in some countries.

Table 17.1 gives the structure of taxes on goods and services for a sample of developed and developing countries. The interesting feature of this data is the importance of taxes on international trade in the developing countries, and the very low emphasis on trade taxes in the developed countries. Some

TABLE 17.1: Indirect taxes as a percentage of total revenue in developed and developing countries

Developed Countries	Domestic Taxes on Goods and Services	General Sales or VAT	Taxes on International Trade
United States (1995)	3.96	–	1.37
Canada (1994)	18.94	13.58	2.32
Japan (1993)	14.4	6.9	1.24
Belgium (1994)	25.0	15.8	–
France (1995)	28.19	19.09	0.01
Germany (1993)	22.7	11.8	–
Italy (1994)	27.7	16.9	0.01
Spain (1993)	20.3	11.7	0.05
Sweden (1995)	29.3	18.7	0.84
Switzerland (1993)	15.7	12.2	6.68
United Kingdom (1995)	32.5	18.2	0.06
Developing Countries			
Botswana (1993)	2.79	2.69	16.14
Ghana (1993)	32.89	4.75	26.76
Zaire (1995)	18.68	5.14	32.64
India (1995)	30.45	0.08	20.43
Indonesia (1994)	33.69	26.42	6.09
Sri Lanka (1995)	52.73	26.74	17.89
Argentina (1992)	26.31	18.32	7.26
Grenada (1995)	41.60	35.00	16.77
St Kitts and Nevis (1994)	10.92	0.42	36.91
St Vincent (1995)	10.67	1.52	40.80

Source: IMF, *Government Finance Statistics Yearbook*, 1996.

Table 17.2: Structure of taxation: Jamaica (percentage of tax revenue)

Tax Group	1991/92	1992/93	1993/94	1994/95
Taxes on International Trade	13.4	14.0	12.5	10.5
Taxes on Goods and Services	44.6	44.0	48.4	47.7
Taxes on Income and Property	42.0	42.0	39.1	41.8
TOTAL	**100.0**	**100.0**	**100.0**	**100.0**

Source: Planning Institute of Jamaica, *Economic and Social Survey of Jamaica*, 1996.

developing countries like Indonesia, Sri Lanka, Argentina, and Grenada show the highest ratios of sales taxes to revenue for developing countries.

Howard (1992) gives a detailed treatment of the tax systems of Jamaica, Barbados, and Trinidad and Tobago before 1990. Our present analysis looks at indirect taxes in three Caribbean countries after 1990 which have been influenced considerably by the tax reforms of the 1990s. These changes are as follows:

1. Taxes on goods and services, especially domestic sales taxes such as the VAT, have become the most important source of revenue in Jamaica. This is shown in Table 17.2 where taxes on goods and services constituted 47.7 percent of revenue in Jamaica in fiscal 1994–95. Taxes on goods and services increased in significance in Barbados, from 32.9 percent in fiscal 1990–91 to 41.0 percent in fiscal 1995–96, and were just as important as income taxes by 1996 (Table 17.3).

Table 17.3: Structure of taxation: Barbados (percentage of tax revenue)

Tax Group	1990–91	1991–92	1993–94	1994–95	1995–96
Taxes on International Trade	23.7	18.2	16.3	17.2	16.4
Taxes on Goods and Services	32.9	35.7	40.3	41.4	41.4
Taxes on Income and Property	43.4	46.1	43.4	41.4	42.6
TOTAL	**100.0**	**100.0**	**100.0**	**100.0**	**100.0**

Source: Central Bank of Barbados, *Annual Statistical Digest*, 1996

2. The decline in import duties, which are the principal component of taxes on international trade, is also noteworthy. This trend is explained by the increased importance of VAT systems, as well as the tax reform movement with its emphasis on trade liberalization (see Tables 17.2, 17.3, and 17.4). Chapter 12 discussed the importance of trade liberalization.

3. Despite the changes in the structure of indirect taxation, the proportion of income taxes in total tax revenue has changed only slightly in Jamaica and Barbados. However, income tax revenue still constitutes the highest proportion of revenue in Trinidad and Tobago (Table 17.4). Trinidad and Tobago is, therefore, a special case. This is due to the high proportion of corporate taxes in the tax revenues of oil producing economies. The ratio of taxes on international trade is much lower in Trinidad and Tobago than in Jamaica and Barbados.

Table 17.4: Structure of taxation: Trinidad and Tobago (Percent of Tax Revenue)

Tax Group	1992	1993	1994	1995	1996
Oil Revenue	29.9	26.8	25.3	30.0	31.4
Non-Oil Revenue	70.1	73.2	74.7	70.0	68.8
(a) Income Tax	29.8	31.1	30.5	31.8	32.3
(b) Property Taxes	0.7	1.1	1.5	0.7	0.6
(c) Taxes on Goods and Services	23.6	24.2	24.2	23.4	22.5
(d) Taxes on International Trade	9.4	9.4	7.7	5.8	5.2
(e) Non-Tax Revenue	6.7	7.5	10.9	8.3	7.9
TOTAL	**100.0**	**100.0**	**100.0**	**100.0**	**100.0**

Source: Central Bank of Trinidad and Tobago, *Annual Economic Survey*, 1997

ISSUES IN INDIRECT TAXATION

The potential impact of taxes on goods and services has been compared with the impact of income taxation. Many of the observations noticed by Due (1977) are still relevant in evaluating indirect taxes today. Our discussion looks at the equity, efficiency, and stabilization features of indirect taxes. We also consider the arguments for levying indirect taxes at differential or uniform rates.

A central issue concerns the regressivity of indirect taxation. Most indirect taxes, especially when levied at uniform rates, tend to fall heavily on the poor. Suggestions have been made by Due (1977) and others that these taxes can be made progressive relative to consumption by imposing higher tax rates on luxuries than on essentials. It appears, however, that direct taxes can reach high concentrations of wealth more efficiently than indirect taxes.

Bird (1987) has commented that studies on the incidence of indirect taxes in developing countries show that though indirect tax systems are not as regressive as previously thought, there was still some regressivity at the bottom of the income scale. Wasylenko (1986) found that the incidence of Jamaica's indirect tax system was roughly proportional. See also McLure (1977) who held the view that indirect taxes were fairly burdensome on the poor.

The extensive literature suggests that direct taxes have a greater disincentive effect on savings and investment than indirect taxes. It is generally argued that the propensity to save is higher for middle income groups who pay higher levels of income taxes. The savings of these groups will be affected more by high income taxes, whereas indirect taxes are levied on consumption. This has led to supply-side theories for reducing high income tax rates.

Indirect taxes do not possess the built-in stabilization properties of direct taxation. The relative yield of indirect taxation may decline during recessions as a result of a reduction in demand for goods and services. Some governments in developing countries often levy increased indirect taxes on a shrinking revenue base as part of stabilization programmes very often recommended by the IMF.

Further, indirect taxes tend to be inflationary especially if the tax is levied early in the distribution process. The tax may tend to pyramid as businesses add profit markups at various stages of production and distribution. Pyramiding as well as cascading of single-stage indirect taxes may cause the final increase in price to the consumer to be much higher than the initial price increase caused by the tax (see Due 1977). Both the inflationary and revenue effects are likely to be greater if the tax is levied on an *ad valorem* basis.

The design of indirect tax structures in developing countries is an important topic discussed in the optimal taxation literature as well the tax reform literature of the 1980s. The first design issue concerns the level of tax rate to achieve an acceptable trade-off between raising revenue from indirect taxes and the principles of equity. The optimal tax theory recommends taxing goods with inelastic demands. If taxes are levied on a broad base of goods used by lower income groups, equity would be sacrificed. In developing countries, lack of information on various elasticities leads to considerable difficulty in balancing revenue and equity objectives. An optimal indirect tax structure may be impossible in developing countries. See chapter 14 for a discussion of optimal taxation.

The second concern is related to the use of indirect taxes to improve the efficiency of resource allocation. Indirect taxes have been used in developing countries to aid import substitution. This is done by imposing taxes that encourage the use of domestic resources, and at the same time, divert spending away from imports. The conflict here is between protection of domestic industry and efficient resource allocation. It is possible that lower taxation on domestic industry may shelter inefficient domestic producers thereby reducing economic efficiency. This point is discussed later when we examine arguments for import duties.

A third issue of tax design deals with differential versus uniform indirect tax rates. Cnossen (1984) puts a strong case against using rate differentials in a general sales tax to achieve distributional goals. He argues that any equity gains from differential tax rates are likely to be more than outweighed by the additional administrative costs incurred. This is a major issue in the design of VAT systems in developing countries. We argue later that it is important to avoid the use of multiple rates, in order to achieve simplicity and neutrality in the design of general sales tax systems.

IMPORT TAXES

This section briefly examines the rationale for import taxes in developing countries, and the concept of effective tariff protection. More elaborate analyses of the theory of tariffs can be found in textbooks on international trade. Tanzi (1991) has remarked that most textbooks on public finance ignore the importance of import duties in developing countries. A possible reason for this is that the ratio of import duties to GDP as well as total tax revenue is very low in the developed countries where most textbooks are written. However, import duties are critically important in the public finances of developing countries because of their contribution to government revenue, and the degree of protection they offer to domestic industry.

Customs duties or trade tariffs are levied on the value of imports. They are easy to collect and administer. They were the most important source of revenue during the colonial period in the Caribbean. However, their importance has declined as income taxes and other domestic sales taxes have become more important. Many developing countries have used customs duties to protect their local industries. For example, a tariff imposed on imported furniture can stimulate the production of local furniture because of reduced competition from abroad. The Caribbean countries have attempted to unify their tariff structures by the imposition of a common external tariff, so that some countries would not be at a disadvantage when trading with countries outside of the region.

Let us examine the infant industry argument for import duties. The rationale for the infant industry argument is that a country may have a potential comparative advantage in an industry if that industry is allowed to develop and attain economies of scale. Temporary protection is needed to allow the industry's competitive position to improve. Protection would be ensured by levying a tax on foreign competitors. Many developing countries have used the infant industry argument to justify extensive import substitution. This has resulted in overprotection of some industries

225

and has fostered economic inefficiency. Industries are sheltered from competition and lack the incentive to pursue further product elaboration and market expansion. High levels of protection have also led to overvalued exchange rates.

Import taxes have also been used to raise revenue. This is so particularly in low income developing countries where internal domestic tax systems are not well developed. Higher tariffs are placed on luxury items and lower tariffs on essentials. Car imports in many countries have been subject to high import taxes. These high valued goods contribute significantly to government revenue. Tariffs for revenue purposes, however, create a wedge between domestic and external prices and may distort the growth process.

The nominal tariff on imports does not give the true rate of protection. The effective tariff or effective rate of protection (ERP) measures the difference in protection on intermediate imports compared with the tariff on final goods. The protective effect of a tariff is larger the lower the import duty on the raw materials used in the production of the final product, and the higher the proportion of value added to output. Further, the greater the difference between the duty on the raw material and the duty on the final product, the higher the rate of effective tariff protection (see Corden 1971).

The ERP can be calculated using the formula:

$$ERP = \frac{t_j - a_y t_i}{1 - a_y}$$

where t_j = nominal rate of duty on final product (j)
t_i = nominal rate of duty on material input (i)
a_{ij} = share of input i in the cost of j.

The example below shows the calculation of the ERP. Let us assume that the nominal duty on raw material imports of wood is 5 percent. Wood imports account for 50 percent of the costs of finished wooden furniture which has a nominal duty of 20 percent. The ERP given by the 20 percent nominal tariff on wooden furniture is as follows:

t_j = 20 percent
t_i = 5 percent
a_{ij} = 50 percent
$(1-a_{ij})$ = 50 percent

Therefore,

$$ERP = \frac{0.20-(0.05)(0.5)}{0.5} \qquad = \textbf{35 percent}$$

The high 35 percent ERP is influenced by the large difference between the low nominal duty of 5 percent on wood imports and the 20 percent duty on finished furniture, as well as value added in final output. Suppose we lowered the nominal duty on finished wood furniture to 15 percent, then the ERP would be 25 percent, a much lower rate of effective protection.

Whitehall's (1984) study of effective protection in Barbados showed that in 1974 and 1980, effective protection was more than twice the nominal rate, largely as a result of high nominal tariffs on final goods. Effective protection on import substitution was much higher than protection on exports. Further, the weighted average of effective protection in manufacturing increased from 133 percent in 1974 to 226 percent in 1980. As we have discussed earlier, the objective of the trade liberalization principle was to reduce high levels of effective protection in the 1980s and 1990s.

EXCISE TAXES

An excise tax is a levy on a single commodity and can be applied on an *ad valorem* or per unit basis. *Ad valorem* taxation means that the tax is imposed on the quoted sales value as distinct from the quantity of the item. Governments prefer *ad valorem* duties because the amount of tax charged increases with inflation. There are various types of excises including sumptuary, service, and benefit excises as well as miscellaneous duties. Sumptuary excises are those imposed on liquor and cigarettes. Service excises include taxes on betting and gambling, airport departure taxes, and so forth. Benefit excises are based on the benefit principle and include taxes on motor vehicles, highway levies, environmental levies, and gasoline taxes. Stamp duties on documents are normally classified as miscellaneous excises (see Due 1977).

One rationale for the use of excises is that they yield large amounts of revenue, especially when levied on goods with inelastic demands. They are easy to collect and administer and provide limited opportunities for evasion (McCarten and Stotsky 1995). Care must be taken not to impose heavy excises on essential goods used by the poor. Some of these excises can be made progressive by levying heavier rates on luxuries and lowering rates on essential goods (see Cnossen 1990: 349). Sumptuary excises are imposed on goods such as cigarettes and liquor, which are considered morally objectionable. These excises are intended to internalize negative externalities generated by the consumer from the consumption of these goods. The demand for these goods are inelastic and their burden tends to be regressive on the poor. However, the health hazards associated with their consumption may be sufficiently disastrous to justify the imposition of heavy indirect taxes (see Cnossen 1990; McCarten and Stotsky 1995 for these views).

Excise taxes on motor fuel and motor cars use can be justified on two grounds. The first reason for taxing motor fuel relates to benefits and resource allocation. Motorists should also be charged for the benefit derived from using the roads. Second, these taxes are justified on the grounds that they control wastage in the use of petroleum resources, as well as internalize negative externalities such as motor vehicle pollution.

Excise taxes are also imposed on services and luxuries. These include taxes on travel, entertainment, betting as well as jewelry. These are justifiable on ability to pay criteria. Other miscellaneous excises include stamp duties on various documents such as mortgages and receipts.

Efficiency is an important consideration in the evaluation of the impact of excise taxes which can have an impact on the economy by reducing consumer welfare. They distort consumer preferences between various goods and services, since they are levied at differential rates. However, governments can use excises to discourage certain types of consumption, or to divert resources to different areas of the economy or to discourage wastage. Certain types of excises may have a beneficial impact on the economy. Excises can favour labour intensive goods over capital intensive goods. In this respect, they can help to promote small-scale industry which is more labour intensive. This last issue has been discussed by Cnossen (1990: 351).

Excises can take the form of specific levies to reduce environmental damage. Our comments on environmental taxes are based on previous work by Nellor (1995). The classic solution to negative ecological externalities is the Pigouvian tax discussed in chapter 2. Pigouvian taxes change the relative prices of activities thereby discouraging participation in the damaging activity. Pigouvian taxes are levied at specific rates per unit of the spillover. That is, the tax is equal to the marginal social cost of the activity. The major shortcoming of applying these taxes stem from the difficulty of measuring the extent of the damage. Environmental taxes are also difficult to administer and may not have the desired effect in reducing the damage.

Environmental taxes can also be levied indirectly on the use of productive inputs or consumption goods used in the production of the damaging activity. This type of excise is levied indirectly on the damage (Nellor 1995: 109). The rationale for taxing inputs arises from the high administrative costs of taxing the damage directly. The efficiency of indirect environmental taxation rests on the ability of policy makers to define a proportional relationship between the productive inputs and the final damage.

SINGLE-STAGE SALES TAXES

There is a tendency by most developing countries to move away from single-stage taxes to VAT systems. Our comments will therefore be brief and rely on the work of Due (1977). The retail sales tax is the most efficient of the single-stage taxes since it does not distort consumer choices by changing relative prices. This is not a feature of other single-stage taxes which are levied early in the distribution channel. Generally speaking, pre-retail sales taxes tend to cascade before they reach the final consumer. Cascading is a process whereby a single product is subject to more than one tax. As a result, the final increase in price to the consumer will be high relative to the initial tax.

The retail sales tax (RST) is applied to the selling price of the good. These taxes are widely used in the United States. The tax has a large base which is equivalent to the final value added of a wide range of goods. The large base encourages a low rate of tax. The main problems with the RST is the large number of retailers which can lead to substantial tax evasion. It is argued that retail sales taxes are collected from the weakest link in the distribution channel and, therefore, the revenue is not protected. Many retailers do not record their transactions by way of invoices. Further, in the underground economy where both legal and illegal transactions exist, tax evasion is at its highest level.

Single-stage taxes are also levied at the wholesale, import, and manufacturing levels. In the case of the wholesale tax, registration is required by all manufacturers and merchants selling at the wholesale stage. Due (1977) has outlined the problem of the wholesale tax. He maintains that firms doing both wholesale and retail business create administrative problems and can evade the tax. Further, retailers may integrate backwards to avoid price increases on the taxed commodity.

A sales tax at the manufacturing and import levels is sometimes known as a consumption tax. This was the form of single-stage tax used in Barbados before it adopted a VAT in 1997. The manufacturer or importer pays the tax. The tax can either be levied on imports net of import duties, or on imports plus import duty, which was the case in Barbados. This type of tax impacts early in the distribution channel. Due (1977) maintains that the manufacturing tax gives manufacturers the incentive to pursue forward integration, by undertaking wholesale and retail activities to free the cost of their business from the base of the tax. As discussed earlier, a consumption tax also leads to tax pyramiding. Further, the consumption tax is usually levied at differential rates thereby distorting production and consumption patterns. Howard (1992) discusses the single-stage sales tax system in Barbados and Jamaica in the 1980s. These systems were highly complex leading to tax evasion and administrative problems.

THE VALUE-ADDED TAX

How the VAT Works

The base of the VAT is gross receipts minus the purchase of intermediate and capital goods. The VAT is a tax on consumption. It is not a tax on businesses even though it is collected from businesses. The invoice/consumption type of VAT deducts all purchases including capital goods and services from the value of gross sales to determine value-added and tax liability. The income type VAT permits only the deduction of depreciation rather than the deduction of the full price of capital goods at the time of purchase (Lent, Casanegra and Guerard 1973). The invoice/consumption VAT is most widely used.

There are three basic methods of calculating the VAT. The first is the addition method which adds the different sources of value added such as wages, interest, and net profit. This method, though useful for the income type of VAT, is not preferred by most countries. Second, the subtraction method subtracts the cost of purchases, including capital goods from gross sales. The rate of VAT is applied to the difference. Third, the invoice method is the most favoured method. Under this method, there are three main steps in the collection of the VAT by a business.

1. The business computes its gross tax, known as output tax, by applying the tax rate to its total sales.
2. The business then deducts the VAT already paid on its purchases, an amount shown on the invoices provided by its suppliers. This

VAT on purchases is known as input tax.

3. In this way, the firm is given a credit for taxes already paid on its purchases. This credit reduces the tax liability computed on its total sales to an amount equal to a tax on its value added. Generally speaking, if input tax exceeds output tax the firm is given a refund.

Table 17.5 shows how the VAT is collected throughout the production and distribution stages. The total VAT paid to the government is $80.00, which is collected from the producer of raw materials ($10.00), the manufacturer ($10.00), the wholesaler ($40.00), and the retailer ($20.00). It should be noted that the total VAT of $80.00 is equivalent to the RST which is the output tax of the retailer in our example. Although we have not included mark-ups in our analysis, the VAT is charged on the cost of the good plus mark-up.

TABLE 17.5: VAT calculation through production stages (10% rate)

Credit Method	Producer of Raw Materials	Manufacturer	Wholesaler	Retailer	Total
1. Sales ($)	100	200	600	800	1,700
2. Output Tax 10% of (1)	10	20	60	80	170
3. Purchases ($)	0	100	200	600	900
4. Input Tax 10% of (3)	0	10	20	60	90
5. VAT ($) (2) minus (4)	10	10	40	20	80

Table 17.6 shows the application of the VAT to a single manufacturer when we assume zero-rating and exemptions. Zero-rating means that sales are exempted from tax, and the firm is also entitled to a credit for taxes already paid on its purchases, so that no element of VAT is included in the price of the final good. When a good or service is exempted, no VAT is charged on gross sales, but the business cannot claim a refund for taxes included in its purchases. Note that all zero-rated and exempt supplies must be identified on a typical tax return form, and they have to be deducted from gross sales. Zero-rated and not exempt supplies are deducted from purchases.

TABLE 17.6: Application of a 10% VAT with zero-rating and exemptions

Category	Manufacturer ($)
(1) Gross Sales	400.00
(2) Zero-rated and exempt supplies included in (1)	25.00
(3) Gross Sales excluding (2) Gross Sales excluding (2)	375.00
(4) Output tax (10% of line (3))	37.50
(5) Purchases	200.00
(6) Zero-rated supplies included in (5)	15.00
(7) Purchases excluding (6)	185.00
(8) Input tax (10% of line (7))	18.50
(9) VAT paid to Government (line (4) less (8))	19.00

Advantages and Limitations of the VAT

The VAT is a neutral tax especially when levied at a single rate. Neutrality means that the VAT will not distort relative prices, consumer choices, or distort economic decisions made in the private sector. This means that no businessman will have an unfair advantage over another as a result of the tax. Multiple rates reduce considerably the neutrality of the VAT.

Another advantage claimed for the VAT is that it is spread over a large number of businesses rather than targetting a particular group. As a result, the VAT "levels the playing field" for doing business. The VAT also reduces the possibility for evasion by the use of the invoice method which is an instrument for cross-checking transactions. Businesses become more careful in their accounting methods as a result of the VAT.

The VAT also contributes substantially to government revenue. This is partly due to its extension to a wide range of services such as telephone and electricity which have inelastic demands. Administrative efficiency is important in order to realize the full revenue potential of the VAT. The high revenue yield of the VAT also increases its ability to regulate consumer demand.

Public finance economists have identified a number of problems associated with the VAT. First, they argue that the VAT is regressive in the sense that a single-rate VAT would be a greater burden on the incomes of the poor than on the rich. This is because consumption becomes a smaller share of income as income rises. Lower income households would pay a larger share of their incomes in taxes.

Second, evasion of the VAT can be accomplished through understatement of sales. This depends, however, on high levels of collusion between traders. Some of these practices can be picked up by auditors. Traders may also collude in the black market to dispose of goods without invoices. Third, the VAT is a more complex tax than other sales taxes, and administrative problems grow with multiple rates and exemptions. Fourth, it is difficult to apply VAT to farmers, small shopkeepers, and small traders who keep no records. This means that the threshold must be set at a high enough level to reduce these problems.

Why should a country adopt a VAT when the RST at the same rate would yield the same amount of revenue? This question has been discussed by Tait (1988) who argues that a VAT is applied to a larger base including services thereby increasing its revenue yield. Further, the VAT provides a better audit trail than the RST because of the use of the invoice system. This enables auditors to check multiple transactions. On the other hand, the RST relies heavily on cash sales and is collected from a large number of heterogeneous retailers. The biggest advantage of the RST is that it is a simpler tax to administer than the VAT.

THE BARBADOS VAT

Rationale for a VAT in Barbados

We now discuss the Barbados VAT as an example of the operation of a VAT system in a developing country. The Barbados government's introduction of the VAT in 1997 stemmed from a philosophy of tax reform which stressed the promotion of economic efficiency, neutrality, and the maintenance of revenue capacity. This reform had started with the simplification of the income tax system in 1992 (see chapter 15). A broad-based indirect tax system was regarded as more efficient than a system with differential rates which is more difficult to administer.

Fiscal authorities in Barbados preferred the VAT because of the inefficiency of the existing consumption tax regime up to 1996. The consumption tax was imposed on imports and manufactured goods at rates ranging from 2 percent to 89 percent. This regime was characterized by a large number of different rates on a narrow selection of goods. Further, a stamp duty which was introduced at 2 percent in 1982 was increased gradually to 20 percent in 1996. The stamp duty was applied to most extra-regional imports.

The negative characteristics of the extended consumption tax and stamp duty regime before 1997 were as follows:

1. The multiple consumption tax rate system was too complicated. This feature interfered with compliance and administration of the system. Some goods were also subject to additional stamp duties and a surcharge.

2. The complicated system distorted prices and consumer choices, leading to inefficient resource allocation.

3. The system led to a drain in foreign reserves since the high prices forced consumers and itinerant merchants to seek cheaper prices in North American markets.

4. The base of the consumption tax system was too narrow. This meant that the taxation of services was too limited in an economy which can be described as a service economy. This caused revenue sacrifices and reduced the elasticity of indirect taxation in Barbados.

5. Cascading was the central element of the pre-VAT system. This meant that double and triple taxation of a single product significantly increased the final price to the consumer. In some cases, the price to the final consumer was three times the import cost of the good.

6. The pre-VAT system also had an anti-export bias since some exports of goods and services carried an element of consumption tax (see Bristow and Wurts 1992).

The VAT was not introduced to achieve a higher level of revenue than the previous consumption tax system. However, despite the argument for revenue neutrality, projections by government on the basis of a 15 percent VAT rate indicated that there would be a small shortfall in revenue yield. Eleven taxes were replaced by the VAT. These were the consumption tax, stamp duty on imports, luxury tax on goods, entertainment tax, hotel and restaurant tax, service tax on pleasure cruises, tax on quarriable minerals, the travel ticket tax, the airline business tax, tax on overseas telephone calls, and the surcharge on rental income.

Scope and Coverage of the VAT in Barbados

The VAT in Barbados is imposed on taxable supplies of goods and services by a registrant, and goods imported into Barbados. Taxable supplies include zero-rated supplies but do not include exempt supplies. A zero-rated supply is a taxable supply on which tax is levied at a zero tax rate. Exempt supplies are not subject to VAT.

The coverage of the VAT is also defined with reference to taxable persons. The VAT legislation distinguishes between a small supplier, whose sales are less than Bds$60,000 a year, and a large supplier whose sales are over Bds$60,000. This figure is described as the registration threshold. A small supplier is not required to register but is eligible to become a registrant.

The Barbados VAT is levied at a rate of 15 percent. The price of the good includes the amount of tax, although a registrant can state separately the amount of tax payable in respect of goods offered for sale. The general practice is that prices in the majority of retail establishments are VAT inclusive. The VAT is levied on the supply of accommodation of guest houses and hotels is 7.5 percent. Therefore, there are really three rates of VAT, namely, a zero rate on zero-rated supplies, 7.5 percent on hotel accommodation, and 15 percent on other supplies and imports.

The Barbados VAT utilizes the invoice system discussed earlier. The invoice system also allows for transactions where discounts are offered at the time of purchase of a good or service. When discounts are given because of the volume purchased or because of a mark-down on sales, VAT is levied on the discounted price. However, if a discount is given because of early payment on an invoice, the VAT is calculated on the original price on the invoice and not on the discounted value. This rule for early payment does not apply to public utilities. In such cases, the VAT is calculated on the discounted amount.

The comptroller of customs is responsible for the administration of the VAT. The powers of the comptroller are extensive, and he can make discretionary assessments of tax outstanding, penalties, and interest payable. The comptroller has the power to make assessments without being bound by any return or information made on behalf of a registrant. If a registrant is dissatisfied with the decisions of the comptroller, the registrant may appeal to a tribunal appointed by the minister of finance. The day-to-day administration of the VAT is carried out by a separate VAT unit.

Three important sectors of the economy are subject to zero-rating or exemption. Exports are zero-rated. This means that materials bought by the exporter are subject to a tax refund, and no output tax is charged on the sale of exports. This measure was designed to assist exporters who previously had to pay consumption tax on certain imported materials. It was also implemented to increase Barbados' international competitiveness in a liberalized trade system.

Certain agricultural supplies are zero-rated. These include live animals, birds, bees, and fish used as a food for human consumption. Additionally, fertilizers, insecticides, and pesticides are zero-rated. This continues the policy of granting tax concessions to the agricultural sector. However, food supplies made to supermarkets and other retail outlets are subject to VAT. The government also zero-rated a basket of basic food items sold in retail outlets.

Financial services are exempt. This means that financial institutions need not register under the VAT system since they cannot charge VAT on their exempt sales of financial services. Financial institutions must, however, pay VAT on their purchases. The implication of this measure is that financial institutions can pass on input taxes to consumers in terms of higher service charges. This applies to legal fees charged to financial institutions, rents, and other capital items.

VAT IMPLEMENTATION EXPERIENCES IN THE CARIBBEAN

It is worthwhile comparing the VAT implementation experiences of Barbados, Jamaica, and Trinidad and Tobago. Our comparisons centre around the following issues: stock-in-trade, zero-ratings and exemption, publicity, the public response to the tax-pricing policies, inflation, and administrative problems of businesses. It should be noted that the VAT was introduced in Trinidad and Tobago in 1990 and the General Consumption Tax (GCT) was implemented in Jamaica in 1991.

One of the most important issues in the implementation phase of these countries was the treatment of stock-in-trade. An imposition of a VAT on stock-in-trade leads to double taxation and a sharp rise in prices immediately after implementation. Jamaica was the only country to grant a stock credit to businessmen. This led to high budgetary costs which were swollen by inflation. The policy of the governments of Barbados and Trinidad and Tobago not to give stock credit was a prudent budgetary decision, even though consumers had to bear the temporary consequential increase in prices.

Of the three countries studied, Jamaica showed the largest number of zero-ratings and exemptions. There existed in Jamaica on implementation day 17 groups of zero-rated items. Barbados, on the other hand, had a much lower level of zero-ratings, with no exemptions or zero-rating of foodstuffs during the first nine months. Zero-rating was also restricted in Trinidad and Tobago and was limited to unprocessed food, a few basic processed food such as flour, bread, milk, and margarine, and specified public utilities and services. However, Jamaica has since reduced the level of zero-ratings and exemptions. The argument is that too high a level of zero-rating undermine the revenue productivity of VAT and reduces its overall efficiency.

In all three countries, there was a fairly intense publicity programme to acquaint firms and the public with the nature of the tax. In Jamaica, the long delay made the public very aware of the tax. In all three countries, there was an advertisement blitz in the media as soon as implementation date was announced.

The public response to the VAT was perhaps more favourable in Jamaica and Trinidad and Tobago than in Barbados. There are a number of reasons for this. First, in Jamaica, the high level of zero-ratings and exemptions as well as stock credit to businessmen by government, restrained the increase in prices and reduced them in some instances. In Trinidad and Tobago, some basic foodstuffs were zero-rated, thereby avoiding public outcry on the price of food. However, according to Due and Greaney (1991), much of the complaint in Trinidad and Tobago was against the 15 percent rate which was regarded as too high. The initial outcry in Barbados against the high price of food diminished gradually during the first few months of implementation.

In all three countries, there was some concern about whether prices should be VAT inclusive or exclusive. In Barbados and Trinidad and Tobago, policy makers required that prices should be VAT inclusive. However, on implementation day many retail outlets in the three countries were showing VAT exclusive prices, but were given some time to shift to VAT inclusive prices. In Trinidad and Tobago, some members of the public showed a preference for VAT exclusive prices. The reason for this was that such a price enabled them to monitor changes in the price of commodities more readily than a VAT inclusive price would have done (see VAT Administrative Centre 1991). In Jamaica many supermarkets and retailers found problems in programming computers to show the VAT component of the price on implementation day.

Another area of concern about the implementation of VAT in these countries was the general impact of the tax on the level of inflation. In every day discussion in Barbados concern was expressed that there was considerable price gouging by businesses before and after the VAT was introduced. Some businessmen increased their mark-ups to retain pre-VAT profit levels. The prices of locally produced food, as well as Caribbean Community (CARICOM) food imports, increased by 15 percent in most cases. The 15 percent rate, however, led to a fall in the price of a wide range of manufactured goods in Barbados.

In the three countries studied, there were problems for businesses of an administrative nature which are too numerous to discuss in detail. These included late filing of returns by some businesses who found difficulty with understanding the returns; late receipt of registration certificates by businesses; compliance costs and various other problems which required judgements by the VAT implementation departments.

COLOMBIA'S EXPERIENCE WITH THE VAT

Colombia's experience with the VAT provides significant lessons for developing countries contemplating the implementation of a VAT. My review of Colombia's experience is informed by the work of Shome (1995b) and Perry and Orozco de Trina (1990). This review outlines chronologically the main changes in the VAT system, and offers an evaluation of this experience.

According to Shome, Colombia was one of the first Latin American countries to adopt a VAT in 1965. The VAT was a basic sales tax at the manufacturing stage. Differential rates were established from the start. The basic rate was 3 percent and other rates were 5 percent, 8 percent, and 10 percent (Perry and Orozco de Trina 1990). Reforms were introduced in 1971, 1974, 1983, 1986, 1990, and 1992. It is appropriate to comment briefly on the content of these reforms.

The reforms of 1971 and 1974 increased the VAT rates and clarified the credit principle of the VAT. In 1971 the basic rate rose to 4 percent and other rates were increased to 10 percent, 15 percent, and 25 percent. In 1974, a refund system was also introduced for taxes paid by manufacturers of zero-rated goods and by exporters of manufactured goods. The result of the reforms of the 1970s led to an excessive list of zero ratings and greater overall complexity of the VAT (see Perry and Orozco de Trina 1990: 181–82).

The VAT reforms of the 1980s broadened the base of the VAT and unified some of the rates. In 1983, the tax was extended to the distributive trades. New services such as hotels, rentals of goods and furniture, financial leasing, and computing services were included in the base. Perry and Orozco de Trina (1990: 182) assert that despite the attempts to improve the VAT, serious administrative problems characterized the VAT system in the 1980s. Differential rates and delays in processing refunds, as well as a long list of zero-rated articles placed a heavy burden on the VAT administration. The distinction between processed and unprocessed food also created administrative problems. The increase in the number of small retailers, as a result of the inclusion of retail services in the VAT base, also created problems for tax administrators.

In 1990, the general rate increased from 10 percent to 12 percent. However, serious defects characterized the system. Exemptions still remained for a number of personal services, mining, electricity, and water. In 1992, the general rate rose to 14 percent. Complete credit for taxes paid on purchases of capital goods was also introduced in 1992, as a credit against the income tax rather than against the VAT paid on sales. The VAT rate was also widened to include more services, and rates of 35 percent to 45 percent were established for luxuries (see Shome 1995b: 4).

Colombia's experience with the VAT demonstrated a lengthy process of trial and error learning. What are the lessons? The first lesson is that differential rates are cumbersome and difficult to administer. The attempt to deal with regressivity with the use of substantial rate differentiation is counterproductive and inefficient. Second, the Colombian experience showed the revenue losses and administrative burden of high levels of zero-ratings and exemptions. Third, developing countries should also learn that a broad VAT base is important for a successful VAT. A broad base not only ensures revenue maintenance, but also a lower VAT rate can be adopted, rather than changing the rates frequently as practised by the Colombian authorities. However, because Colombia established the VAT much earlier than other developing countries, the Colombian government did not benefit from the cumulative experiences of other countries with the VAT. These experiences are now available to other countries planning the implementation of the VAT.

VAT Lessons from Developing Countries

The introduction of the VAT has led to a major change in tax policy in developing countries. We have discussed the VAT experiences of some Caribbean countries and Colombia. However, no attempt is made in this section to discuss the VAT experiences of other developing countries. It is more meaningful to analyse other important lessons learnt from these experiences. The discussion is informed by the work of Gillis, Shoup and Sicat (1990). We are interested in the impact of the VAT on revenue, prices, tax administration, and income distribution.

Gillis, Shoup and Sicat (1990) indicate that there are certain consensus issues in evaluating the impact of the VAT. First, the VAT has the reputation of being a "money machine". Most studies have shown that revenues from the VAT increased substantively after its implementation. The inclusion of services in the base of the VAT is an important factor augmenting revenues. The revenue impact varies with the degree of zero-ratings and exemptions.

Second, the view that the VAT may generate inflation seems not to be supported by the evidence. Tait (1990) examined changes in prices for 35 countries including developed and developing countries and found that in most countries the VAT had little or no effect on prices. Although the VAT may lead to a once-and-for-all increase in the price level, inflation may be due to other factors in the economy.

Third, the analysis of Latin America indicates that tax evasion may be a major problem in administering the VAT (see IDB 1996). This means that a high level of resources must be invested in VAT administration to curb tax evasion. Administrative tax reform is discussed in chapter 20.

Fourth, there is no firm consensus on a number of VAT issues. Gillis et al (1990) have shown that there is no consensus on the treatment of farmers. Further, there is no definitive analysis on the impact of the VAT on the income distribution and due to the fact that the VAT is so comprehensive in its scope, it is difficult to measure its efficiency and equity. One prevailing view discussed earlier is that the VAT is a regressive tax. However, this is a feature of other indirect taxes.

SUMMARY

Indirect taxation is an important instrument of fiscal policy in developing countries which in recent years have shown a preference for sales taxation especially the VAT. Import taxes, though still important, have declined in terms of their contribution to tax revenues in developing countries.

Our analysis concentrated heavily on the VAT. It was shown that the VAT has a number of advantages in terms of its significant contribution to revenue and levelling the playing field for doing business. Tax evasion and other administrative problems were characteristic of the VAT. These problems will be discussed in chapter 20.

Chapter Eighteen

Taxation of Productive Sectors in Developing Countries

Most textbooks on public sector economics place considerable emphasis on the well-known broad-based taxes such as personal income, corporation, sales, property, and payroll taxes. However, there is a growing literature on various taxes and levies imposed on productive sectors in developing countries. Taxes on exports were important in the 1970s but have declined as revenue earners in many developing countries. Other taxes on mineral rents, agricultural land, tourism, and the financial sector have a significant influence on resource allocation. We need to consider the traditional arguments and main issues involved in taxes on productive sectors in developing countries. The presentation will focus on the incidence and efficiency of these forms of taxation, as well as their impact on government revenues. References will be made to specific developing countries.

EXPORT TAXES

Rationale for Export Taxes

Tanzi (1991) has outlined a number of traditional arguments to explain why countries impose export taxes. An export tax can be levied to keep down the internal price of the product. This is equivalent to an implicit subsidy to consumption of the product at home. He cites the case of rice in Thailand and meat in Argentina. In this case, an export tax can redistribute income to low income consumers.

An export tax can also be used to stimulate local production, or exports of more highly processed products which use domestic raw materials as inputs. This approach encourages local manufacturing. Export taxes can also be used to promote better crops especially when several grades are produced. This is achieved by taxing lower grades at higher rates than high quality grades.

Other reasons for export taxes include sterilizing windfall gains as a result of high prices. Extracting the surplus from the agricultural sector for use in capital formation is also a rationale for export taxation. In some countries, export taxes are considered as advanced payments for income taxes, or as substitutes for land taxes. The above arguments had some justification in the 1970s for countries at earlier stages of development.

Goode (1984) shows that export taxes constituted a substantial proportion of revenue in many developing countries in the 1970s. Export duties as a percentage of revenue for 31 developing countries ranged from an average of 5 percent for the Philippines to 28 percent for Ghana. Goode, however, predicted that these taxes would decline in importance.

Our analysis in Table 18.1 supports Goode's prediction. We compared data for 1992 to 1994 with Goode's data for 1973–79. The analysis shows

TABLE 18.1: Exports duties as percentage of total revenue in selected developing countries

Country	Average 1973–79	1992 (%)	1993 (%)	1994 (%)
Ghana	28	6.1	5.4	–
El Salvador	26	0.5	0.1	0.003
Zaire	25	5.0	9.4	9.4
Rwanda	23	4.5	–	–
Sri Lanka	19	1.0	0.05	–
Malaysia	16	4.0	3.7	2.5
Guatemala	15	0.01	–	–
Guyana	14	n.a.	n.a.	n.a.
Mauritius	12	3.6	3.5	2.8
Bolivia	11	–	–	–
Dominican Republic	11	0.01	–	–
Colombia	10	–	–	–

Sources: For years 1973–79, see R. Goode, *Government Finance in Developing Countries* (Washington DC: The Brookings Institution, 1984); IMF, *Government Finance Statistics Yearbook*, vol. 19, 1995.

a sharp decline in the ratio of export taxes to total revenue in all developing countries surveyed. Export taxes are most important in Ghana and Zaire. No export taxes were reported for Bolivia and Colombia after 1992, and they disappeared in Guatemala after 1993. Export taxes in Malaysia are mainly on petroleum exports, while for Sri Lanka, tea is the main export.

There are two main reasons for the decline of export taxation in the 1990s. First, many of these countries have sought to diversify their economies away from staple exports and have pursued structural adjustment programmes to achieve this goal. Second, developing countries now place more reliance on internal taxes such as the VAT. As a result of these trends, the arguments advanced for export taxes by Tanzi (1991) and others have less importance in the calculus of decision making by most governments. The emphasis on the earning of foreign exchange in the pursuit of balance of payments equilibrium outweighs the arguments for taxing exports in developing countries.

Incidence of Export Taxes

The incidence of export taxes has been analysed in relation to the degree of monopoly power exercised by the export producers, the various demand and supply elasticities of the export product, and the relative size and bargaining power of the country in the world economy. These conditions have been analysed previously by Goode (1984), Tanzi (1991), Sanchez-Ugarte and Modi (1990), and Goode, Lent and Ojha (1966).

An export tax may be shifted to foreign consumers if a country has a monopoly or if its production is a large part of world output. If the price elasticity of supply of the foreign producers is low, the more the tax will be shifted to foreign consumers. Similarly, if the elasticity of demand by foreign consumers is high, the more difficult it is to shift the export tax to foreigners. Even though a country may supply a large part of the world market, price increases resulting from export taxes may stimulate production by producers in other countries.

A country's size also determines the incidence of export taxes. A small country with no influence on world prices is unable to shift export taxes to the rest of the world. Tanzi (1976) showed how the burden of heavy taxation of Haiti's coffee exports in the 1970s fell on the domestic economy.

TOURISM TAXATION

Main Issues in Taxing Tourism

Tourism taxation is not given much attention in the public finance literature. I am not aware of any published studies examining quantitatively the incidence and efficiency of tourism taxes. An article by Bird (1992) is a lucid analysis of the rationale for taxing tourism, as well as the relative merits of various types of tourism taxes. A study by the Caribbean Tourism Organization (1996) also provides a survey of tourism taxes in the Caribbean.

One reason for the difficulty of analysing the incidence of tourism taxation is a result of the heterogeneous character of the tourism industry. Taxes on the hotel sector are easy to identify for statistical purposes, but other taxes on ancillary tourist services cannot be separated from tax revenues collected from other consumers in the economy.

Second, the tourism industry in most developing countries benefits from a wide range of tax incentives, making the net incidence of taxes on tourists and businesses difficult to determine. Most incentives take the form of relief from import duties and profit taxes. These include exemptions up to 15 years in Jamaica and St Lucia.

It is also difficult to determine the efficiency costs of tourism taxes, that is, the impact of taxes on resource allocation. It has been suggested that tax incentives to promote tourism investment are inefficient. A study sponsored by the Organization of American States and the Caribbean Tourism Organization (1990) found that there was no discernible link between the level of incentives and the increase in hotel investment measured by available room capacity. Incentives were more useful in attracting local investors. International investors were much less swayed by fiscal incentives alone. The Caribbean Tourism Organization study (1996), while recognizing the above arguments, still recommended that incentives should be oriented towards lowering input costs such as lower import duties on food and beverages, lower property taxes, and tax credits for training.

I do not support the view of Bird (1992) that subsidizing private investment in tourism is counterproductive. One must also examine the foreign exchange, employment and output benefits of such investment. Tourism certainly contributes to economic growth. Some level of subsidization is required to maintain international price competitiveness. However, the nature of the incentives must change to decrease the emphasis on new construction and reward refurbishing, training, marketing, and employment generation. McIntyre, Arthur and Charles (1993) have

TABLE 18.2: Hotel Room Tax for Caribbean Countries in 1994

Country	Room Tax Rate %	Total Revenue (US$ million)
Aruba	5	8.0
Bahamas	4	6.1
Barbados*	5	8.1
Jamaica	GCT 5.9	10.0
St Lucia**	8	4.1

*Barbados adopted a 7.5 percent VAT on hotel rooms in 1997.
**For 1993.
GCT is the General Consumption Tax.

Source: Caribbean Tourism Organization, *Caribbean Tourism Sector Taxation*, January 1996. (Prepared by Deloitte and Touch)

TABLE 18.3: Departure Tax for Caribbean Countries in 1994

Country	Departure Tax Rates US$	Total Revenue US$m
Aruba	12.50 (Through September) 20.00 (Thereafter)	5.8
Bahamas	15.00 (Air and Sea)	51.0
Barbados*	12.50 (Air) 6.00 (Sea)	6.9
Jamaica	14.28 (Air) 10.00 (Sea)	n.a.
St Lucia**	10.00 (Air) 4.00 (Sea)	5.1

*Barbados replaced these taxes by a 15 percent VAT in 1997.
**For 1993.

Source: As for Table 18.2

proposed that 90 percent of profits should be exempted rather than 100 percent. This may be one way of decreasing slightly the level of subsidization, rather than completely eliminating subsidies.

Nature of Tourism Taxes

Taxes on tourism comprise general sales taxes such as VAT, import duties, corporation, and property tax. Other levies include hotel room occupancy tax, departure taxes and, in some countries, casino taxes. According to the Caribbean Tourism Organization study (1996), occupancy and departure taxes, as well as taxes on cruise ship passengers, are common in the Caribbean. Property taxes on hotel real estate are a major source of revenue in the Bahamas. Bird (1992) contends that the hotel accommodation tax is the most important tourist tax since it is easily identifiable as a source of revenue.

Tables 18.2 and 18.3 provide estimates of revenue collected from room occupancy and departure taxes in five Caribbean territories. These taxes, except in the case of the Bahamas departure tax, are small in relation to total tax revenues in these countries. It is argued that given the high levels of tax incentives in Caribbean tourism, duty-free spending, and low property taxes with the exception of the Bahamas, it is entirely possible that the effective tax rate on tourism is negative.

LAND TAXATION

Reasons for Taxing Agricultural Land

The two leading arguments advanced to support the taxation of agricultural land in the past is that such taxation raises productivity in the agricultural sector, as well as transfers resources from agriculture to industry. These views have been discussed by public finance economists including Goode (1984), Bird (1974) and Skinner (1991). Our analysis reconsiders these arguments noting particularly the critique by Skinner (1991).

It was sometimes believed that a tax on agricultural land would induce farmers to improve the productivity of their land or sell unproductive land to small farmers. This thesis has been applied to Japan in the nineteenth century where heavy taxation on the gross income of land forced farmers to work harder and more efficiently. The weakness of this thesis is that other factors including the growth of markets and land reform may have induced improvements in agriculture (Skinner 1991). Further, heavy taxation of agricultural land lowers land values and may have an opposite effect on work effort.

The second argument is that agricultural taxation transfers surplus food, labour, and capital to the non-agricultural sector. This role is emphasized in the work of Lewis (1955) on the surplus labour economy. Lewis maintained that the continuous growth of the capitalist sector required heavy taxation of agriculture in order to feed the non-farmers. Agricultural taxation was also required to accelerate capital formation in the capitalist sector. These arguments obviously applied to economies at early stages of development. As an economy grows, other sources of finance become more important. These include foreign borrowing, taxation of other sectors as well as domestic borrowing. In some developing economies, agriculture is no longer the largest sector and therefore cannot provide a substantial source of taxation for economic development. If governments want to maximize foreign exchange from agriculture, heavy taxation of agricultural land clearly becomes counterproductive and should not be used to attain development goals. Further, land value taxes produce little revenue and are costly to administer (Strasma et al. 1990).

Methods and Incidence of Land Taxation

Bird (1974) has identified four methods of assessing taxes on agricultural land: (1) an *in rem* tax based on land area; (2) a tax based on the gross or net income from land; (3) a tax based on rental value; and (4) betterment levies on increments in land values. Economists also distinguish between a tax based on the capital value of the land and improvements, and a site value tax based on land value only. We now discuss the various merits and demerits of these methods in developing countries.

A tax on land area is usually easy to administer, and is levied at a uniform rate according to the area of the farm or each taxpayer's landholdings, without regard to the capacity of the land to produce income (Bird 1974). Despite the administrative advantage of this tax, it is a limited way to raise revenue for the central government (Skinner 1991). It may be more suitable to finance local government.

Taxes on gross or net income from production have also been utilized in some countries. The tax imposed on gross income from the harvest is known as a tithe. Generally speaking, it is difficult to assess agricultural income since many farmers keep no records. In many countries, including Barbados, net income from agriculture is included in assessable income for income tax purposes.

The method mostly used for assessing agricultural land taxes is taxation of rental value. Rental value is based on the view that rent for any given parcel of land is determined by the excess of its yield over the yield on marginal or poor quality land. The rental value can be expressed as a rate of payment for the use of land or as the capital value of the land. Land taxes are usually imposed on the capital value of the land which is a notional value determined by assessors (Bird 1974). In many cases, the land tax is imposed on the site value which is equivalent to the capital value minus improvements. In many countries, the site value of agricultural land is taxed at a preferential rate compared with the general property tax on improved capital value.

The biggest problem of the capital value tax is the administrative difficulty of determining market value. As a result, some economists such as Holland and Follain (1990) have recommended site value taxation as a more efficient means of taxing land. For a long period, Jamaica used a site value tax which continued at progressive rates after the reform of 1986. However, a flat site value tax is more efficient than a progressive tax, which may lead to artificial divisions of ownership among family members to reduce the rate base of the tax (Goode 1984). The main weakness of the site value tax is that it narrows the tax base and, therefore, requires a higher rate to raise the same revenue (see Stotsky and Yucelik 1995).

Another method of taxing land is through betterment levies. These are equivalent to capital gains taxes on increments in land values. Sometimes betterment levies may be earmarked for specific projects benefiting taxpayers (Bird 1974). One variation of the betterment levy is the valorization tax that was applied in Colombia. This tax was used by municipalities to recoup the cost of municipal projects. The levy contributed significantly to the improvement of infrastructural projects in Colombia (see Stotsky and Yucelik 1995: 187).

The valorization tax in Colombia has been regarded as a pure form of earmarking. The reasons for this are that there is substantial overlap of taxpayers and beneficiaries, the use of benefit-cost considerations, and the strong link in the areas of valorization, revenue and expenditure. Further, valorization revenues follow expenditures, whereas in most earmarking schemes, revenue drives levels of expenditures. These points are made by McCleary (1991: 93).

The valorization tax in Colombia has certain drawbacks. McCleary (1991: 94) suggests three problems. First, collections fall short of 100 percent partly because of cost overruns, generous exemptions, and generous accommodation for the poor with liquidity problems. Second, some beneficiaries fall outside the zone allocated for the tax, and taxpayers within the zone are unwilling to bear an additional tax burden. Third, administrative deficiencies exist in the implementation and planning of projects, leading to an unstable growth of revenue.

Economic theory informs us that if agricultural land is fixed in supply in a perfectly competitive market, the tax will be borne by the landowner. We have mentioned in chapter 16 that this case is even stronger if the tax is capitalized. The tax reduces the capital value of agricultural land at the time of its imposition. As a result, the current landowner bears the full burden since future buyers of the agricultural land will pay only the reduced capital value. A general conclusion is that high land taxes reduce the capital value of agricultural land as well as the rate of return to investment in land. The implications of this analysis for small Caribbean economies is that heavy taxes on agricultural land may not spur improvements, but may induce farmers to sell their land, thereby encouraging land speculation, and the conversion of land into non-agricultural uses such as commercial real estate.

Stotsky and Yucelik (1995: 187) maintain that effective implementation of land taxes requires information on all property including the physical size, area, ownership, land value, and improvements. This requires a cadastral survey. A cadastre is an official record of the location, size, and ownership of each parcel of land as well as the value of land. A good cadastre is important for efficient land tax administration. In the case of uniform property, a block valuation may apply to all property within a block.

TAXING THE FINANCIAL SECTOR

Financial sector taxation is not usually discussed in public finance textbooks. Taxation of the financial sector comprises both explicit and implicit taxes. Explicit taxes include corporation taxes, taxes on loans, interest income, and taxes on assets. In many countries, the financial sector is exempt from VAT on financial services. This means that even though the financial sector cannot charge VAT on financial services, the sector still has to pay VAT on purchases (see Stotsky (1995) for a discussion of explicit taxes on financial institutions). In Barbados, for example, explicit taxes include a 12.5 percent withholding tax on deposit interest and a tax on commercial bank assets. In the financial sector, it is difficult to determine the incidence and efficiency of this wide range of taxes on the users of financial services.

Implicit taxes are a prominent feature of government policy towards commercial banks. They consist of reserve requirements, interest rate ceilings, and lending targets at below market rates. They are regarded as instruments of financial repression, which exists when government taxes and other restrictions on financial transactions reduce the growth of the financial sector relative to the non-financial sector. Interest rate ceilings and reserve requirements restrict the flow of resources to the private sector and divert funds to the public sector (Fry 1988). Even though the effective rate of tax of such instruments is difficult to determine, these taxes constitute an important source of government revenue.

Chamley (1991) has attempted to measure the efficiency costs of implicit taxes. He identifies different types of efficiency in the taxation of financial assets in developing countries. The first is the reduction of the level of financial assets in the banking system and a diversion of these assets to foreign financial markets and the informal sector. Second, these taxes distort the allocation of available assets and reinforce existing imperfections in credit markets. Third, implicit taxes reduce the level of savings and the intertemporal allocation of resources.

Chamley attempts to measure the efficiency costs of implicit taxes using partial equilibrium analysis. He found that efficiency costs are higher when the inflation rate is high. The limitation of Chamley's analysis is that the large number of variables affected by financial repression would necessitate a general equilibrium analysis.

Proponents of financial liberalization have argued that it is necessary to reduce the level of implicit taxes, or remove them altogether to improve the efficiency of the financial system. There is a vast literature on financial liberalization (see, for example, Williams 1996). However, Stiglitz (1994) has argued that market failure necessitates government intervention in financial markets, and governments in developing countries should tread cautiously in their attempts to liberalize regulated banking systems.

TAXATION OF THE MINERAL SECTOR

Mineral Rents and Taxation

According to Palmer (1980), the central problem of mineral tax policy in developing countries is that, in the context of high risks, the government attempts to ensure a high tax share from mineral rents while guaranteeing a favourable return to the investor. Mineral taxation involves the assessment of the economic rent of mineral resources, and the appropriate rate of tax to be levied on the investor (Garnaut and Cluneis-Ross 1983).

The mineral rent of a resource is the excess profits after deducting the costs of production that corresponds to the minimum returns to capital to induce investment into new projects. This minimum return can be regarded as the supply price of investment. The risks involved in mining determines the supply price of investment. These risks include geological risks arising from exploration uncertainty, sovereign risks which stem from uncertainty over future treatment by the State, and commercial risks related to construction lags, market availability, and so forth. Monopoly rents may also arise because of exclusive access to the resource. The existence of these various risks requires that investors be compensated with a risk premium in terms of additional profit to undertake the investment. If the supply price of investment is low, the greater the resource rents available for taxation (Palmer 1980; Garnaut and Cluneis-Ross 1983).

Types of Taxes on Mineral Rents

The efficiency of taxation on mineral rents can be judged by a number of criteria. First, the tax should be neutral to avoid distortions in patterns of production and consumption. Second, the tax should reduce investor risks. Third, the tax should capture a high share of resource rents for the government. Fourth, tax revenues should be predictable over the life of the project. Some taxes are more efficient than others in achieving these objectives.

Garnaut and Cluneis-Ross (1983) identify six basic forms of taxation on the mineral sector. These are as follows:

1. Fixed Fee (FF)
2. Specific or *Ad Valorem* Duty (SAVD)
3. Higher Rates of Proportional Income Tax (HRIT)
4. Progressive Rent Tax (PRT)
5. Resource Rent Tax (RRT)
6. Brown Tax (BT).

The FF is a lump sum payable by the investor after obtaining mining rights. SAVD is a specific tax on output and includes royalties and various types of levies. The Jamaican bauxite levy of 1974 falls into this category. According to Goode (1984), specific levies and taxes are easier to apply than ad valorem ones, which require the verification of prices. Further, *ad valorem* duties fluctuate with prices and may be unstable over time. HRIT and PRT are corporation taxes and other taxes on income. Corporation tax is a prominent method of taxing the petroleum industry in Trinidad and Tobago.

The RRT and the BT are more controversial proposals for taxing mineral rents than the other methods mentioned above. These taxes were originally proposed to deal with the risks faced by investors. The RRT was proposed by Garnaut and Cluneis-Ross (1975). It constitutes a profits tax that is collected after a certain threshold internal rate of return is realized on cash flow. "There is a tax-free period until the threshold return has been earned, with a high proportional tax rate being applied to all net cash flows in excess of this return" (Palmer 1980: 527). Garnaut and Cluneis-Ross (1983) note that the RRT has less distortionary effects on investment than the SAVD, the PRT, and the HRIT, to the extent that the RRT taxes only positive net present values. However, the RRT delays the receipt of government revenue and, therefore, is an increased risk to the government. Palmer (1980) argues that the RRT is not likely to be politically acceptable in developing countries because of the extended tax-free period. A version of the RRT was adopted for Papua New Guinea (Goode 1984).

The BT is a term coined by Garnaut and Cluneis-Ross (1983) to describe a tax proposed by E. Cary Brown (1948). Under this tax, "the authorities would tax all cash flows generated by the project at a constant proportional rate collecting positive taxes in years in which there are positive net cash flows and paying subsidies (negative) taxes in years in which net cash flows are negative" (Garnaut and Cluneis-Ross 1983: 100). This would be a completely neutral tax but would incur a possible financial loss to the government.[1]

Both the RRT and BT proposals are high-risk taxes for the government. The author is not aware of any widespread application of these taxes. It is arguable that in countries where large MNCs dominate the mining industry, most governments should reject the RRT and BT as being antidevelopmental. The RRT and BT reinforce the neoclassical theory based on maximizing the net profit of the mining firm at the expense of the developing country.

Our critique of the literature on mineral taxation leans heavily on Francis (1981). I agree with Francis that the neoclassical approach focuses heavily on the negative effects of taxation for the mining firm. Both profit taxes and output royalties are regarded as distortionary taxes which reduce rates of return and distort the time path of production. The neoclassical literature stresses that output royalties are less desirable than profit taxes, because royalties force firms to shift the pattern of their preferred output from present to future. This is because a royalty per unit of output leads to a reduction in the rate of extraction. Further, Jenkins (1990) argues that a flat rate royalty on production leads to bypassing high-cost ores in production that would have been utilized in the absence of a tax. Francis cites Gillis and McLure (1975) among the proponents of this view. This literature has scant regard for the needs of developing countries to maximize their foreign exchange through appropriate taxation of the MNCs.

Francis (1981) examines the low level of taxation on bauxite firms in Jamaica before the imposition of the bauxite levy in 1974. This levy of 7.5 percent of the realized price of alumina was widely criticized as a punitive tax on mining companies which reduced the competitiveness of Jamaican bauxite. However, the imposition of the levy must be regarded as a reaction to years of exploitation of the Jamaican economy by mining firms (Girvan 1984). Further, it must be realized that vertical integration helps the MNC to shift taxable income between countries by transfer pricing. It is therefore more difficult to use income taxes to appropriate mineral rents. The output royalty is, therefore, a more sensible choice in small open economies.

SUMMARY

This study has surveyed the main issues relating to the taxation of productive resources in developing countries. These economies have diminished the importance of taxes on exports and agricultural land as instruments of development. In the past, these taxes were used mainly to mobilize the surplus from the agricultural sector to finance the non-agricultural sectors. Taxes on tourism are generally offset by generous tax incentives leading to heavy subsidization of tourism in developing countries. There is an argument for modifying the form of these incentives to favour training, marketing, and refurbishing rather than new construction. Heavy implicit taxes on the financial sector are regarded as instruments of financial repression, channelling scarce financial resources into undesirable areas. However, to the extent that such taxes are a response to market failure, it is advised that some measure of regulation is still necessary in developing economies with inefficient financial markets. The analysis of mining taxes raised the view that the neoclassical model of intertemporal profit maximization for the mining firm pays scant attention to the crucial needs of the developing economy; these include the earnings of foreign exchange, the generation of employment, and the need for government to retain high levels of mineral rents.

Chapter Nineteen

International Taxation

Internatonal taxation is highly significant in open developing economies seeking to attract foreign investment from abroad. The issues which concern us here are the problems related to tax incentives, tax havens and offshore banking as well as transfer pricing. We also examine some of the arrangements to avoid double taxation. The final topic of the chapter is fiscal harmonization in common markets.

TAX INCENTIVES FOR FOREIGN INVESTMENT

An important fiscal strategy by governments in developing countries has been the use of tax incentives to stimulate the inflow of foreign investment. Major tax incentives include income tax holidays, investment tax credits, accelerated depreciation allowances, and exemptions from import duties. The neoclassical argument for tax incentives is that they reduce the cost of capital and the risks associated with investment. Income tax holidays and accelerated depreciation allowances are the most widespread forms of incentives, and enable investors to recover the cost of their initial investment.

This section makes no attempt to survey the extensive literature on tax incentives in developing countries. Howard (1992) and McIntyre, Arthur and Charles (1993) have reviewed the work on tax incentives in the Caribbean. Studies on other developing countries can be found in Bird and Oldman (1990: 151–201). An early work by Lent (1967) also provides a good evaluation of tax incentives in developing countries.

Chua (1995) outlines some of the main characteristics of tax incentives. Income tax holidays provide the investor with an exemption from the payment of profit tax for periods ranging from 5 to 15 years or longer. One problem with the tax holiday is the erosion of the tax base because tax revenue has to be foregone. Further, there is no guarantee that the firm will remain in the country after the tax holiday period has expired. However, a tax holiday may also increase the desirability of equity financing if dividends distributed by tax-exempt firms are also exempt from the personal income tax (Chua 1995: 166).

Investment tax credits and accelerated depreciation allowances reduce capital costs. Accelerated depreciation allowances allow the firm to write off its investment expenditures at a faster rate. Tax credits permit the firm to reduce its tax liability by some percentage of the initial investment. The main criticism of these incentives is that they lead to a bias in favour of capital intensive investments. Relief from import duties on raw material imports may also encourage capital intensity. If firms are export-oriented, the increased earnings of foreign exchange may compensate for the capital intensity bias.

The most important conclusions emerging from the literature on tax incentives in developing countries are as follows:

1. Tax incentive programmes are very generous and governments tend to overconcede to foreign investors, who are able to recover significantly the cost of their investment before being subject to tax. This point has been made by Lim (1983) who argues that developing countries try to compensate for their lack of incentives by offering generous incentives.

2. Although tax incentives help to reduce the cost of investment, other factors such as the availability of natural resources, adequate infrastructure, low wage costs, and political stability are perhaps more important in attracting foreign investors. Much of the literature supports the view that tax incentives per se are not effective in moving foreign investment from abroad.

3. Overconceding leads to significant revenue losses for the government, and may create distortions in the economy by encouraging high levels of capital intensity and low levels of local value added. The literature on the Caribbean advanced empirical data to support these points (see Howard 1992: 127).

4. It can be argued that most critics have not advanced viable alterna-tive strategies of industrialization or alternative fiscal prog-rammes (Howard 1992: 128). This implies that more research needs to be directed towards improving the beneficial impact of tax incentives on the country receiving the investment.

TAX HAVENS AND OFFSHORE CENTRES

This section relies on analyses by Casenegra de Jantscher (1976), McCarthy (1979), and ECLAC (1995). Tax avoidance is the major reason why companies invest in tax havens and offshore centres.

A tax haven is a place where foreigners may receive income or own assets without paying high rates of taxes (Casenegra de Jantscher 1976). Tax relief is usually in the form of exemption from income, estate, or gift taxes. Generally speaking, the main characteristic of a tax haven is a very low effective tax rate on foreign income. Major tax havens are the Bahamas, Bermuda, Cayman Islands, Hong Kong, Panama, and Singapore. Most tax havens are developing countries where governments believe that tax haven status would accelerate their rate of economic growth.

Tax havens are used by the foreign investor to establish legal entities, such as trusts, personal holding companies, offshore banks or corporate subsidiaries. Income earned elsewhere is taxed at the low effective tax rate in the tax haven. Transfer pricing, which is discussed later, is one method whereby the prices of goods and services traded between a parent company and its foreign subsidiaries are manipulated in order to increase global profits.

Policy makers in developing countries believe that the main benefits of tax havens would be higher employment and investment, as well as revenue from licences and fees. Tax havens do not generate high levels of employment because many transactions are bookkeeping type operations. Most benefits are derived from licences especially when there is a large number of offshore banks. Tax havens are sensitive to international and internal political developments. Political stability is a necessary condition for a country to be a successful tax haven.

Tax havens are hosts to offshore financial institutions. These offshore centres facilitate financial transactions between non-residents by means of low taxation and relief from exchange controls. The main characteristics of offshore centres are low licence fees and low or no relevant taxes on trans-actions. Other institutions found in offshore centres are captive insurance companies which are subsidiaries of large corporations. They are used to insure the parent company against high risks at more attractive rates than can be offered by the insurance industry in the home country. International business companies, ship registries, mutual funds, trusts, and holding companies are also established in offshore centres to conduct operations in the context of lower taxes, fees, and licences than exist in their countries of origin.

McCarthy (1979) outlines the various advantages and disadvantages of offshore centres. Licence fees are the most important benefit to governments in these centres. In most "paper" centres employment generation is low. One office may administer the affairs of several banks. These centres, however, provide some employment for lawyers and accountants because of the legal nature of many transactions. The costs incurred in establishing an offshore centre include expenditure on infrastructure as well as advertising and marketing programmes by the host country government.

The ECLAC (1995: 8) gives a detailed analysis of the activities of offshore banks and tax havens in the Caribbean. Tax revenues varied considerably in these centres between 1992 and 1994. Government revenues from offshore centres, as a percent of current government revenue, were as follows: the Bahamas (3 percent), Barbados (2 percent), Bermuda (7 percent), Netherland Antilles (28 percent), Cayman Islands (16 percent), and the British Virgin Islands (38 percent).

Transfer Pricing and Taxation

We briefly referred to transfer pricing in our discussion of tax havens. Transfer pricing is designed to reduce the overall tax liability of the MNC. The transactions between MNC subsidiaries are not only in the form of trade flows, but interest payments, dividend payments, and fees for specific services such as management contracts and payments for head office expenses.

The manipulation of internal prices by MNCs is determined by a number of factors. First, there is the overall objective of the MNC to maximize global profits. Costs may be overstated in a jurisdiction where the corporation tax is high, in order to shift profits to a subsidiary in a low-tax jurisdiction. Second, other factors such as exchange controls on the expatriation of profits may also provide a motivation for transfer pricing. There may also be an incentive to reduce internal prices in a particular subsidiary for purposes of wage bargaining.

Plasschaert (1979) has identified a number of constraints on the use of transfer pricing. The imposition of centrally planned transfer prices reduces the autonomy of managers in local subsidiaries, thereby eroding their initiative. The centralized management approach to transfer pricing conflicts with the concept of a subsidiary as an autonomous profit centre. Plasschaert also contends that the administration costs of running an optimizing transfer pricing system are high because the MNCs, activities and facilities are scattered over a wide range of countries.

It has been suggested by some analysts that governments in the Caribbean and other developing countries should seek to enforce "arm's length" pricing to control the MNCs' pricing strategies. The "arm's length" price is the price that actually exists on the market, or that would be charged in similar transactions by an independent seller to an independent buyer. "Arm's length" pricing is difficult to implement. First, some goods are specific to the enterprise because the intermediate good can serve as an input only in the subsidiary's production function. Second, the prices of services may be difficult to control because of the heterogeneity of many services (Plasschaert 1979).

Transfer pricing poses considerable problems for taxation policy. McCarten (1995) has suggested that revenue officials in countries where subsidiaries reside should explore opportunities for international cooperation, designed to facilitate the exchange of tax information with tax authorities in the countries of the parent companies. He recommends that developing countries enforce legal provisions to combat manipulative transfer pricing. Many developing countries have not been able to devise appropriate legislation to deal with transfer pricing. The imposition of withholding taxes on royalties and fees paid abroad is perhaps the most aggressive methods adopted by some developing countries.

DOUBLE TAXATION, WITHOLDING TAXES, AND TAX TREATIES

Double taxation arises when an individual or business acquiring income in a foreign country is required to pay taxes on that income in both the foreign country as well as the country of origin. For example, an American company operating in a developing country, in the absence of a tax treaty between the two countries, may have to pay a withholding tax to the government of the developing country, as well as corporation tax to the

United States government. Relief from taxes may be given on a unilateral basis in the absence of a double taxation agreement.

Withholding taxes are usually at the centre of discussions on double taxation agreements between countries. A withholding tax is a tax levied on dividends and interest paid by a subsidiary or foreign company to an overseas host country government. The tax is usually levied on profits or income earned by the foreign subsidiary before the income is repatriated. Sometimes a withholding tax is imposed by the host country government to induce the foreign firm to reinvest part of its surplus in the host country. Many developing countries employ withholding taxes. The term withholding tax can also be used to describe an income tax levied on the interest on dividends of a resident individual. In this case, the tax is deducted by the bank paying the interest or by the company paying the dividends, and thereafter, submitted to the government.

Two important concepts in evaluating double taxation and the formulation of double taxation agreements are the residence and source principles of direct taxation. The residence principle states that individuals should be taxed in their country of residence regardless of the sources of income. This principle calls for a precise definition of residence. The source principle states that income of an individual should be taxed in relation to the source of that income. This principle supports the taxing of income earned in foreign countries.

Developing countries have applied these principles on grounds of expediency. For instance, some developing countries have not taxed the foreign income of residents because it may not be administratively efficient to do so or because of the low level of income. Many countries have foregone taxing the domestic income of non-residents because of the need to give tax incentives to foreign investors (Faria 1995a).

Faria (1995b) examines two methods used by developing countries in giving unilateral foreign tax relief. The first of these is the income deduction method where the foreign source income is exempted from tax, or such income is assessed net, after the deduction of foreign taxes. Faria contends that revenue gains would accrue to the home country under this method, if the home country's tax rate was equal to, or higher than, the foreign country's tax rate.

The second approach to foreign tax relief is where a partial or full tax credit is offered by the home country in respect of tax paid in the source country. This implies, from a tax incidence point of view, that a resident in his home country would be taxed according to the residence principle applied to his worldwide income. The two principles above effectively reduce double taxation.

Many developing countries, including Barbados, Jamaica, and Trinidad and Tobago, have treaty withholding tax agreements with developed countries. For details of withholding tax agreements for other developing countries see Ernst and Young (1995). A tax treaty becomes necessary when "the inherent conflict between the residence and source principles of income is not unilaterally resolved through a residual tax crediting or an income deduction approach" (Faria 1995c: 218). Tax treaties are often complicated documents stating the tax treatment of dividends, interest, royalties, and capital gains.

FISCAL HARMONIZATION

My primary concern in this section is an examination of the conceptual issues in tax harmonization with special reference to CARICOM. Fiscal harmonization analysis is highly complex, theoretically as well as practically. Fiscal harmonization includes both public expenditure harmonization and tax harmonization (Dosser 1967). Although expenditure harmonization will be discussed briefly, most of the issues raised here will relate to tax harmonization.

Following Kopits (1992: 1), a distinction can be made between "concerted" tax harmonization, which denotes a formal agreement for convergence not necessarily equalization of tax structures, and "spontaneous" tax harmonization. The later term indicates convergence of tax structures in response to competitive pressures without formal agreement. Concerted harmonization will be the assumption of the analysis.

This section discusses the main issues involved in fiscal harmonization and differentiates between various economic scenarios such as fixed and flexible exchange rates, customs unions and common markets, uniform and differential taxation, and the origin and destination principles of taxation. I also indicate how the issues raised here should help to inform the scope of fiscal harmonization in CARICOM. The work also speaks to some of the tax base constraints on fiscal harmonization in CARICOM. The analysis concludes with proposals for tax harmonization.

Criteria for Tax Harmonization
The chief criteria for the analysis of tax harmonization are those of efficiency,

growth, stabilization, and income distribution. Most work on tax harmonization has been concerned with the achievement of efficiency in resource allocation. In pursuit of efficiency, tax harmonization theory has stressed the removal of tax distortions affecting commodity and factor movements, to strengthen the integration process (Kopits 1992). Tax harmonization is therefore seen as convergence towards a uniform effective tax regime across member countries. Uniform taxation leads to greater neutrality in the burden distribution, thereby creating a "level playing field" for investors and consumers. In this regard, tax harmonization reduces the incentive for factors of production to move from high-tax to low-tax countries.

Harmonization analysis must also consider equity or fairness. Kopits (1992) advances the following points. It is important to note that equity relates not only to taxpayers but also to fairness in the distribution of tax revenue among countries. In particular, the theory of harmonization suggests that the benefit principle should be used to allocate tax revenues arising from tax harmonization. Tax revenues should accrue to the country which provides the services connected with the economic activity. The value added generated by the activity in the member country is a rough proxy for the benefit provided. In practice, it is quite difficult to calculate the incidence of tax harmonization on member countries.

Dosser (1967) suggests that harmonization through the tax equalization approach may improve or worsen a member country's trade balance. Therefore, it is difficult to predict the stabilization policy effects of tax harmonization. Even if convergence of tax rates is desirable, differential rates of indirect taxes between countries may be necessary at times to achieve the stabilization goal. For these reasons, economists have concentrated on the efficiency aspects of tax harmonization, rather than the stabilization implications.

In order to appreciate the above criteria for tax harmonization, a consideration of the major principles of international taxation is necessary. The first principle is the destination principle. Under this criterion, commodities are taxed in the country of destination, that is, the country in which consumption of the goods takes place, regardless of where they are produced. This principle ensures that imports are taxed at the same rate as domestic substitute goods. The destination principle guarantees international neutrality, because differential tax rates distort consumption.

Under the origin principle, commodities should be taxed where they are produced, regardless of the country of consumption. The origin principle ensures neutrality if a uniform tax is imposed on goods produced in a country, either for domestic consumption or export.

The two other principles guaranteeing neutrality for direct taxation of capital income are the residence principle of taxation and the source principle. These principles have been defined previously in our analysis of double taxation. Kopits (1967) asserts that the destination principle is widely accepted for commodity taxation by international convention. However, there is no consensus regarding the principle that should govern capital income.

Harmonization of Indirect and Direct Taxes

Robson (1984) presents a number of scenarios to illustrate the operation of the destination and origin principles in the context of tax harmonization. These scenarios will aid our analysis of the scope of fiscal harmonization in CARICOM.

First, following Robson (1984), let us assume two countries, say Jamaica and Barbados. Further, assume that each country has flexible exchange rates and no tariffs. Jamaica exports clothes and Barbados has a comparative advantage in sugar. Assume that Jamaica has a uniform VAT of 10 percent on all goods and Barbados' VAT rate is 20 percent on all goods. Robson (1984) shows that given these internally uniform, but internationally different rates of VAT, the choice between the destination and origin principle has no effect on the composition and level of trade.

Robson's model works as follows: if the tax is imposed on the destination principle, and exports are exempt from the tax, the relative costs of clothes and sugar will not be affected by the VAT. There are no trade or exchange rate effects. If the VAT is imposed on the origin principle, all exports of both products will pay the tax, but the relative costs of clothes and sugar will remain unchanged. Therefore, under a system of flexible exchange rates and complete free trade, uniform VAT rates in both countries lead to neutrality and will not hinder efficient resource allocation. There is considerable difficulty of achieving neutrality in CARICOM because of the existence of differential rates of indirect taxation.

Second, if differential VAT rates are imposed in the two countries on various goods, relative consumer prices will be distorted, leading to a distortion of trade patterns. In this case, Robson shows that differential indirect taxes lead to sub-optimal trade patterns in a common market, regardless of whether the origin or destination principle is chosen.

The principle issue in the harmonization of direct taxes concerns the effect of differential direct tax rates on factor mobility between countries, the problem of double taxation, and the problem of the international distribution of tax revenues. The effects of differential tax rates on capital income in a union depend on the degree of factor mobility between countries and the incidence of the corporation tax within member countries. If factors are not mobile and direct taxes are not shifted, capital taxation will play only a minor role and harmonization will not be a major issue.

Capital will normally flow from high-tax to low-tax countries. In the context of CARICOM, the most important harmonization instrument to promote a favourable distribution of foreign investment is the harmonization of fiscal incentives. This instrument prevents polarization of foreign investment. Further, the equalization of effective corporation taxes in each country where the source principle applies is one way of reducing the tendency of capital to flow from high- to low-tax areas.

Criticisms of the Equalization Approach

One criticism of the equalization of statutory rates of taxes, whether direct or indirect, is that this approach will not unify effective rates, that is, the effective burden of tax. This is attributable to the fact that effective tax burdens vary according to domestic conditions and the type of market structures in various countries. Further, unless harmonization is accompanied by some form of budgetary integration, the overall budgetary incidence will differ significantly from the effective tax burden in member countries.

Due and Robson (1967) have identified other disadvantages of uniformity of nominal rate structures. Budget inflexibility is likely to arise, since policy makers' adherence to uniformity is likely to slow down changes in the tax structures in response to changing economic needs. Agreement between countries is necessary for changes to take place, whereas autonomous national action is needed if a member country is experiencing a stabilization problem.

The equalization approach is easier to implement for corporate taxation. It is argued that it is possible to harmonize income tax structures, although it may not be feasible to equalize all rates since the latter are largely determined by internal levels of income, and other factors such as whether the economy is agrarian, service-oriented, or petroleum-based.

The equalization of internal indirect tax rates in CARICOM would probably be an exercise in futility. First, the VAT in the Caribbean is not a completely neutral tax because of the high levels of exemptions and zero-rated goods. However, the zero-rating of exports in Jamaica, Barbados, and Trinidad and Tobago implies that the present VATs will not distort export prices, and therefore, no further equalization of VAT rates is warranted. Other CARICOM countries have differential indirect taxes which are incompatible with the VAT and, therefore, cannot be harmonized with VAT rates.

The above analysis does not indicate much optimism for fiscal harmonization. Further analysis on the scope for fiscal harmonization in CARICOM will suggest a "minimum approximation" to convergence with respect to the harmonization of statutory corporate tax rates, despite the weaknesses of this approach.

Expenditure Harmonization

Joint-benefit public expenditure is necessary to strengthen an economic union. Such expenditure may include the financing of public enterprises or regional institutions which yield advantages of economies of scale to two or more member countries. A prominent example of cost-sharing efforts in CARICOM is the University of the West Indies. The problem of joint-benefit expenditures is the calculation of the benefits involved. The benefits are measurable in some cases such as educational output of students, but other services may be more difficult to assess. Further, the distribution of costs must be related to ability to pay considerations, probably measured by per capita income levels of member countries, the ratio of the fiscal deficit to GDP, and so forth.

SCOPE FOR FISCAL HARMONIZATION IN CARICOM

The scope for fiscal harmonization in CARICOM is limited by certain economic conditions facing the region. These include flexible exchange rates in some countries and fixed exchange rates in others, controls on the movements of capital and labour, widely varying withholding taxes on capital income, and highly differential indirect tax rates in most countries. Given these factors, it can be argued that the most promising area of harmonization is the equalization of the corporate tax rate. First, we look at the areas where some success has been achieved in harmonization. Second, some proposals are advanced for a minimum approximation to fiscal convergence.

CARICOM has made some progress in fiscal harmonization in the following areas:
1. Harmonization of fiscal incentives
2. Joint-benefit public expenditures (e.g., University of the West Indies)
3. Common External Tariff (CET)
4. Some agreement on the phased equalization of tariff rates

Our analysis here will not describe the details of CARICOM's harmonization of fiscal incentives. Readers can consult McIntyre, Arthur and Charles (1993) who discuss some of the work on the harmonization of fiscal incentives in CARICOM. They make the point that some governments have overconceded to foreign investors. Harmonization of fiscal incentives has helped to divert some foreign investment to the less developed countries in CARICOM. The institution of the CET and reduction of tariff rates were intended to liberalize trade within the region, as well as encourage regional production.

Should statutory tax rates be harmonized in CARICOM? According to Musgrave (1967), for purposes of tax harmonization, it is the effective tax rate rather than the statutory rate which is of interest. Musgrave describes the effective tax rate on capital as the percentage by which taxation reduces net capital income defined as total receipts less total costs. A simple statutory rate may yield different effective tax rates depending on different concepts of taxable income, reflecting depreciation allowances for tax purposes, stock valuation, and the type of firm under consideration. Musgrave suggests a concept called the "effective apparent tax rate" which is equal to reported taxes paid divided by reported profits. This rate can be calculated for CARICOM and compared with the nominal statutory rate.

Musgrave (1967) further maintains that a truly neutral profits tax would apply the same effective rate to all investments in depreciable assets in member countries. This implies that the equalization of effective rates between countries would require the same set of neutral depreciation schedules in all countries. Equalization also requires application of the same jurisdictional principle (for instance, the residence principle) for all corporations. Musgrave further warns that if monetary conditions promote asymmetrical shifting of the profit tax, tax harmonization would require a common monetary union.

Estimating a regional average weighted personal tax rate on dividends is more difficult. This involves estimating the percentage distribution of dividends by size-of-income class for each country. There are no available statistics for this purpose. However, it is suggested that the dividend tax rate should converge to an average of 15 percent withholding tax throughout the region. Countries with higher rates than 15 percent should be induced to lower their high dividend tax rates.

Tax harmonization depends heavily on tax base considerations in various countries. Divergent tax bases are a constraint on fiscal harmonization. There has been an unconcerted attempted to harmonize the objectives of income tax reform in keeping with the world tax reform movement, even though tax rates and bases remain widely divergent. Income tax bases differ with respect to the varying treatments of insurance premiums, interest income, pensions, mortgage interest, and prerequisites. It is difficult to harmonize effective income tax rates in the Caribbean, unless tax bases are harmonized. This means that various forms of income should be subject to the same tax treatment in each country.

Indirect tax bases are even more widely divergent. These bases have been influenced considerably by devaluations in various countries. Therefore, even if statutory rates are equalized, effective rates will remain divergent and no effective harmonization will take place. In this scenario, the various territories would have to adopt a common currency to avoid sharp fluctuations in tax bases. Further, common practices in respect of the valuation of goods should become operational.

In Jamaica and Trinidad and Tobago, the overall effective VAT rate is determined by the different exemptions and zero-ratings applied to various goods. This also reduces the neutrality of the VAT internally. For harmonization to take place, countries need to agree on a common policy toward exemptions and zero-ratings.

Concluding Suggestions on Fiscal Harmonization in CARICOM

The most fruitful area for harmonization is the harmonization of corporate tax rates. Capital income is more mobile, and foreign investment flows can be influenced by the level of the effective corporate tax rates.

Musgrave's methodology has been suggested for the calculation of an effective corporate rate, but the main problem would be the existing deficiencies in the national income data in CARICOM countries. In the light of these problems, it is suggested that the statutory rates of member countries should converge to a common statutory rate of 35 percent.

Further, any attempt to harmonize effective rates should be accompanied by the adoption of the same depreciation schedules and the same jurisdictional principles for each country. Tax laws governing the movement of capital income would also have to be harmonized.

It is more feasible to harmonize income tax structures rather than equalize all income tax rates. That is, the principles of neutrality, simplicity and base broadening can be applied to the design of the tax structure. Further, the same tax treatment can be applied to various sources of income such as interest and pensions. However, overall minimum and maximum statutory income tax rates can be allowed to vary, depending on the income base in the various countries.

The various regimes of flexible and fixed exchange rates in the region suggest that it may be impossible to harmonize highly differential indirect tax rates. Internal VATs in Jamaica, Barbados, and Trinidad and Tobago are not neutral, given the number of zero-ratings and exemptions. Therefore, equalizing VAT rates would not guarantee fiscal harmonization. Again, all countries may not be willing to move to VAT in an attempt to bring more neutrality to their internal indirect tax structures. Overall, I am not optimistic about the scope of tax harmonization in CARICOM, beyond the harmonization of fiscal incentives.

SUMMARY

This chapter has surveyed the principal aspects of international taxation. The analysis has not been exhaustive. International taxation is a discipline which incorporates international tax law and accounting principles beyond the scope of this work. There are many legal issues involved in the areas of tax treaties, double taxation, and tax incentive agreements. It can be argued that the tax issues discussed should be related to the need to promote economic development. In this regard, tax incentives should be designed to maximize the benefits to host countries especially employment generation, the earning of foreign exchange, and the promotion of exports. Similarly, tax haven and offshore financial legislation should attempt to minimize the outflow of dividends and profits from the host country. Fiscal harmonization is a challenging area of research. In regional groupings with substantially different rates of development and divergent exchange rates, it may be difficult to harmonize effective rates of income and commodity taxation.

Chapter Twenty

Tax Administration

Tax policy cannot achieve the goal of efficient resource allocation unless the tax system is well administered. This chapter is about tax administration in both developed and developing countries. The latter countries have less efficient tax administration systems than the former. Most public finance textbooks either ignore tax administration issues, or relegate their discussion to footnotes. In the context of the tax reforms of the 1980s and 1990s, many tax planners and public finance economists have realized that tax reforms cannot work effectively unless a country improves its tax administration.

Increasing attention has been devoted to models of tax evasion, compliance costs, tax amnesties, and the reform of tax administration systems. The implementation of the VAT in many countries has also increased the cost of tax administration in an effort to improve administrative efficiency. It is necessary to assess the importance and scope of tax administration, and evaluate some of the work on tax evasion and compliance costs.

It should be noted that most research on tax administration has been carried out in developed countries. However, policy makers in developing countries can learn important lessons from this work. Our survey looks at the general issues involved in tax administration, as well as administrative tax reform. The chapter closes with some observations on the nature of VAT administration.

IMPORTANCE AND SCOPE OF TAX ADMINISTRATION

My analysis of the general importance of tax administration draws heavily on the work of Mansfield (1988) and Frampton (1993). Mansfield (1988: 181) regards tax administration as "a loosely defined area that embraces law, public administration, sociology, and psychology as well as economics". Tax administration can be regarded as an eclectic discipline designed to facilitate fiscal policy and influence resource allocation.

Tax administration requires that tax policy be translated into a set of laws which represent the tax system. Such legislation enables government to enforce the collection of revenue. Tax administrators need to monitor the tax laws in order to encourage voluntary compliance, facilitate the workings of self-assessment systems, and reduce tax evasion. Mansfield (1988) indicates that the failure to administer the tax laws effectively can result in a substantial gap between tax law and actual taxation, which implies negative consequences for government revenues.

Frampton (1993) has identified certain prerequisites for a sound tax administration. He discusses these under the headings of law, enforcement, personnel, simplicity, information technology, public acceptance, the right attitude, and malpractices. I discuss Frampton's criteria because they seem comprehensive enough as guides to evaluating tax administration in both developed and developing countries.

I have already mentioned the role of law in tax administration. The legislation for each tax is embodied in a separate tax act which outlines in detail potential taxpayers, the goods or types of income subject to tax, powers of enforcement, collection dates for the tax, and penalties for non-compliance. The tax act should minimize loopholes which encourage tax avoidance. Reform of the tax system leads to changes in the fiscal legislation.

The second criterion for a good tax administration is the ability to enforce the law. The main problems of enforcement are identifying the taxpayers, controlling the known taxpayer, criminal and other investigations, and methods to deal with tax offences. Tax enforcement incurs additional costs which must be borne by the government. Frampton (1993: 12) argues that carrying enforcement too far will produce additional revenue to government, but at a high cost. This cost factor can be measured not only in terms of resources employed, but reflects an increased burden to delinquent taxpayers, and a possible loss of voluntary compliance.

Efficient tax administration depends on the skills and experience of the civil servants in the inland revenue departments. Such workers should be trained in the relevant techniques required for tax collection, enforcement, and auditing. Training in accounting, tax law, information technology, and public administration is essential. One of the most important functions is audit. Workers have to make checks on samples of taxpayers to identify discrepancies in the completion of tax forms. With the development of self-assessment procedures for income tax and the VAT, audit has become more limited in scope, because the cost of auditing large numbers of returns would be very high.

Some of the skills discussed above are scarce in many developing countries. Governments in these countries need to recruit specialists in their tax departments while retaining other experienced workers. Developed countries have assisted in the training of tax specialists though technical assistance schemes. In the implementation of tax reform exercises in developing countries, workers in tax administration offices are usually supervised by foreign experts, in order to learn to manage the reformed system.

A previous chapter discussed the simplicity of taxation. According to Frampton (1993: 27), simplicity leads to a reduction in administrative costs, resulting in greater efficiency. Simplicity also increases taxpayer compliance. Simplicity can be applied to administrative procedures. For example, self-assessment places a greater responsibility on the taxpayer, and reduces the burden of the inland revenue department in calculating the tax liability for all taxpayers.

Tax administration has benefited significantly from information technology. Automated data processing (ADP) systems have been implemented in developing countries in customs and other tax departments. According to Corfmat (1990: 471), ADP systems in customs departments are designed "to produce external trade statistics, special summaries and studies, such as analyses of import and export prices, and insurance and freight studies". ADP systems are also used in inland revenue departments to process returns and payments, compile statistics, generate delinquent account notices, and also in PAYE systems (see Byam 1992: 197–98 for a listing of other tax related activities).

Frampton's last three prerequisites for good administration are generally acceptable. First, the public must generally accept the payment of tax. Failure to do this results in massive tax evasion which undermines the system. Second, the administration must be friendly to taxpayers. This means that administrators must be willing to advise taxpayers in preparing tax forms. Third, a good administration depends on the reduction of internal malpractices. This means that officers of a tax department must uphold the department's code of conduct. Malpractice undermines secrecy and, in the case of criminal offences, the morale of workers may decline considerably. The efficiency of revenue departments can be improved by internal audit which not only checks the work of officers, but also their tax returns especially the verification of expenses and allowances which they claim (Byam 1992: 194).

The administrative issues discussed above vary in their complexity from one developing country to another. Some developing countries have not fully computerized their tax systems, and may suffer from significant lags in tax collection. Other countries have a poor database which is a constraint on sound administration. Corruption and malpractice exist in the third world, and there are great possibilities for tax evasion. The deficiency of research in developing countries on problems, such as tax evasion and tax compliance costs, imposes a constraint on efforts to reform their tax administration systems.

TAX EVASION

Tax evasion is perhaps the most serious problem facing administrators worldwide. The theoretical literature on tax evasion is concerned with the motivation of taxpayers to evade taxes. At the empirical level, attempts have been made to measure the extent of tax evasion. My analysis examines these approaches and summarizes some of the main findings in the field.

The Theoretical Approach to Tax Evasion

The theoretical approach to tax evasion "treats the tax evader as a rational economic agent contemplating an economic crime and making decisions under uncertainty, given assumed probabilities of detection, conviction, and levels of punishment" (Mansfield 1988: 184). The tax evader maximizes an expected utility function which is dependent on his income. He divides his income into two components, that is, declared and undeclared income. The tax evader will choose the level of evasion which depends on the probability of being caught or not being caught. This approach suggests that if the taxpayer can increase expected utility without declaring some income, then the rational decision is to evade. On the other hand, a penalty is imposed on the undeclared income of the taxpayer if he is caught. The penalty is assumed to be greater than the tax rate. The tax evader will weigh the probability of not getting caught by declaring part of his income, and the probability of not declaring his income and paying the penalty rate. The theoretical approach uses models to analyse the taxpayer's decisions under uncertainty.[1]

The theoretical approach to tax evasion has numerous shortcomings as outlined by Mansfield (1988). He argues that the expected utility approach makes no allowance for institutional mechanisms such as withholding which could interfere with the decision to evade. Generally speaking, the majority of taxpayers are honest and not criminally motivated. Further, some taxpayers prefer the route of tax avoidance by using legal loopholes in the tax law. The theoretical approach also ignores compliance costs. These models also need to be supported by more empirical work. Sample surveys of taxpayer attitudes as well as studies of individual tax returns are among the methods used to gauge the motivation to evade taxes.[2]

Measurement of Tax Evasion

Empirical analysis attempts to measure the extent of tax evasion. Richupan (1984: 38) suggests that estimates of the underground economy can be used as proxies for tax evasion. This is so because the underground economy approach can be used to measure income unreported or under-reported in tax returns.[3] Estimates of the underground economy based on GNP data will generate biased estimates of income. He identifies a number of approaches to the measurement of tax evasion. Three of these are the "monetary approach", the "gap approach" and the "survey approach". These approaches are summarized below.

The monetary approach assumes that there is a ratio of currency to demand deposits which would have remained constant over time, without the presence of the underground economy. This approach selects a period in the past when the currency ratio was constant, and compares it with a period when the underground economy existed. If the currency ratio is higher in the latter period, the excess money is assumed to have resulted from the growth of the underground economy implying an increase in tax evasion. The criticism of this approach is that the currency ratio cannot be assumed to be constant in many countries, and forms of tax evasion can exist which have nothing to do with the underground economy (Richupan 1984: 38–39).

The gap approach compares income reported in tax returns with income in the national income accounts. The measure deducts exemptions and allowances from personal income in the national accounts and compares the net personal income with that reported in tax returns. The "gap" or difference between net personal income and income reported in the tax returns is a measure of tax evasion. The weakness of this approach is that in many countries, national income is derived from tax data.

The survey approach simply surveys the income of taxpayers by means of a sample survey, and compares this income with that reported in tax returns. This approach is subject to statistical problems such as sample bias and data problems (Richupan 1984: 40).

A study by Alm, Bahland and Murray (1991) estimated the extent of tax evasion by self-employed persons in Jamaica prior to the tax reform of 1986. According to these authors, the major form of tax evasion by the self-employed in Jamaica was non-filing. Given the high level of non-filing, it was difficult to estimate precisely the revenue loss from tax evasion. Their study used "gap analysis" discussed previously to gauge potential taxable income. In 1980, it was estimated that the revenue loss from tax evasion was 50 percent compared with 39 percent in 1983.

The pattern of evasion was further investigated by considering a "professional sample" of more than 2,000 names comprising accountants, architects, doctors, attorneys, veterinarians and optometrists. A random sample of 572 names was drawn. No tax reference number was found for 30 percent of this sample, and another 26 percent had no returns filed for any year between 1980 and 1983. Overall, 22 percent only of the sample were within the tax net. It was concluded that 30 percent of income tax revenue was lost due to non-filing and underreporting. In an extended sample of 43,985 self-employed persons in 1982, 36,360 were non-filers (Alm, Bahland and Murray 1991).

Alm, Bahland and Murray (1991) also tested the degree of under-reporting of tax by means of an audit sample of 482 persons. About half of the undeclared income for these taxpayers was in the top marginal tax brackets, supporting the theory that taxpayers facing high marginal rates are more likely to evade taxes. This conclusion was supported by regression analysis.[4]

Policies to Curb Tax Evasion

The policy measures advocated to reduce levels of tax evasion include improved registration of taxpayers, effective withholding schemes, penalties, audits, and tax amnesties.[5] First, it is necessary to register more self-employed workers. The discussion of the Jamaican case before 1986 showed that many highly paid professionals were non-filers. Second, even though penalties are necessary, many countries do not enforce criminal penalties. Third, an effective withholding system is important. According to Mansfield (1988: 188), withholding removes the element of free choice. It can be applied to wages, dividends, and interest, but not to rental income or incomes of professionals or small businesses. Fourth, regular audits are necessary to increase compliance, even though they can be quite time-consuming. Generally speaking, policies to curb tax evasion should emphasize the simplicity of tax collection and administration.

Hasseldine (1998: 303) notes that tax amnesties have several advantages in reducing tax evasion. First, tax amnesties allow delinquent taxpayers to return to the system and disclose previously hidden tax information. Second, tax agencies benefit from the collection of outstanding taxes. A third benefit is that tax amnesties may increase future voluntary compliance. Finally, tax amnesties allow for a transition period prior to a strengthened enforcement regime.

However, certain obvious disadvantages are associated with amnesties. Hasseldine (1998: 303) writes that "honest taxpayers may be upset by them. If the bulk of taxpayers already voluntarily comply with the tax laws, then these taxpayers may take offence at a 'soft option' being given to tax evaders". Further, taxpayers may expect amnesties in the future and may decide to reduce their compliance. Finally, an amnesty may not be economically viable as a result of the administrative costs involved in the process.[6] Hasseldine reports that there is very little research into the effects of amnesties. Much of the research has been carried out in the United States rather than developing countries.

ADMINISTRATION AND COMPLIANCE COSTS OF TAXATION

According to Sandford (1995a: 89), administrative costs are "the official costs of administering an existing tax code". These include salaries, wages, accommodation, postage, telephone and other current cost of running an office. Compliance costs are "costs which taxpayers (or third parties, notably businesses) incur in order to meet the requirements laid on them by the tax legislation and the revenue authorities" (Sandford 1995a: 90).

Talib (1996) divides compliance costs into two components, namely, computational costs and planning costs. Computational costs are unavoidable. These consists of payments to professional advisors, postage, telephone, and accounting for taxes on goods for sale. Planning costs are avoidable in theory, but must be undertaken by companies. The literature does not seem to place much emphasis on planning costs in practice.

Our analysis notes the observation of Talib (1996) that research on compliance costs was neglected until very recently, possible due to the costs and length of time in conducting surveys. Talib asserts that there has been an upsurge in literature in this area and lists a number of studies to support this observation.[7] Compliance costs are usually measured by surveys. For the United Kingdom, Sandford, Goodwin and Hardwick (1989) used mail questionnaires to estimate the compliance costs of PAYE and the British VAT system.

How can government reduce administrative and compliance costs? Our discussion draws heavily on Sandford (1995a) who outlines a number of ways in which administrative and compliance costs can be minimized. First, government must reduce the frequency of tax changes because frequent tax changes create confusion and resentment in the minds of taxpayers. From an administrative point of view these tax changes generate a new set of paper work, and extra time is needed to explain tax forms. Second, a simple tax system helps to minimize administrative and compliance costs. Simplicity is one of the major principles of tax reform in the 1990s. Third, accessible and readable tax literature, as well as short and clear tax forms also increase the cost effectiveness of the tax system. Further, fewer taxes on a broader base lead to lower administrative and compliance costs.

ADMINISTRATIVE TAX REFORM

Many developing countries have attempted to improve their tax administration systems to support the tax reforms of the 1980s. I now examine the rationale and nature of administrative tax reform. An edited work by Bird and Casanegra de Jantscher (1992) provides detailed country studies of administrative tax reforms in Jamaica, Columbia, Trinidad and Tobago, and Guatemala. Space constraints do not allow us to reproduce the details of these studies. This section also looks at the administrative issues associated with the introduction of VAT systems. Many of these issues apply to developed countries as well.

Bahl and Martinez-Vazquez (1992: 66–67) argue that tax administration is poor in developing countries largely because of the use of

275

antiquated procedures, badly trained staff, and complicated tax systems. Some governments do not want high levels of enforcement and are willing to accept a certain amount of evasion. As stated earlier, a simplified tax system is easier to administer and leads to a higher level of compliance. This suggests that there is a close relationship between tax policy and tax administration. Tax administrative procedures need to be simplified in developing countries in order to enforce a reformed tax system.

How can tax administration be reformed? Bahl and Martinez-Vazquez (1992: 104–6) answer this question by distinguishing between three different views of the administrative constraints to tax structure reform. First the "incremental view" is that tax reform should be gradualist or incremental, and it that is easier for the tax administration to deal with these reforms because tax administration changes very slowly. The second view is that tax administration can be improved quickly if there are enough resources to administer the process of tax structure changes. This "insufficient resources view" implies that poorly trained staff is a serious constraint on tax administration reform. The third view, known as the "policy first" view, is that tax administration projects, which are implemented without tax policy reforms, are likely to fail. They refer to the Jamaican tax reform where changes in tax policy preceded administrative changes.

Administrative reforms can be extensive. They relate to the abolition of certain procedures, improving the efficiency of revenue collection and data processing, information gathering about taxpayers, enforcement of rules relating to penalties, the revision of penalty systems, and organizational changes. McLure and Pardo (1992) discuss the administrative reforms implemented by the Colombian government in 1986. They show that tax administration became much more efficient in Colombia. For example, they observe how the fiscal authorities were able to access information relevant to identifying taxpayers and assessing liabilities. Banks were legally required to file information returns identifying individuals or companies having accounts over a certain money value of transactions annually. This information helped to identify non-filers. Further, institutions issuing credit cards were obligated to provide information on wealthy holders of credit cards (McLure and Pardo 1992: 133).

Privatization of tax administration also became a topic under discussion in the 1990s. Acuna (1992: 379–92) examines the feasibility of contracting out certain tax administration tasks to the private sector. These include collection of tax receipts, audit, and the collection of delinquent accounts. For example, tax return forms can be printed by the private sector rather than by the government's printing office. The same companies printing the forms can distribute them to taxpayers. Another example of privatizing tax administration mentioned by Acuna is the practice of withholding tax at source. We have already discussed how withholding can reduce tax evasion. Acuna indicates that payment for tax administration services by the private sector can be controversial. He discusses the various ways by which banks and other agencies can be remunerated.

VAT administration is very important because the VAT is a new tax in most developing countries. The introduction of the VAT entails significant reforms in tax administration, because procedures for administering a large number of old indirect taxes have to be replaced by a system for administering a single tax. Tait (1988) discusses the details of VAT administration and staffing. Our analysis summarizes briefly some important VAT administration issues.[8]

One of the first considerations in VAT administration is which tax administration office should be responsible for the VAT. A separate VAT office leads to greater specialization, whereas the integration of the VAT office and the income tax office may create less duplication of resources. However, the resolution of this issue depends on the circumstances facing the particular country (Tait 1988: 234–45).

Staffing of the VAT office is a significant aspect of VAT administration. The staffing requirement is a function of a large number of variables, including the tax treatment of various sectors of the economy, the extent of exemptions, the frequency of returns, the complexity of tax rates, and the existing computer systems. For example, the higher the level of transactions omitted from the VAT, the more staffing needs are reduced. Further, if a large amount of the VAT is collected by the customs at the import stage, this reduces the demands for staff in the VAT office. Finally, the more complex the VAT, the greater is the need for staff to administer it. A multiple rate VAT requires more staff than a single rate VAT (Tait 1988: 245–51).

Another important area of VAT administration is audit to reduce evasion. Tait distinguishes between two types of audits: field audit and office audit. A field audit takes place at the taxpayer's place of business. An office audit is limited to the checking of returns for accuracy. Audit manuals are sometimes used to standardize the auditing process. Audits are sometimes accompanied by physical checks on the delivery and supply of goods.

We have already discussed the general aspects of tax evasion. Tait (1988: 306–15) lists the various forms of VAT evasion. These include traders who are liable to VAT but do not register, exaggerated refund claims, unrecorded cash purchases, credit claimed for taxable supplies used in exempt activities, and under-reported sales. The reduction of evasion depends heavily on the efficiency of audit, physical checks and visits to business places, and powers of entry and search under warrant.

One way of dealing with VAT evasion is the imposition of penalties. Tait (1988: 318) identifies four forms of VAT penalties: automatic financial, automatic non-financial, criminal financial, and criminal non-financial. Automatic financial penalties apply to offenses resulting from negligence or forgetfulness including late filing. These penalties can take the form of fines as a percentage of the tax. Automatic non-financial penalties may involve the closure of the business for a specified time period. Criminal penalties include fines resulting from prosecution in a court of law or imprisonment. Criminal prosecution can take a long time and conviction relies on high standards of evidence. Tax authorities are usually cautious before initiating criminal prosecutions.

SUMMARY

I have discussed the main areas of tax administration. My analysis was not intended to be exhaustive. A lot of work needs to be done on tax evasion in developing countries as well as the administrative costs of tax systems such as the VAT and PAYE. Further, tax legislation in developing countries must be well drafted to reduce levels of tax avoidance. The chapter looked briefly at some of the features of VAT administration. My analysis stated general principles and approaches which can be applied to both developed and developing countries.

Notes

CHAPTER ONE

1. Koopmans (1957) maintains that a competitive equilibrium, even if it is Pareto optimal, may involve an unequal distribution of income. He argues that the concept of Pareto optimality is not sensitive to this condition, and in this sense the term "optimum" is a misnomer. Allocative efficiency may be a better term. Atkinson and Stiglitz (1980) use the term Pareto efficiency.
2. The literature on MNCs is extensive. For their impact on foreign investment in developing countries see Gillis, Perkins and Roemer (1992).
3. The characteristics of the informal economy in Jamaica are explored by Witter and Kirton (1990).

CHAPTER THREE

1. Tanzi and Zee (1997: 180) assert that a country's growth is determined by three factors, namely, the state of technical know-how in the country, the accumulation of productive resources including human capital, and technological progress. They further argue that the premise of the endogenous growth literature is that a country's growth performance in the long run is endogenously determined by a set of variables affected by fiscal policy (p. 181).
2. Lewis (1955) maintained that the three proximate causes of growth are the will to economize, increasing knowledge and capital accumulation. His work was concerned with identifying the type of institutions and environments which favour these proximate causes.
3. For an analysis of the role of property rights in economic development, see World Bank (1997). The report states that the legal system must buttress property rights in areas such as land titling, the securities markets, the protection of intellectual property and anti-monopoly legislation.

4. Krueger (1985) outlines many advantages of export promotion. These include foreign exchange growth, economies of scale, avoidance of overvalued exchange rates and the reduction of protectionism.

CHAPTER FIVE

1. This discussion does not pretend to survey the literature on political business cycles in developed countries. A comprehensive survey can be found in Persson and Tabellini (1990). For further reading see Rogoff and Siebert (1988), Cukierman and Meltzer (1986) and Lindbeck (1976).

CHAPTER SEVEN

1. The literature on the Maharashtra Scheme is extensive. See, for example, work by Ravallion (1991), Ravallion et al. (1993) and Ravallion and Datt (1995). This work in part expresses the view that although employment schemes help to reduce the poverty gap, only a few people actually escaped poverty.

CHAPTER TEN

1. The literature on Ricardian equivalence deals with theoretical as well as empirical issues. We rely heavily on Barro (1989), Bernheim (1989), and Seater (1993). Seater provides a comprehensive review of the literature which can be used as a foundation for further work.
2. For a detailed discussion of the issues raised in this paragraph, see Seater (1993). He argues that besides the altruistic motive for bequests, other motives include strategic behaviour by donors, mutual insurance by family members, and accidents arising from uncertain lifetimes. Seater also contends that recent empirical evidence for developed countries supports the Ricardian equivalence.

CHAPTER ELEVEN

1. These issues are well covered in the articles by Killick (1984). See also the critique by Payer (1974).
2. There is an extensive literature on the monetary approach. A good explanation of this school of thought is provided by Kreinin and Officer (1978).
3. Economists of this school adopted a historical structural approach to development. Many of them were also supporters of dependency economics. The term

"old structuralists" is borrowed from Sutton (1984).

4. The data used in this paragraph were drawn from Central Bank of Barbados, *Annual Report*, 1996.

5. See Blejer and Cheasty (1988) for an extensive discussion of these issues as well as the impact of the inflation tax on the budget deficit.

6. For further details on the IMF intervention in Korea, for example, see IMF (1998b). This report states that the two objectives of the IMF Stand-by Arrangement of December 1997 for Korea was the restoration of confidence in the basic soundness of the Korean economy, and the fundamental restructuring of the financial and corporate sectors.

CHAPTER TWELVE

1. The financial liberalization theory owes much to McKinnon (1973) and Shaw (1973). They argue that interest rate liberalization leads to "financial deepening" by making capital markets more efficient.

2. For a discussion of financial regulation in the Caribbean context, see Williams (1996).

3. For a more detailed analysis of this experience, the reader is referred to Rodriguez (1992).

4. The Jamaican experience with stabilization policy is well documented. See Howard (1992) and Polanyi-Levitt (1991).

5. This paragraph is based on information contained in Planning Institute of Jamaica, *Economic Survey of Jamaica*, 1997, p. iii.

6. For these data see Planning Institute of Jamaica, *Economic Survey of Jamaica*, 1997, p. iii.

7. We have not considered political and strategic factors in analysing Turkey's performance. See Aricanli and Rodrik 1990 for a discussion of these factors.

8. For details of the structural adjustment experience of sub-Saharan Africa see analyses by Nsouli 1993; Lensink 1996; and Hadjimichael, Ghura and Muhleisen 1995.

9. Ghana's experiences with structural adjustment has been evaluated by Nowack, Basanti and Horvath (1996).

CHAPTER FOURTEEN

1. The literature on incidence, excess burden, and optimal tax theory is extensive. For supplementary reading the following books and articles are insightful: Musgrave 1959; Musgrave and Musgrave 1973; Rosen 1992; Auerbach 1985; Harberger 1962, 1974; Break 1974; Stern 1984; Mirrlees 1971; and Krelove 1995.

CHAPTER FIFTEEN

1. The broad provisions summarized here can be found in Auerbach and Slemrod (1997). TRA86 also made changes in the provisions for allowances for individuals, and other miscellaneous business tax changes.

2. See Sandford (1993: 132). He argues that one of the complexities was the distinction between active and passive income.

3. For details on the provisions related to fringe benefits, depreciation, tax incentives, and the tax treatment of pensions and insurance see Gillis (1985: 237–40).

4. For details of the VAT, see Asher (1997: 145–49).

5. The report of the Inter-American Development Bank, *Economic and Social Progress in Latin America 1996*, lists these objectives of tax reform in Latin America. The points in this paragraph are drawn from the IDB 1996 Report, pages 125–128.

6. See the IDB Report 1996 mentioned above for this observation.

7. For further analysis of administrative tax reform in Colombia, see McLure and Pardo (1992).

CHAPTER SIXTEEN

1. Goode (1977) has indicated that American tax specialists prefer to describe this concept as the Haig-Simons concept of income. However, Georg von Schanz (1853–1931) was a German economist who advanced a similar concept before Haig (1921) and Simons (1938). Schanz's definition can be found in *Finanz-Archiv*, 13, no. 1 (1896). Haig (1921) defined income as the money value of the next accretion to economic power between two points of time.

2. For a good summary of itemized deductions in developing countries, see Ernst and Young (1997). Some developing countries continue to deduct social security contributions, medical insurance payments, and so forth.

3. Our analysis of the mechanics of these systems in this section draws heavily on the work of Cnossen (1993) and King (1995a). It should be noted that most countries have combinations of these various systems developed to suit their own economic environment. Additionally, the systems are complicated by the use of various tax credits and allowances defined in the tax legislation for different types of economic activities.

Chapter Eighteen

1. Brown's (1948) proposal had broad applicability outside the mineral sector. He considered the direct effect of a "business-income tax" on incentives to invest in "durable producers' goods" and how the type of depreciation would effect the incidence of the tax. He argued that a proportional tax levied on business income could be neutralized if government paid for losses of the firm at the same rate as it taxed the firm's income.

Chapter Twenty

1. See, for example, models by Allingham and Sandmo (1972) and Pyle (1993).
2. For a discussion of the issues in this paragraph see Pyle (1993). He argues that the paucity of empirical studies on tax evasion stems from the absence of good data to perform tests.
3. For an analysis of the underground economy in developed countries, see Tanzi (1982b). This work is also concerned with the measurement of tax evasion.
4. Alm, Bahland and Murray (1992) regressed the logarithm of underreported income and underreported taxes on taxable income, the marginal tax rate on taxable income and other dummy variables such as family size, gender, and tax credits. The results showed that the coefficients of the income variable and the marginal tax rate were positive and significant, implying that tax evasion rises with income and high marginal tax rates.
5. Discussions of these approaches can be found in Gordon (1990), Mansfield (1988), Pyle (1993), and Hasseldine (1998). Our analysis leans heavily on these works.
6. For a more detailed discussion of tax amnesties, the reader is referred to Alm and Beck (1990) and Dubin, Graetz and Wilde (1992).
7. See Talib (1996: 21) for references to articles on compliances costs in Singapore, Australia, Canada, New Zealand and the United States.
8. There are other issues not dealt with here. These include taxpayer identification, invoicing and bookkeeping requirements, filing and payment requirements, administration of refunds and the costs of VAT administration. For further reading on these issues see Casanegra de Jantscher (1990: 175–79).

References

Aaron, H. J. 1975. *Who Pays the Property Tax?* Washington, DC: The Brookings Institution.

Acuna, L. F. 1992. "Privatization of tax administration". In *Improving Tax Administration in Developing Countries*, edited by R. Bird and M. Casanegra de Jantscher. Washington, DC: International Monetary Fund.

Ahluwalia, M. S. 1974. "The scope for policy intervention". In *Redistribution and Growth*, edited by H. Chenery et al. New York: Oxford University Press.

Ahluwalia, M. S. 1976. "Inequality, poverty and development". *Journal of Development Economics* 3, no. 4 (December).

Alam, A., and S. Rajapatirana. 1993. "Trade reform in Latin America and the Caribbean". *Finance and Development* 30, no. 3 (September).

Albrecht, W. P. 1983. *Economics*. Englewood Cliffs, NJ: Prentice Hall.

Alderman, H., and K. Lindert. 1998. "The potential and limitations of self-targeted food subsidies". *World Bank Research Observer* 13, no. 2 (August).

Alesina, A. 1989. "Politics and business cycles in industrial democracies". *Economic Policy* 8 (April).

Alesina, A., and J. Sachs. 1988. "Political parties and the business cycle in the United States 1948–1984". *Journal of Money, Credit and Banking* 20, no. 1 (February).

Alesina, A., and L. Summers. 1993. "Central Bank independence and macroeconomic performance: some comparative evidence". *Journal of Money, Credit and Banking* 25, no. 2 (May).

Ali, S. M., and R. H. Adams, Jr. 1996. "The Egyptian food subsidy systems operation and effects on income distribution". *World Development* 24, no. 11 (November).

Alleyne, D. 1991. "An analysis of the structure and burden of the post reform tax system of Jamaica, fiscal year 1988/89". Mimeograph. Consortium Graduate School, Faculty of Social Sciences, University of the West Indies, Mona, Jamaica.

Alleyne, D. 1996. "Testing for Wagner's law in Jamaica, Guyana and Barbados: Is there a spurious relationship?" Presented at Annual Review Seminar, Research Department, Central Bank of Barbados, Bridgetown, July 17–19.

Alleyne, D. 1997. "Taxation and labour supply: Evidence from Jamaica". Central Bank of Barbados Working Papers, Vol. 1, Bridgetown, Central Bank of Barbados.

Allingham, M., and A. Sandmo. 1972. "Income tax evasion: A theoretical analysis". *Journal of Public Economics* .

Alm, J., R. Bahland, and M. Murray. 1991. "Income tax evasion". In *The Jamaican Tax Reform*, edited by R. Bahl. Cambridge, Mass.: Lincoln Institute of Land Policy.

Alm, J., and W. Beck. 1990. "Tax amnesties and tax revenues". *Public Finance Quarterly* 18: 433–53.

Altimir, O. 1982. *The Extent of Poverty in Latin America*. World Bank Staff Working Paper, no. 522, Washington, DC: World Bank.

Anand, S., and S. M. Kanbur. 1993. "The Kuznets process and the inequality-development relationship". *Journal of Development Economics* 40, no. 1 (February).

Anderson, P., and M. Witter. 1994. "Crisis, adjustment and social change: A case study of Jamaica". In *Consequences of Structural Adjustment: A Review of the Jamaican Experience*, edited by E. LeFranc. Mona, Jamaica: Canoe Press.

Aricanli, T., and D. Rodrik. 1990. "An overview of Turkey's experience with economic liberalization and structural adjustment". *World Development* 18, no. 10.

Asher, M. 1997. "Reforming the tax system in Indonesia". In *Tax Reform in Developing Countries,* edited by W. Thirsk. Washington, DC: World Bank.

Atkinson, A. 1995. "On targeting social security: Theory and Western experience with family benefits". In *Public Spending and the Poor*, edited by D. Van de Walle and K. Nead. Washington, DC: World Bank

Atkinson, A. B., and J. E. Stiglitz. 1980. *Lectures on Public Sector Economics*. New York: McGraw-Hill.

Auerbach, A. J. 1985. "The theory of excess burden and optimal taxation". In *Handbook of Public Economics*, Vol. 1, edited by A. J. Auerbach and M. Feldstein. Amsterdam: North Holland.

Auerbach, A. J., and J. Slemrod. 1997. "The economic effects of the tax reform act of 1986". *American Economic Review* 35, no. 2 (June).

Bahl, R. (ed.). 1992. *The Jamaican Tax Reform*. Cambridge, Mass.: Lincoln Institute of Land Policy.

Bahl, R., and J. Martinez-Vasquez. 1992. "The nexus of tax administration and tax policy in Jamaica and Guatemala". In *Improving Tax Administration in Developing Countries*, edited by R. Bird and M. Casanegra de Jantscher. Washington, DC: International Monetary Fund.

Balassa, B. 1974. "Estimating the shadow price of foreign exchange in project appraisal". *Oxford Economic Papers* 26, no. 2 (July).

Balassa, B. 1982. "Disequilibrium analysis in developing economies: An overview". *World Development* 10, no. 12 (December).

Baldwin, G. B. 1972. "A layman's guide to Little–Mirlees". *Finance and Development* 9, no. 1.

Barro, R. J. 1989. "The Ricardian approach to deficits". *Journal of Economic Perspectives* 3, no. 2 (Spring).

Bartlett, B. 1987. "The case for tax cuts". *Economic Impact,* no. 57.

Batra, R., and S. Guisinger. 1974. "A new approach to the estimation of the shadow exchange rate in evaluating development projects in less developing countries". *Oxford Economic Papers* 26, no. 2 (July).

Baumol, W. 1967. "Macroeconomics of unbalanced growth". *American Economic Review* 57, no. 3 (June).

Becker, G. S. 1983. "A theory of competition among pressure groups for political influence". *Quarterly Journal of Economics* 98, no. 3 (August).

Belgrave, A., and R. Craigwell. 1997. "The impact of government expenditure on economic growth in Barbados: A disaggregated approach". In *Macroeconomics and Finance in the Caribbean: Quantitative Analyses*, edited by D. Worrell and R. Craigwell. Trinidad: Caribbean Centre for Monetary Studies.

Bergstrom, T. C., and R. P. Goodman. 1973. "Private demands for public goods". *American Economic Review* 63, no. 2 (May).

Bernheim, B. D. 1989. "A neoclassical perspective on budget deficits". *Journal of Economic Perspectives* 3, no. 2 (Spring).

Besley, T., and R. Kanbur. 1988. "Food subsidies and poverty alleviation". *Economic Journal* 92.

Bird, R. 1974. *Taxing Agricultural Land in Developing Countries*. Cambridge, Mass.: Harvard University Press.

Bird, R. 1987. "A new look at indirect taxation in developing countries". *World Development* 15, no. 9.

Bird, R. 1992. "Taxing tourism in developing countries". *World Development* 20, no. 8.

Bird, R. M., and B. D. Miller. 1986. "The incidence of indirect taxes on low-income households in Jamaica". Jamaica Tax Structure Examination Project, Staff Paper no. 26, Metropolitan Studies Program, Maxwell School, Syracuse University (April).

Bird, R. M., and O. Oldman. 1990. *Taxation in Developing Countries*. Baltimore: Johns Hopkins University Press.

Bird, R. M., and L. De Wulf. 1973. "Taxation and income distribution in Latin America: A critical review of empirical studies". *IMF Staff Papers* 20 (November).

Bird, R. M., and M. Casanegra de Jantscher. 1992. *Improving Tax Administration in Developing Countries*. Washington, DC: International Monetary Fund.

Blackman, C. N. 1992. "An analytical framework for the study of Caribbean public enterprise". *Social and Economic Studies* 41, no. 4 (December).

Blejer, M. I., and A. Cheasty. 1988. "High inflation, heterodox stabilization, and fiscal policy". *World Development* 16, no. 8 (August).

Blinder, A. S. 1975. "Distribution effects and the aggregate consumption function". *Journal of Political Economy* 83.

Boadway, R., and D. Wildasin. 1984. *Public Sector Economics*. Boston: Little, Brown.

Bonbright, J. C., A. L. Davidsen, and D. R. Karmerschen. 1988. *Principles of Public Utility Rates*. Arlington: Public Utilities Reports.

Borcherding, T. E. 1977. "The sources of growth of public expenditures in the United States 1902–1970". In *Budgets and Bureaucrats: The Sources of Government Growth*, edited by T. E. Borcherding. Durham: Duke University Press.

Borcherding, T. E. 1985. "Causes of government expenditure growth: A survey of the US evidence". *Journal of Public Economics* 28.

Borcherding, T. E., and R. T. Deacon. 1972. "The demand for services of non-federal governments". *American Economic Review* 62 (December).

Boskin, M. J. 1978. "Taxation, saving and the rate of interest". *Journal of Political Economy* 86, no. 2 (April).

Boyd, D. A. C. 1984. "Jamaica: Pay as you earn taxation". *Bulletin for International Fiscal Documentation* 38, no. 12.

Break, G. F. 1957. "Income taxes and incentives to work: An empirical study". *American Economic Review* 47 no. 2 (September).

Break, G. F. 1974. "The incidence and economic effects of taxation". In *The Economics of Public Finance*, edited by A. Blinder, R. Solow and G. Break. Washington, DC: The Brookings Institution.

Bristow, J., and B. Wurts. 1992. "Barbados: reform of indirect taxation". Mimeograph. Washington DC: International Monetary Fund.

Brittain, J. 1957. *The Payroll Tax for Social Security*. Washington, DC: The Brookings Institution.

Brown, C. V., and P. M. Jackson. 1990. *Public Sector Economics*. Oxford: Martin Robertson.

Brown, E. 1948. "Business income taxation and investment incentives". *Income, Employment, and Public Policy: Essays in Honour of Alvin H. Hansen*. New

York: W. W. Norton. This article has been reproduced in R. A. Musgrave, and C. S. Shoup (eds). *Readings in the Economics of Taxation*. Homewood, Ill.: Richard D. Irwin, 1959.

Browning, E. K. 1994. *Public Finance and the Price System*. Englewood Cliffs, NJ: Prentice Hall.

Buchanan, J. M. 1958. *Public Principles of Public Debt*. Homewood, Ill.: Richard D. Irwin.

Buchanan, J. M. 1965. "An economic theory of clubs". *Economics* 32 (February).

Buchanan, J. M. 1966. "Joint supply, externality and optimality". *Economica* 33 (November).

Buchanan, J. M., and M. R. Flowers. 1975. *The Public Finances*. Homewood, Ill.: Richard D. Irwin.

Buchanan, J. M., and C. J. Goetz. 1972. "Efficiency limits of fiscal mobility: An assessment of the Tiebout model". *Journal of Public Economics* 1 (April).

Buchanan, J. M., and G. Tulloch. 1962. *The Calculus of Consent*. Ann Arbor: University of Michigan Press.

Buchanan, J. M., and R. Wagner. 1977. *Democracy in Deficit: The Political Legacy of Lord Keynes*. New York: Academic Press.

Burgess, R., and N. Stern. 1993. *Taxation and Development. Journal of Economic Literature* 31, no. 2 (June).

Byam, R. 1992. "The administrative aspects of tax reform". In *Tax Reform in the Caribbean*, edited by K. Theodore. Mona, Jamaica: Institute of Social and Economic Research.

Cagan, P. 1956. "The monetary dynamics of hyperinflation". In *Studies in the Quantity Theory of Money*, edited by M. Friedman. Chicago: University of Chicago Press.

Caribbean Tourism Organization. 1990. *Impact of Tourism Investment Incentives in the Caribbean Region*. Sponsored by the Organization of American States and the Caribbean Tourism Organization.

Caribbean Tourism Organization. 1996. *Caribbean Tourism Sector Taxation*. January (prepared by Deloitte and Touch).

Cardoso, E., and R. Dornbusch. 1987. "Brazil's tropical plan". *American Economic Review* 77, no. 2 (May).

Cardoso, E., and A. Helwege. 1992. "Below the line: Poverty in Latin America". *World Development* 20, no. 1.

Casenegra de Jantscher, M. 1976. "Tax havens explained". *Finance and Development* 13, no. 1 (March).

Casenegra de Jantscher, M. 1990. "Administering the VAT". In *Value-Added Taxation in Developing Countries*, edited by M. Gillis, C. S. Shoup and G. P. Sicat. Washington, DC: World Bank.

Chamley, C. 1991. "Taxation of financial assets in developing countries". Working Paper Series, Country Economics Department, World Bank.

Chang, H. 1997. "The economics and politics of regulation". *Cambridge Journal of Economics* 21.

Chelliah, R. J. 1971. "Trends in taxation in developing countries". *IMF Staff Papers* 18 (July).

Chrystal, K. A., and J. E. Alt. 1981. "Some problems of formulating and testing a politico-economic model of the United Kingdom". *Economic Journal* 91 (September).

Chua, D. 1995. "Tax incentives". In *Tax Policy Handbook*, edited by P. Shome. Washington, DC: International Monetary Fund.

Cnossen, S. 1984. "Jamaica's indirect tax system: The administration and reform of indirect taxes". Metropolitan Studies Programme Staff Paper, no. 8, Syracuse.

Cnossen, S. 1990. "The case for selective taxes on goods and services in developing countries". In *Taxation in Developing Countries*, edited by R. Bird, and O. Oldman. Baltimore: Johns Hopkins.

Cnossen, S. 1993. "What kind of corporation tax". In *Key Issues in Tax Reform*, edited by C. Stanford. Bath, England: Fiscal Publications.

Coase, R. 1960. "The problem of social choice ". *Journal of Law and Economics* 3.

Corden, W. M. 1971. *The Theory of Protection*. London: Oxford University Press.

Corfmat, F. 1990. "Computerizing revenue administrations in LDCs". In *Taxation in Developing Countries*, edited by R. M. Bird and O. Oldman. Baltimore: Johns Hopkins University Press.

Corlett, W. J., and D. C. Hague 1953. "Complementarity and the excess burden of taxation". *Review of Economic Studies* 21.

Craigwell, R. 1992. "Government deficits and spending in Barbados: An empirical test of the Buchanan-Wagner hypothesis". *Public Finance* 47, no. 3

Craigwell, R., C. Mascoll, and H. Leon. 1994. "Government revenue and expenditure causality in the presence of seasonality in Barbados". *Social and Economic Studies* 43, no. 4 (December).

Craigwell, R., and C. Mascoll. 1995. "On unbalanced productivity growth in Barbados". *Money Affairs* 7, no. 2 (July–December).

Cukierman, A., and S. Webb. 1994. "Political influence on the central bank: international evidence". Paper prepared for the American Political Science Association Meeting, New York (August 31 – September 4).

Dasgupta, A. K., and D. W. Pearce. 1978. *Cost-Benefit Analysis: Theory and Practice*. London: Macmillan.

David, W. L. 1985. *The IMF Policy Paradigm: The Macroeconomics of Stabilization, Structural Adjustment and Economic Development*. New York: Praeger.

Demsetz, H. 1967. "Towards a theory of property rights". *American Economic Review* (Papers and Proceedings), May.

De Wulf, L. 1975. "Fiscal incidence studies in developing countries: survey and critique". *IMF Staff Papers* 22, no. 1 (March).

Diamond, J. 1990. "Government expenditure and growth". *Finance and*

Development 27, no. 4.

Diamond, P. 1987. "Optimal tax theory and development policy: Directions for future research". In *The Theory of Taxation for Developing Countries*, edited by D. Newbery and N. Stern. New York: Oxford University Press.

Diaz-Alejandro, C. 1985. "Goodbye financial repression, hello financial crash". *Journal of Development Economics* 19, no. 1/2 (September).

Diez de Medina, R. 1997. "Poverty and income distribution in Barbados 1996". Mimeograph. Inter-American Development Bank.

Dosser, D. 1967. "Economic analysis of tax harmonization". In *Fiscal Harmonization in Common Markets*, edited by C. Shoup. New York: Columbia University Press.

Downes, A. S. 1987. "The distribution of household income in Barbados". *Social and Economic Studies* 36, no. 4 (December).

Downes, A. S. 1994. "The impact of the prices and incomes policy on the economic climate of Barbados". *Social and Economic Studies* 43, no. 4 (December).

Downs, A. 1957. *An Economic Theory of Democracy*. New York: Harper and Row.

Dubin, J. A., M. J. Graetz, and L. L. Wilde. 1992. "State income tax amnesties: Causes". *Quarterly Journal of Economics* 107.

Due, J. F. 1960. "Net worth taxation". *Public Finance* 14.

Due, J. F. 1977. *Indirect Taxation in Developing Countries*. Baltimore: Johns Hopkins University Press.

Due, J. F., and F. Greaney. 1991. "Trinidad and Tobago: The development of a value-added tax". *Bulletin for International Fiscal Documentation* (June).

Due, J. F., and P. Robson. 1967. "Tax harmonization in the East African common market". In *Fiscal Harmonizatin in Common Markets*, edited by C. Shoup. New York: Columbia University Press.

Easterly, W., and S. Rebelo. 1993. "Fiscal policy and economic growth: An empirical investigation". *Journal of Monetary Economics* 32 (December).

Economic Commission for Latin America and the Caribbean. 1989. *Extent of Poverty in Eight Countries in Latin America*. Santiago: United Nations.

Economic Commission for Latin America and the Caribbean. 1995. *Offshore Financial Centres in the Caribbean* (March).

Economic Commission for Latin America and the Caribbean. 1996. *Economic Survey of Latin America and the Caribbean 1995–1996*. Santiago: United Nations.

Edwards, S. 1994. "The political economy of inflation and stabilization in developing countries". *Economic Development and Cultural Change* 42, no. 2 (January).

Eichengreen, B., and M. Mussa. 1998. "Capital account liberalization and the IMF". *Finance and Development* 35, no. 4 (December).

Ernst and Young. 1995. *Worldwide Corporate Tax Guide and Directory*. New York:

Ernst and Young International.

Ernst and Young. 1997. *1998 Worldwide Executive Tax Guide*. New York: Ernst and Young International.

Evans, O. 1983. "Tax policy and the interest elasticity of saving, and capital accumulation". *American Economic Review* 73.

Faria, A. G. 1995a . "Source versus residence principle". In *Tax Policy Handbook*, edited by P. Shome. Washington, DC: International Monetary Fund.

Faria, A. G. 1995b. "Relief from double taxation". In *Tax Policy Handbook*, edited by P. Shome. Washington, DC: International Monetary Fund.

Faria, A. G. 1995c. "Aspects of tax treaties". In *Tax Policy Handbook*, edited by P. Shome. Washington, DC: International Monetary Fund.

Farrell, T. W. 198 1. "The government budget and the money supply in open petroleum economies: Trinidad and Tobago, 1973–1980". Mimeograph. Central Bank of Trinidad and Tobago.

Feldstein, M. S. 1980. "International difference in social security and savings". *Journal of Public Economics* 14.

Fischer, S. 1987. "The Israeli stabilization programme, 1985–86". *American Economic Review* 77, no. 2 (May).

Fischer, S. 1998. "The Asian crisis and the changing role of the IMF". *Finance and Development* 35, no. 2 (June).

Frampton, D. 1993. *Practical Tax Administration*. Bath, England: Fiscal Publications.

Francis, A. A. 1981. *Taxing the Transnationals in the Struggle over Bauxite*. Research Report Series, no. 9. The Hague: Institute of Social Studies.

Frey, B. S. 1978. "Politico-economic models and cycles". *Journal of Public Economics* 9.

Frey, B. S., and Schenider, F. 1978. "A politico-economic model of the United Kingdom". *Economic Journal* 88 (June).

Fry, M. 1988. *Money Interest and Banking in Economic Developing*. Baltimore: Johns Hopkins University Press.

Furubotn, E., and S. Pejovich. 1972. "Property rights and economic theory: A survey of the recent literature". *Journal of Economic Literature* 10 (December).

Gandhi, V. 1987a. "Tax reform: some considerations and limits (Lessons from experiences of developing countries)". Seminar paper, University of the West Indies, St Augustine, Trinidad, November 1987.

Gandhi, V. 1987b . "Tax structure for efficiency and supply side economics in developing countries". In *Supply Side Tax Policy: Its Relevance to Developing Countries*, edited by Ved P. Gandhi. Washington, DC: International Monetary Fund.

Garfield, P. J., and W. F. Lovejoy. 1964. *Public Utility Economics*. Englewood Cliffs, NJ: Prentice-Hall.

Garnaut, R., and A. Cluneis-Ross. 1975. "Uncertainty, risk aversion and the taxing of natural resource projects". *Economic Journal* 85 (June).

Garnaut, R., and A. Cluneis-Ross. 1983. *Taxation of Mineral Rents*. Oxford: Clarendon Press.

Ghatak, S. 1978. *Development Economics*. London: Longman.

Gillespie, W. I. 1976. "On the redistribution of income in Canada". *Canadian Tax Journal* 24.

Gillis, M. 1985. "Micro and macroeconomics of tax reform: Indonesia". *Journal of Development Economics* 19, no. 3 (December).

Gillis, M. 1989. "Tax reform: lessons from postwar experience in developing nations". In *Tax Reform in Developing Countries*, edited by M. Gillis. London: Duke University Press.

Gillis, M., and C. McLure. 1975. "Taxation of natural resources: Incidence of world taxes on natural resources with special reference to bauxite". *American Economic Review* 65, no. 2 (May).

Gillis, M., D. Perkins, and M. Roemer. 1992. *Economics of Development*. New York: Norton.

Gillis, M., C. S. Shoup, and G. P. Sicat. 1990. "Lessons for developing countries". In *Value-Added Taxation in Developing Countries*, edited by M. Gillis et al. Washington, DC: World Bank.

Girvan, N. 1971. "Making the rules of the game: Country–company agreements in the bauxite industry". *Social and Economic Studies* 20, no. 4 (December).

Girvan, N. 1984. "The Jamaican production levy: A view of the past, a vision of the future". *JBI Journal* 3, no. 1.

Goffman, J. J., and D. J. Mahar. 1971. "The growth of public expenditures in selected developing nations: Six Caribbean countries". *Public Finance* 26, no. 1.

Goode, R. 1977. "The economic definition of income". In *Comprehensive Income Taxation*, edited by J. Pechman. Washington, DC: Brookings Institution.

Goode, R. 1984. *Government Finance in Developing Countries*. Washington, DC: The Brookings Institution.

Goode, R., G. E. Lent, and P. Ojha. 1966. "Role of export taxes in developing countries". *International Monetary Fund Staff Papers* 13, no. 3 (November).

Gordon, R. K. 1990. "Income tax compliance and sanctions in developing countries". In *Taxation in Developing Countries*, edited by R. Bird and O. Oldman. Baltimore: Johns Hopkins University Press.

Gordon, S. 1976. "The new contractarians". *Journal of Political Economy* 84, no. 3.

Great Britain, Ministry of Overseas Development. 1977. *A Guide to the Economic Appraisal of Projects in Developing Countries*. London: Her Majesty's Stationery Office.

Griffith, W. 1987. "Can CARICOM countries replicate the Singapore experience?" *Journal of Development Studies* 24, no. 1 (October).

Grosh, M. E. 1995. "Towards quantifying the trade-off: Administrative costs and incidence in targeted programmes in Latin America". In *Public Spending and the Poor*, edited by D. Van de Walle and K. Nead. Washington, DC: World Bank.

Hadjimichael, M. T., D. Ghura, and M. Muhleisen. 1995. *Sub-Saharan Africa: Growth, Savings, and Investment, 1986–93*. Occasional Paper, no. 118 (January). Washington, DC: International Monetary Fund.

Haig, R. M. 1921. "The concept of income: Economic and legal aspects". In *The Federal Income Tax*, edited by R. M. Haig. New York: Columbia University Press.

Haindl, E., D. Dunn, and O. Schenone. 1995. "Income tax issues". In *Comprehensive Tax Reform: The Colombian Experience*, edited by P. Shome. Washington, DC: International Monetary Fund.

Handa, S., and D. King. 1997. "Structural adjustment policies, income distribution and poverty: A review of the Jamaican experience". *World Development* 25, no. 6.

Hanke, S. 1987. "The necessity of property rights". In *Privatization and Development*, edited by S. Hanke. San Francisco: Institute for Contemporary Studies.

Harberger, A. C. 1962. "The incidence of the corporation income tax". *Journal of Political Economy* 78 (June).

Harberger, A. C. 1974. *Taxation and Welfare*. Boston: Little, Brown.

Hasseldine, J. 1998. "Tax amnesties: An international review". *Bulletin for International Fiscal Documentation* 52, no. 7 (July).

Hausman, J. A. 1981. "Labour supply". In *How Taxes Affect Economic Behaviour*, edited by H. J. Aaron and J. A. Pechman. Washington, DC: The Brookings Institution.

Haynes, C. 1997. "Lessons from Barbados' experiment with the International Monetary Fund". In *Central Banking in Barbados: Reflections and Challenges*, edited by H. Codrington, R. Craigwell and C. Haynes. Barbados: Central Bank of Barbados.

Head, J. G. 1972. "Public goods: The polar case". In *Modern Fiscal Issues*, edited by R. Bird, and J. G. Head. Toronto: University of Toronto Press.

Head, J. G. 1990. "Public goods and public policy". In *Readings in Public Sector Economics*, edited by S. Baker and C. Elliott. Lexington, Mass.: D.C. Heath.

Hemming, R., and A. Mansoor. 1988. "Is privatization the answer?" *Finance and Development* 25, no. 3.

Henry, Z. 1972. *Labour Relations and Industrial Conflict in Commonwealth Countries*. Trinidad: Columbus Publishers.

Heymann, D. 1987. "The austral plan". *American Economic Review* 77, no. 2 (May).

Hibbs, D. 1977. "Political parties and macroeconomic policy". *American Political Science Review* 71, no. 4 (December).

Holland, D., and J. Follain. 1990. "The property tax in Jamaica". In *The Jamaican Tax Reform*, edited by R. Bahl. Cambridge, Mass.: Lincoln Institute of Land Policy.

Howard, M. 1979. *The Fiscal System of Barbados*. Occasional Papers Series, no. 12. Cave Hill, Barbados: Institute of Social and Economic Research, University of the West Indies.

Howard, M. 1982. "Post-war public policy in Barbados 1946–1979". *Social and Economic Studies* 31, no. 3 (September).

Howard, M. 1989a. "Public sector financing in Jamaica, Barbados and Trinidad and Tobago 1974–1984". *Social and Economic Studies* 38, no. 3.

Howard, M. 1989b. *Dependence and Development in Barbados 1945–1985*. Bridgetown, Barbados: Carib Research and Publications.

Howard, M. 1992. *Public Finance in Small Open Economies: The Caribbean Experience*. Westport, Conn.: Praeger.

Howard, M. 1995. "Theoretical aspects of fiscal harmonization in CARICOM". *Bulletin of Eastern Caribbean Affairs* 20, no. 3 (September).

Howard, M., and C. Mascoll. 1994. "Barbados tax reform of 1992 compared with 1986". *Bulletin of Eastern Caribbean Affairs* 19, no. 3 (September).

Hye, A. H. 1993. "Designs for poverty alleviation programmes in South Asia: Experience and lessons". In *Strategies for Poverty Reduction*, edited by C. Easter. London: Commonwealth Secretariat.

Inter-American Development Bank. 1981. In *Estimating Accounting Prices for Project Appraisal*, edited by T. Powers. Washington, DC: Inter-American Development Bank.

Inter-American Development Bank. 1996. *Economic and Social Progress in Latin America*. Washington, DC: Inter-American Development Bank (November).

International Monetary Fund Staff. 1998a. "The Asian crisis: Causes and cures". *Finance and Development* 35, no. 2 (June).

International Monetary Fund. 1998b. *IMF Economic Reviews*. May–August, no. 2. Washington, DC: International Monetary Fund.

Inman, R. P. 1987. "Markets, governments and the new political economy". In *Handbook of Public Economics* 11, edited by A. J. Auerbach and M. Feldstein. Amsterdam: North Holland.

Jackson, P. M. 1993. "Taxation, public choice and public spending". In *Current Issues in Public Sector Economics*, edited by P. M. Jackson. London: Macmillan.

Jarvis, M. T., and R. J. Sampson. 1973. *Public Utilities Regulation, Management and Ownership*. Boston: Houghton Mifflin.

Jenkins, G. P. 1990. "How to tax mineral extraction". In *Taxation in Developing Countries*, edited by R. Bird, and O. Oldman. Baltimore: Johns Hopkins University Press.

Jha, R. 1994. *Macroeconomics for Developing Countries*. New York: Routledge.

Johnston, R. B. 1998. "Sequencing capital account liberalization". *Finance and Development* 35, no. 4 (December).

Jones, E. 1987. *Coalitions of the Oppressed*. Mona, Jamaica: Institute of Social and Economic Research, University of the West Indies.

Jones, E. 1992. *Development Administration: Jamaican Adaptation.* Kingston, Jamaica: CARICOM Publishers.

Jones-Hendrickson, S. B. 1985. *Public Finance and Monetary Policy in Open Economies.* Mona, Jamaica: Institute of Social and Economic Research, University of the West Indies.

Kanbur, R., M. Keen, and M. Tuomala 1995. "Labour supply and targeting in poverty-alleviation programmes". In *Public Spending and the Poor*, edited by D. van de Walle and K. Nead. Washington, DC: World Bank.

Keen, M. J. 1992. "Needs and targeting". *Economic Journal* 102.

Keleher, R. 1982. "Supply-side tax policy: Reviewing the evidence". In *Viewpoints on Supply-Side Economics*, edited by T. J. Hailstones. Reston, Va.: Reston Publishing.

Khan, M., and M. D. Knight. 1982. "Some theoretical and empirical issues relating to stabilization in developing countries". *World Development* 10, no. 9 (September).

Kiguel, M., and N. Liviatan. 1992. "When do heterodox stabilization programmes work?" *World Bank Research Observer* 7, no. 1 (January).

Killick, T. 1984. "IMF stabilization programmes". In *The IMF and Stabilization: Developing Country Experience*, edited by T. Killick. London: Heinemann Educational Books.

King, J. R. 1995a. "The mechanics of integration". In *Tax Policy Handbook*, edited by P. Shome. Washington, DC: International Monetary Fund.

King, J. R. 1995b. "Taxation of capital gains". In *Tax Policy Handbook*, edited by P. Shome. Washington, DC: International Monetary Fund.

King, M. A. 1974. "Taxation and the cost of capital". *Review of Economic Studies* 41.

Kogan Page. 1995. *World Business and Economic Review 1995.* London: Kogan Page and Walden.

Kogiku, K. C. 1971. *Microeconomic Models.* New York: Harper and Row.

Koopmans, T. 1957. *Three Essays on the State of Economic Science.* New York: McGraw-Hill.

Kopits, G. 1992. "Overview". In *Tax Harmonization in the European Community: Policy Issues and Analysis*, edited by G. Kopits. Occasional Paper 94 (July). Washington, DC: International Monetary Fund.

Kreinin, M. E., and L. H. Officer. 1978. *The Monetary Approach to the Balance of Payments: A Survey, Princeton Studies in International Finance*, no. 43, Princeton University.

Krelove, R. 1995. "General equilibrium incidence of taxes". In *Tax Policy Handbook*, edited by P. Shome. Washington, DC: International Monetary Fund.

Krelove, R, and J. Stotsky. 1995. "Business assets and receipts taxes". In *Tax Policy Handbook*, edited by P. Shome. Washington, DC: International Monetary Fund.

Krueger, A. O. 1985. "Import substitution versus export promotion". *Finance and Development* 22, no. 2 (June).

Krzyzaniak, M., and R. A. Musgrave. 1963. *The Shifting of the Corporation Income Tax*. Baltimore: Johns Hopkins University Press.

Kuznets, S. 1955. "Economic growth and income inequality". *American Economic Review* 45, no. 1 (March).

Lal, D. 1974. *Methods of Project Analysis A Review*. World Bank Staff Occasional Paper, no. 16, Baltimore: Johns Hopkins University Press, Mona.

Lefranc, E. 1994. *Consequences of Structural Adjustment: A Review of the Jamaican Experience*. Jamaica: University of the West Indies Press.

Lensick, R. 1996. *Structural Adjustment in Sub-Saharan Africa*. London: Longman.

Lent, G. E. 1967. "Tax incentives for investment in developing countries". *IMF Staff Papers* 14, no. 2 (July).

Lent, G. E. 1977. "Corporation tax in developing countries". *IMF Staff Papers* 24.

Lent, G. E., M. Casanegra, and M. Guerard. 1973. "The value-added tax in developing countries". *IMF Staff Papers* 30 (July).

Leuthold, J. 1991. "Tax shares in developing countries: A panel study". *Journal of Development Economics* 35, no. 1 (January).

Lewis, W. A. 1955. *The Theory of Economic Growth*. London: Allen and Unwin.

Lim, D. 1983. "Fiscal incentives and direct foreign investment in less developed countries". *Journal of Development Studies* 19, no. 2 (January).

Lindbeck, A. 1976. "Stabilization policy in open economies with endogenous politicians". *American Economic Review* 66 (May).

Lipsky, J. 1998. "Asia's crisis: A market perspective". *Finance and Development* 35, no. 2 (June).

Little, I. M. D., and J. Mirrlees. 1974. *Project Appraisal and Planning for Development*. London: Heinemann.

Lotz, J. R., and E. R. Morss. 1967. "Measuring tax effort in developing countries". *IMF Staff Papers* 14, no. 3 (November).

Lovejoy, R. M. 1963. "The burden of Jamaican taxation, 1958". *Social and Economic Studies* 12, no. 4.

Lowenstein, L. 1995. "Capital gains tax cuts a better way". *Washington Post*, 30 April.

Macrae, C. D. 1977. "A political model of the business cycle". *Journal of Political Economy* 85, no. 2 (April).

Maithani, B. P. 1993. "Poverty-specific policy approaches: The Indian experience". In *Strategies for Poverty Reduction*, edited by C. Easter. London: Commonwealth Secretariat.

Mansfield, C. Y. 1972. "Elasticity and buoyancy of a tax system: A method applied to Paraguay". *IMF Staff Papers* 19, no. 2 (July).

Mansfield, C. Y. 1988. "Tax administration in developing countries". *IMF Staff Papers* 35.

Marsden, K. 1990. "Taxes and economic growth". In *Taxation in Developing*

Countries, edited by R. M. Bird, and O. Oldman. Baltimore: Johns Hopkins University Press.

Martinez, G. O. 1998. "What lessons does the Mexican crisis hold for recovery in Asia". *Finance and Development* 35, no. 2 (June).

Mascoll, C. 1989. "The growth of government rxpenditure in three Caribbean countries, 1955–85: A test of two supply-side hypotheses". *Working Papers*, Central Bank of Barbados (December), Bridgetown, Barbados.

Mascoll, C. 1991. "Trends in effective tax rates of representative individuals in Barbados during the 1980s". Central Bank of Barbados, *Economic Review* 18, no. 3, Bridgetown, Barbados.

Mathieson, D. J., A. Richardson, and S. Sharma. 1998. "Financial crises in emerging markets". *Finance and Development* 35, no. 4 (December).

McCarten, W. 1995. "International transfer pricing and taxation". In *Tax Policy Handbook*, edited by P. Shome. Washington, DC: International Monetary Fund.

McCarten, W., and J. Stotsky. 1995. "Excise taxes". In *Tax Policy Handbook*, edited by P. Shome. Washington, DC: International Monetary Fund.

McCarthy, I. 1979. "Offshore banking centres: Benefits and costs". *Finance and Development* 16, no. 4 (December).

McClean, A. W. A. 1995. "Regulation of public utilities". *Barbados Advocate*, December 4–8.

McCleary, W. 1991. "The earmarking of government revenue: A review of some World Bank experience". *The World Bank Research Observer* 6, no. 1 (January).

McIntyre, A.,O. Arthur, and S. Charles. 1993. "Proposals for a harmonized system of incentives for industry, tourism and services for CARICOM". Mimeograph. Guyana: CARICOM Secretariat.

McKinnon, R. I. 1973. *Money and Capital in Economic Development*. Washington, DC: The Brookings Institution.

McLure, C. E. 1975. "General equilibrium incidence analysis: The Harberger model after ten years". *Journal of Public Economics* 4, (February).

McLure, C. E. 1977. "The incidence of Jamaica taxes, 1971–72". *Working Paper*, no. 16. Mona, Jamaica: Institute of Social and Economic Research, University of the West Indies

McLure, C. E. 1989. "Lessons for LDCs of US income tax reform". In *Tax Reform in Developing Countries*, edited by M. Gillis. London: Duke University Press.

McLure, C. E., and S. Pardo. 1992. "Improving the administration of the Colombia income tax". In *Improving Tax Administration in Developing Countries*, edited by R. Bird and M. Casanegra de Janscher. Washington, DC: International Monetary Fund.

McLure, C. E., and G. Zodrow. 1997. "Thirty years of tax reform in Colombia". In *Tax Reform in Developing Countries*, edited by W. Thirsk. Washington, DC: World Bank.

297

Meerman, J., and P. Shome. 1980. "Estimating counterfactual incomes in studies of budget incidence". *Public Finance* 35, no. 2.

Mesa-Lago, C. 1997. "Social welfare reform in the context of economic-political liberalization: Latin American cases". *World Development* 25, no. 4 (April).

Mieszkowski, P. M. 1967. "On the theory of tax incidence". *Journal of Political Economy* 75 (June).

Mieszkowski, P. M. 1972. "The property tax: An excise tax or a profits tax". *Journal of Public Economics* 1.

Mirrlees, J. A. 1971. "An exploration in the theory of optimum income taxation". *Review of Economic Studies* 38, (April).

Moffit, R. L. 1992. "Incentive effects of the US welfare system". *Journal of Economic Literature* 30.

Morgan, D. 1979. "Fiscal policy in oil exporting countries 1972–78". *IMF Staff Papers* 26 (March).

Morley, S. A. 1995. *Poverty and Inequality in Latin America: The Impact of Adjustment and Recovery in the 1980s*. Baltimore: Johns Hopkins University Press.

Morrison, T. K. 1982. "Structural determinants of government budget deficits in developing countries". *World Development* 10, no. 6.

Mueller, Dennis C. 1987. "The growth of government: A public choice perspective". *IMF Staff Papers* 34, no. 1 (March).

Munday, S. C. 1996. *Current Developments in Economics*. London: Macmillan.

Murthy, N. R. 1993. "Further evidence of Wagner's law for Mexico: An application of cointegration analysis". *Public Finance* 48, no. 1.

Musgrave, P. 1967. "Harmonization of direct business taxes: A case study". In *Fiscal Harmonization in Common Markets*, edited by C. Shoup. New York: Columbia University Press.

Musgrave, R. A. 1959. *The Theory of Public Finance*. New York: McGraw-Hill.

Musgrave, R. A. 1969a. "Provision of social goods". In *Public Economics*, edited by J. Margolis and H. Gritton. New York: St Martin's Press.

Musgrave, R. A. 1969b. *Fiscal Systems*. New Haven: Yale University Press.

Musgrave, R. A. 1976. "Optimal taxation, equitable taxation and second-best taxation". *Journal of Public Economics* 6 (July–August).

Musgrave, R. A. 1985. "A brief history of fiscal doctrine". In *Handbook of Public Economics*, Vol. 1, edited by A. J. Auerbach, and M. Feldstein. Amsterdam: North Holland.

Musgrave, R. A., K. E. Case, and H. B. Leonard. 1974. "The distribution of fiscal burdens and benefits". *Public Finance Quarterly* 2.

Musgrave, R. A., and P. B. Musgrave. 1973. *Public Finance in Theory and Practice*. New York: McGraw-Hill.

Musgrave, R., and A. T. Peacock. 1964. *Classics in the Theory of Public Finance*. London: Macmillan.

Muten, L. C. 1995. "Capital gains tax: gaining ground". In *More Key Issues in Tax Reform*, edited by C. Stanford. Bath, England: Fiscal Publications.

Nellor, D. C. 1995. "Environmental taxes". In *Tax Policy Handbook*, edited by P. Shome. Washington, DC: International Monetary Fund.

Niskanen, W. A. 1971. *Bureaucracy and Representative Government*. Chicago: Aldine-Atherton.

Niskanen, W. A. 1978. "Deficits, government spending, and inflation: What is the evidence?" *Journal of Monetary Economics* 4:591–602.

Nordhaus, W. D. 1975. "The political business cycle". *Review of Economic Studies* 42 (January).

North, D. C. 1985. "The growth of government in the United States". *Journal of Public Economics* 28.

North, D. C., and J. J. Wallis 1982. "American government expenditures: A historical perspective". *American Economic Review* 72 (May).

Nowak, M., R. Basanti, and S. Horvath. 1996. "Ghana, 1983–91". In *Adjustment for Growth: The African Experience*, edited by M. Hadjimichael et al. Occasional Papers 143 (October). Washington, DC: International Monetary Fund.

Nozick, R. 1974. *Anarchy, State and Utopia*. Oxford: Basil Blackwell.

Nsouli, S. 1993. "Structural adjustment in Sub-Saharan Africa". *Finance and Development* 30, no. 3 (September).

Nsouli, S., and M. Rached. 1998. "Capital account liberalization in the Southern Mediterranean". *Finance and Development* 35, no. 4 (December).

Nurse, L. 1992. *Trade Unionism and Industrial Relations in the Commonwealth Caribbean*. Westport: Greenwood Press.

Oakland, W. H. 1972. "Congestion, public goods and welfare". *Journal of Public Economics* 1.

Oakland, W. H. 1987. "Theory of public goods". In *Handbook of Public Economics*, Vol. 11, edited by A. J. Auerbach and M. Feldstein. Amsterdam: North Holland.

Odle, M. A. 1975. "Public policy". In *Caribbean Economy*, edited by G. L. Beckford. Mona, Jamaica: Institute of Social and Economic Research, University of the West Indies.

Odle, M. A. 1976. *The Evolution of Public Expenditure*. Mona, Jamaica: Institute of Social and Economic Research, University of the West Indies.

Organization for Economic Cooperation and Development. 1992. *OECD Economic Surveys: Mexico*. Paris: OECD.

Organization for Economic Cooperation and Development. 1995. *OECD Economic Surveys: Mexico*. Paris: OECD.

Orchard, L., and H. Stretton. 1997. "Public choice". *Cambridge Journal of Economics* 21, no. 3 (May).

Orzechowski, W. P. 1982. "Monetary aspects of supply-side economics". In *Supply-*

Side Economics: A Critical Appraisal, edited by R. H. Fink. Frederick, Md.: University Publications of America.

Palmer, K. F. 1980. "Mineral taxation policies in developing countries: An application of resource rent tax". *IMF Staff Papers* 27, no. 3 (September).

Payer, C. 1974. *The Debt Trap: The International Monetary Fund and the Third World*. New York: Monthly Review Press.

Peacock, A. 1979. *The Economic Analysis of Government and Related Themes*. Oxford: Martin Robertson.

Peacock, A. T., and J. Wiseman. 1961. *The Growth of Public Expenditure in the United Kingdom*. National Bureau of Economic Research, Princeton: Princeton University Press.

Pechman, J. A. 1989. *Tax Reform, The Rich and the Poor*. London: Harvester Wheatsheaf.

Pechman, J. A., and B. Okner. 1974. *Who Bears the Tax Burden*. Washington, DC: The Brookings Institution.

Peltzman, S. 1976. "Towards a more general theory of regulation". *Journal of Law and Economics* 19 (August).

Perry, G., and A. Orozco de Trina. 1990. "The VAT in Colombia". In *Value-Added Taxation in Developing Countries*, edited by M. Gillis, C. S. Shoup, and G. P. Sicat. Washington, DC: World Bank.

Persson, T., and G. Tabellini. 1990. *Macroeconomic Policy, Credibility and Politics*. New York: Harwood Academic.

Pigou, A. C. 1920. *The Economics of Welfare*. London: Macmillan.

Plasschaert, S. R. 1979. *Transfer Pricing and Multinational Corporations: An Overview of Concepts, Mechanisms and Regulations*. London: Gower.

Polanyi-Levitt, K. 1991. *The Origins and Consequences of Jamaica's Debt Crisis, 1970–1990*. Mona, Jamaica: Consortium Graduate School of Social Sciences, University of the West Indies.

Posner, R. 1974. "Theories of economic regulation". *Bell Journal of Economic and Management Science* 5, no. 2.

Premchand, A. 1983. *Government Budgeting and Expenditure Controls: Theory and Practice*. Washington, DC: International Monetary Fund.

Premchand, A. 1993. *Public Expenditure Management*. Washington, DC: International Monetary Fund.

Prest, A. R. 1975. *Public Finance in Developing Countries*. London: Weidenfeld and Nicolson.

Prest, A. R. 1978. "The taxable capacity of a country". In *Taxation and Economic Development*, edited by J. F. J. Toye. London: Frank Cass.

Psacharopoulos, G. 1993. *Poverty and Income Distribution in Latin America: The Story of the 1980s*. Washington, DC: World Bank.

Pyhrr, P. 1973. *Zero Base Budgeting*. New York: Wiley.

Pyle, D. J. 1993. "The economics of taxpayer compliance". In *Current Issues in*

Public Sector Economics, edited by P. M. Jackson. London: Macmillan.

Ramanadham, V. V. 1989. *Privatization in Developing Countries*. New York: Routledge.

Ramsaran, R. 1994. "The theory and practice of structural adjustment". In *Structural Adjustment, Public Policy and Administration in the Caribbean*, edited by J. Laguerre. St Augustine, Trinidad: University of the West Indies, School of Continuing Studies.

Ramsey, F. P. 1927. "A contribution to the theory of taxation". *Economic Journal* 37.

Rao, C. H. 1993. "Integration of poverty alleviation programmes into overall development strategies: The case of India". In *Strategies for Poverty Reduction*, edited by C. Easter. London: Commonwealth Secretariat.

Ravallion, M. 1991. "Reaching the rural poor through public employment: Arguments, evidence, and lessons from South Asia". *World Bank Research Observer* 6, no. 2 (July).

Ravallion, M., et al. 1993. "Does Maharashtra's employment guarantee scheme guarantee employment? Effects of the 1988 wage increase". *Economic Development and Cultural Change* 41, no. 2 (January).

Ravallion, M., and G. Datt. 1995. "Is targeting through a work requirement efficient? Some evidence for rural India". In *Public Spending and the Poor: Theory and Evidence*, edited by D. van de Walle and K. Nead. Baltimore: Johns Hopkins University Press.

Rawls, J. 1971. *A Theory of Justice*. Cambridge, Mass. : Harvard University Press.

Richupan, S. 1984. "Measuring tax evasion". *Finance and Development* 21, no. 4 (December).

Robson, P. 1984. *The Economics of International Integration*. London: Allen and Unwin.

Rochjadi, A., and J. Leuthold. 1994. "The effect of taxation on labour supply in a developing country: Evidence from cross-section data". *Economic Development and Cultural Change* 42, no. 2 (January).

Rodney, W. 1972. *How Europe Underdeveloped Africa*. London: Bougle-L'Ouverture.

Rodriguez, F. 1992. "The Mexican privatization programme: An economic analysis". *Social and Economic Studies* 41, no. 4 (December).

Rodrik, D. 1990. "How should structural adjustment programmes be designed?" *World Development* 18, no. 7.

Roemer, M., and J. Stern. 1975. *The Appraisal of Development Projects*. New York: Praeger.

Rogoff, K., and A. Sibert. 1988. "Elections and macroeconomic policy cycles". *Review of Economic Studies* 55, no. 1 (January).

Romer, T., and H. Rosenthal. 1979. "Bureaucrats versus voters: On the political economy of resource allocation by direct democracy". *Quarterly Journal of Economics* 93: 563–87 (November).

Rosen, H. S. 1992. *Public Finance*. Homewood, Ill: Irwin.

Rubinfeld, D. L. 1987. "The economics of the local public sector". In *Handbook of Public Economics*, Vol. 2, edited by A. J. Auerbach and M. Feldstein Amsterdam: North Holland.

Sachs, J. 1987. "The Bolivian hyperinflation and stabilization". *American Economic Review* 77, no. 2 (May).

Sackey, J. A. 1980. "Underdevelopment disequilibrium and growth in government expenditures: Some empirical generalizations". *Social and Economic Studies* 29, no. 4.

Samuelson, P. A. 1954. "The pure theory of public expenditure". *Review of Economics and Statistics* 36 (November).

Samuelson, P. A. 1955. "Diagrammatic exposition of a theory of public expenditure". *Review of Economics and Statistics* 37.

Samuelson, P. A. 1969. "Contrast between welfare conditions for joint supply and public goods". *Review of Economics and Statistics* 51 (February).

Sanchez-Ugarte, F., and J. R. Modi. 1990. "Export taxes in theory and practice". In *Taxation in Developing Countries*, edited by R. M. Bird and O. Oldman. Baltimore: Johns Hopkins University Press.

Sandford, C. 1995a . "Minimising administrative and compliance costs". In *More Key Issues in Tax Reform*, edited by C. Sandford. Bath, England: Fiscal Publications.

Sandford, C. 1993. "Successul tax reforms in six countries". Bath, England: Fiscal Publications.

Sandford, C. 1995b. "Taxing wealth". In *More Key Issues in Tax Reform*, edited by C. Sandford. Bath, England: Fiscal Publications.

Sandford, C., M. Goodwin, and P. Hardwick. 1989. *Administrative and Compliance Costs of Taxation*. Bath, England: Fiscal Publications.

Sandler, T., and J. T. Tschirhart. 1980. "The theory of clubs: A survey". *Journal of Economic Literature* 18 (December).

Sandmo, A. 1976. "Optimal taxation: An introduction to the literature". *Journal of Public Economics* 6 (July/August).

Schanz, G. von. 1896. *Finanz–Archiv* 13, no.1.

Schick, A. 1978. "The road from zero base budgeting". *Public Administration Review* 38.

Schuknecht, L. 1996. "Political business cycles and fiscal policies in developing countries". *Kyklos* 49, Fasc. 2.

Seater, J. J. 1993. "Ricardian equivalence". *Journal of Economic Literature* 31, no. 1 (March).

Sen, A. 1995. "The political economy of targeting". In *Public Spending and the Poor*, edited by D. van de Walle, and K. Nead. Washington, DC: World Bank.

Shah, A., and J. Whalley 1991. "Tax incidence analysis of developing countries: An alternative view". *World Bank Economic Review* 5, no. 3 (September).

Shaw, E. S. 1973. *Financial Deepening in Economic Development*. New York: Oxford University Press.

Shaw, J. 1993. "Poverty-specific policy approaches". In *Strategies for Poverty Reduction*, edited by C. Easter. London: Commonwealth Secretariat.

Shome, P. 1978. "The incidence of the corporation tax in India: A general equilibrium analysis". *Oxford Economic Papers* 30 (March).

Shome, P. 1995a. "Tax reform in Latin America". *Finance and Development* 32, no. 1 (March).

Shome, P. 1995b. "Value-added tax issues". In *Comprehensive Tax Reform: The Colombian Experience*, edited by P. Shome. Washington, DC: International Monetary Fund.

Shoup, C. S. 1990. "A growth-oriented tax system". In *Taxation in Developing Countries*, edited by R. M. Bird and O. Oldman. Baltimore: Johns Hopkins University Press.

Shoven, J. B., and J. Whalley. 1972. "A general equilibrium calculation of the effects of differential taxation of income from capital in the USA". *Journal of Public Economics* 1 (November).

Shultze, C. L. 1968. *The Politics and Economics of Public Spending*. Washington, DC: The Brookings Institution.

Simons, H. C. 1938. *Personal Income Taxation: The Definition of Income as a Problem of Fiscal Policy*. Chicago: University of Chicago Press.

Skinner, J. 1991. "Prospects for agricultural land taxation in developing countries". *World Bank Economic Review* 5, no. 3 (September).

Steiner, P. O. 1974. "Public expenditure budgeting". In *The Economics of Public Finance*, edited by A. S. Blinder, R. Solow, and C. Break. Washington, DC: Brookings Institution.

Stern, N. 1984. "Optimum taxation and tax policy". *IMF Staff Papers* 31, no. 2 (June).

Stigler, G. 1971. "The theory of economic regulation". *Bell Journal of Economic and Management Science* 2, no. 1.

Stiglitz, J. E. 1973. "Taxation, corporate financial policy, and the cost of capital". *Journal of Public Economics* 2.

Stiglitz, J. E. 1994. "The role of the state in financial markets". *Proceedings of the World Bank Annual Conference on Development Economics 1993*. Washington, DC: World Bank.

Stiglitz, J. E. 1996. "The role of government in economic development". In *Annual World Bank Conference on Development Economics*, edited by M. Bruno, and B. Pleskovic. Washington, DC: World Bank.

Stotsky, J. 1995. "Taxation of the financial sector". In *Tax Policy Handbook*, edited by P. Shome. Washington, DC: International Monetary Fund.

Stotsky, J., and M. Z. Yucelik. 1995. "Taxation of land and property". In *Tax Policy Handbook*, edited by P. Shome. Washington, DC: International Monetary Fund.

Strasma, J. et al. 1990. "Taxing the agricultural sector". In *Taxation in Developing Countries*, edited by R. Bird and O. Oldman. Baltimore: Johns Hopkins University Press.

Summers, L. H. 1983. "The after tax rate of return affects private savings". *American Economic Review* 74.

Sutton, M. 1984. "Structuralism: The Latin America record and the new critique". In *The IMF and Stabilization: Developing Country Experiences*, edited by T. Killick. London: Heinemann Educational Books.

Tait, A. 1988. *Value-Added Tax: International Practice and Problems*. Washington, DC: International Monetary Fund.

Tait, A. 1990. "VAT revenue, inflation, and the foreign trade balance". In *Value-Added Taxation in Developing Countries* edited by M. Gillis, C. S. Shoup and G. P. Sicat. Washington, DC: World Bank.

Talib, A. A. 1996. "The compliance costs of taxation". *Bulletin for International Fiscal Documentation* 50, no. 9 (September).

Tanzi, V. 1976. "Export taxation in developing countries: Taxation of coffee in Haiti". *Social and Economic Studies* 25 (March).

Tanzi, V. 1978. "Inflation, real tax revenue, and the case for inflationary finance: Theory with an application to Argentina". *IMF Staff Papers* 25, no. 3 (September).

Tanzi, V. 1982a. "Fiscal disequilibrium in developing countries". *World Development* 10, no. 12 (December).

Tanzi, V. (ed.). 1982b . *The Underground Economy in the United States and Abroad*. Lexington: Lexington Books.

Tanzi, V. 1990. "Quantitative characteristics of the tax systems of developing countries". In *Taxation in Developing Countries*, edited by R. Bird and O. Oldman. Baltimore: Johns Hopkins.

Tanzi, V. 1991. *Public Finance in Developing Countries*. Vermont: Edward Elgar.

Tanzi, V., and H. Zee. 1997. "Fiscal policy and long-run growth". *IMF Staff Papers* 44, no. 2 (June).

Taylor, L. 1987. "Macro policy in the tropics: How sensible people stand". *World Development* 15, no. 12 (December).

Thorn, R. S. 1967. "The evolution of public finance during economic development". *Manchester School of Economic and Social Studies* 35 (January).

Thurow, L. 1971. "The income distribution as a pure public good". *Quarterly Journal of Economics* 85 (May).

Thurow, L. C. 1984. *Dangerous Currents: The State of Economics*. New York: Vintage Books.

Tiebout, C. 1990. "A pure theory of public expenditure". Reprinted in *Readings in Public Sector Economics*, edited by S. Baker, and C. Elliott. Lexington, Mass.: D. C. Heath.

Tietenberg, T. 1996. *Environmental and Resource Economics*. New York: HarperCollins.

Tollison, R. D. 1982. "Rent seeking: A survey". *Kyklos* 35, no. 4.

Ture, N. B. 1982. "The economic effects of tax changes: Neoclassical analysis". In *Supply Side Economics: A Critical Appraisal*, edited by R. H. Fink. Frederick: University Publications of America.

United Nations Industrial Development Organization. 1980. *Manual for Evaluation of Industrial Projects*. New York: United Nations.

United Nations Development Programme. 1997. *Human Development Report*. London: Oxford University Press.

van de Walle, D. 1998a. "Assessing the welfare impacts of public spending". *World Development* 26, no. 3 (March).

van de Walle, D. 1998b. "Targeting revisited". *World Bank Research Observer* 13, no. 2 (August).

VAT Administration Centre. 1991. *VAT Information Bulletin* 1 (June).

Vernon-Wortzel, H., and L. Wortzel. 1989. "Privatization: Not the only answer". *World Development* 17, no. 5.

Wade, R. 1998. "The Asian debt-and-development crisis of 1997". *World Development* 26, no. 8.

Wade, R., and F. Veneroso. 1998. "The resources lie within". *Economist* (November): 7–13.

Wasylenko, M. 1986. "The distribution of tax burden in Jamaica: Pre-1985 reform". Staff Paper no. 30 Jamaican Tax Examination Project, Syracuse University and Government of Jamaica.

Weisner, E. 1985. "Latin American debt crisis". *Finance and Development* 22, no. 1 (March).

Weissman, S. R. 1990. "Structural adjustment in Africa: Insights from the experiences of Ghana and Senegal". *World Development* 18, no. 12.

Whalley, J. 1984. "Regression or progression: The taxing question of tax incidence analysis". *Canadian Journal of Economics* 17.

Whitehall, P. 1984. "Protection in the manufacturing sector of Barbados 1960–80". Central Bank of Barbados, *Economic Review* 11, no. 2 (September).

Wildavsky, A. 1979. *The Politics of the Budgetary Process*. Boston: Little, Brown.

Williams, M. 1996. *Liberalising a Regulated Banking System: The Caribbean Case*. Brookfield, Vt.: Ashgate Publishing.

Williamson, J. G. 1961. "Public expenditure and revenue: An international comparison". *Manchester School of Economic and Social Studies* (January).

Wiltshire, K. 1987. *Privatisation: The British Experience*. Melbourne: Longman Cheshire.

Witter, M., and C. Kirton. 1990. *The Informal Economy in Jamaica: Some Empirical Exercises*. Working Paper no. 36. Mona, Jamaica: Institute of Social and Economic Research, UWI.

Wood, A. 1994. "Improving the contribution of finance to the growth process in Barbados: Is financial intermediation a desirable option?" *Social and Economic*

Studies 43, no. 4 (December).

World Bank. 1990. *World Development Report 1990*. London: Oxford University Press.

World Bank. 1996. *Caribbean Countries Poverty Reduction and Human Resource Development in the Caribbean*. Report no. 15342–LAC.

World Bank. 1997. *World Development Report 1997: The State in a Changing World*. New York: Oxford University Press.

Worrell, D. 1992. *Economic Policies in Small Open Economies: Prospects for the Caribbean and Latin America*. London: Commonwealth Secretariat, Commonwealth Economic Papers, no. 23.

Worrell, D., and A. Belgrave. 1997. *The Treasury and the Central Bank: Independence or Consensus*. Central Bank of Barbados, *Working Papers* 1997, Vol. 1. Bridgetown, Central Bank of Barbados.

Yucelik, Z. M. 1995. "Taxation of bequests, inheritances and gifts". In *Tax Policy Handbook*, edited by P. Shome. Washington, DC: International Monetary Fund.

Zee, H. H. 1995. "Theory of optimal commodity taxation". In *Tax Policy Handbook*, edited by P. Shome. Washington, DC: International Monetary Fund.

Index